HUME, NEWTON, AND THE DESIGN ARGUMENT

HUME, NEWTON,

AND

THE DESIGN ARGUMENT

By Robert H. Hurlbutt III

Revised Edition

UNIVERSITY OF NEBRASKA PRESS • LINCOLN & LONDON

First Landmark Edition printing: 1985

The material in Chapter Nine first appeared in different form in "David Hume and
Scientific Theism," *Journal of the History of Ideas,* Vol. VII, No. 4 (October, 1956).

Library of Congress Cataloging in Publication Data
Hurlbutt, Robert H.
    Hume, Newton, and the design argument.
    "The material in chapter nine first appeared in different form in 'David Hume and
scientific theism,' Journal of the history of ideas, vol. VII, no. 4 (October 1956)"—T.p.
verso.
    Bibliography: p.
    Includes index.
    1. Teleology—History. 2. Newton, Isaac, Sir,
1642–1727. 3. Hume, David, 1711–1776. I. Title.
BD541.H8 1985   212'.1   85-8618
ISBN 0-8032-2337-4

For my wife, Laurie

Preface to the Revised Edition

With this new edition of *Hume, Newton, and the Design Argument,* I still feel secure in its main thesis concerning Hume and Newtonianism: that in the *Dialogues Concerning Natural Religion* one of Hume's deepest concerns was to refute the attempts made in eighteenth-century versions of the design argument to exploit Newtonian science for religious purposes. I still believe that his refutation of those attempts was conclusive. I have, however, come to hold a different view of certain aspects of the *Dialogues,* and this is the topic of the new supplementary essay, "The *Dialogues* as a Work of Art."

One of my predictions, really a comment, that revealed religion was on the rise, has, unfortunately, been amply confirmed. However, given the dialectical features of religious concepts that Hume uncovered in the *Dialogues,* I suppose the present worldwide horrors in connection with religion should occasion no surprise. They certainly provide a depressing vindication of Hume's profound fear of superstition and religious enthusiasm, a vindication that would afford him no joy.

Were I to rewrite Chapter 11, I would be less critical of the attempts of ordinary language philosophers to salvage something of religion; and in other chapters I would add sections on Kant's treatment of natural religion, and on similar efforts by Thomist thinkers. Fortunately, these subjects have been taken up by others.

In the preparation of the supplementary essay, I have been aided greatly by colleagues. I thank Robert Audi, Albert Casullo, Nelson Potter, and Robert Fendel Anderson. I am also grateful to Arlene Rash, who has typed the essay thrice over.

Acknowledgments

It is very nearly impossible for an author to thank properly those who have provided him with inspiration. I should like, however, to state my special indebtedness to Professor E. W. Strong, who first introduced me to the critical history of ideas and to the influences of Newtonian science. His constant encouragement through ten years of research and writing provided the stimulation without which this book could not have been produced.

In addition I should pay special tribute to numerous authors whose works on Early Modern and modern thought were of great help to me. Among them are L. T. More, E. A. Burtt, E. C. Mossner, John Orr, S. G. Hefelbower, F. L. Baumer, and Frederick Ferré.

The laborious but essential task of reading the manuscript and discovering many mistakes was performed with good humor by colleagues at the University of Nebraska: Professors Charles Patterson, Robert Dewey, and Cedric Evans from the Philosophy department; and Professor William Bowsky from the History department. The errors that remain are uniquely my own.

And finally I wish to thank my wife, Laurie, for unceasing encouragement.

Contents

Preface to the Revised Edition   vii

Acknowledgments   ix

Introduction   xiii

PART ONE. NEWTONIANISM: SCIENCE AND THEOLOGY
IN THE EIGHTEENTH CENTURY

1. Newton's Scientific Theism   3
2. Other Contemporary Scientists   27
3. Philosophers and Theologians   43
4. Deists   65
5. Conclusions to Part One   79

PART TWO. THE ANCIENT AND MEDIEVAL CONTEXT
OF THE DESIGN ARGUMENT

6. In Classical Thought: Plato, Aristotle, Stoicism, Philo   95
7. In Medieval Thought: Augustine, Aquinas, and Others   116
8. Conclusions to Part Two   127

PART THREE. THE DENOUEMENT: HUME AND THE
DESIGN ARGUMENT

9. Hume's Critique of Natural Theology   135
10. The Curtain Call   169
11. Epilogue: The Contemporary Context of Natural Theology   189

The *Dialogues* as a Work of Art   213

Index   247

Introduction

The period in Europe spanning the seventeenth and eighteenth centuries was an exciting and formative one. This is true for not only those whose actions, high and low, graced or disgraced its stage, but for its admiring observers also. Its intellectual life, so drab a subject in other periods as to be of interest only to specialized scholars, displays a dynamic and dramatic ferment, perhaps because the twentieth-century onlooker realizes that the tapestry whose warp and woof contain so many of his own ideas, attitudes, and institutions was woven during these times.

This book concerns the interrelationships of two main threads in this tapestry—science and theology—in particular as they are epitomized in the work of two of the period's great figures, Isaac Newton and David Hume. And while it is impossible to avoid selection and abstraction in the treatment of these materials, it should nevertheless be remembered that the eighteenth century was a period of great political and religious upheaval. During the lives of Newton and Hume, the old conception of the divine right of kings gasped out its life on the battlefields of England. While Newton and other scientists were peering through their microscopes and telescopes, or looking at the pretty colors thrown on walls by prisms, or formulating new mathematical theorems, kings were killed or deposed, and generals ruled Britain for a time. While Hume and other philosophers fretted over the laws which govern human experience and thought, or analyzed causation and substance, or criticized religion, the foundations of parliamentary government and religious freedom were laid.

Our subject is less spectacular, but not without its own drama. Newton's work in physics and mathematics formed the ground from which modern science and engineering developed. Hume's philosophical ideas and arguments are the proximate source of a significant part of modern critical and analytical philosophy. Thus the works of Newton and Hume have been of profound and increasing interest to philosophers and historians in recent years.

Specifically, this book is concerned with the ways in whicn the theological and philosophical views of these two major thinkers came into conflict in the eighteenth century, and with tracing the issues generated by this conflict through the nineteenth century on into the contemporary theological and philosophical scene.

There are a number of reasons for making such a study. For one thing, it is of interest to see how a new and epoch-making system of ideas— Newtonian science—effected other intellectual currents during a formative period of the Age of Reason. And some important consequences of the emergence of science have been neglected. Thus only a limited and not always respectful attention has been paid to Newton's theological ideas, mainly because they were so overshadowed by his scientific masterpieces, *Mathematical Principles of Natural Philosophy*, and the *Optics*. Consequently, the significance of Newtonian theology, which in the works of Newton himself and his followers played an important role in eighteenth-century thought, has been unappreciated. This in turn has led historians of ideas and philosophers to underrate the philosophical and theological significance of this "Newtonian" or "scientific" theism, as it will be called. The importance of "Newtonian theism" lies in the fact that it was the first concerted attempt to square modern experimental science with Christianity.

Another reason for the study relates to the proper understanding of Hume's work. While considerable effort has been devoted to Hume's criticism of religion and theology, in particular to his *Dialogues Concerning Natural Religion*, the typical abstract treatment has failed to note that his attack was aimed primarily at the Newtonian attempt to bring about a rapprochement between science and religion. Realization that this was the specific axe being ground by Hume gives an important insight into the character of the arguments he used in his critique, and in turn makes possible their proper evaluation.

And finally, there is the design argument: the argument that since the world exhibits order and design, it must have had a designer. Newton and his followers reformulated this ancient argument in terms of scientific laws of nature. Its historical importance has not been appreciated. Arguments for the existence and attributes of God are, of course, legion; and the major ones have names as famous as philosophy itself: there are ontological, cosmological, moral arguments; there are arguments from faith, from scriptures, from revelation, and from authority. There are others. But when the theological chips are down, and when all other means of subduing the skeptic have failed, the devotee will always, as does Cleanthes in Hume's

Dialogues, remonstrate impatiently "... but look round the world ...," and deal out the design argument. This argument, in some form or another, is and always has been the most universally accepted and commonly used argument for the existence, power, intelligence, and goodness of God. Therefore the design argument deserves the extensive treatment it receives herein, particularly since Newton builds his scientifically oriented theology upon it, and since, in addition, it is the main target of Hume's skeptical attack against natural theology.

In the following pages the subject is divided, mainly for topical reasons, into three sections. The prime consideration throughout has been to understand scientific theism in terms of its nature, its sources or origins, and its fate and validity. Part One, Newtonianism, is devoted to a description and analysis of the ways in which Newton and his scientific, philosophical, and theological contemporaries reformulated the classical design argument in terms of the methods and conclusions of the new physics and optics. In addition this scientific theism is carefully compared with and distinguished from other current theological views. Among the major thinkers considered are Bacon, the Cambridge Platonists, Boyle, Locke, the Deists, Berkeley, and Butler.

Part Two, The Ancient and Medieval Context of the Design Argument, inquires into classical origins of Newtonian theism, and finds them in the design argument, whose ancestry reaches into the dim past. The design argument, along with its attendant logical formula, argument by analogy, is traced from Plato to Galileo. Included is an analysis of the ways in which the traditional formulations of the argument differ from and agree with those of the Newtonians. Two purposes are served by this investigation: the one to which we have just referred, understanding the origins of Newtonian theism; the other, to provide a description of one of Hume's targets in the *Dialogues*, for he attacks this classical formulation of the design argument as well as that of Newton.

The historical analysis of Newtonian and classical natural theology gives way to the consideration of Hume's critique. And thus Part Three has both historical and critical functions, with the latter receiving increasing emphasis as the material develops. The opening portion is devoted to proving the thesis that Hume was directly interested in refuting the Newtonian or scientific formulations of natural theology, as well as those derived from classical sources. Then a detailed evaluation and criticism of Hume's refutation of natural theology is undertaken, wherein each of his arguments is submitted to scrutiny. It is concluded that his refutation of the design argument and of natural theology is logically devastating and conclusive.

Nevertheless, neither the design argument nor its scientific formulations disappeared from the philosophical and theological scene. They were not only alive, indeed they were popular in the nineteenth century, many of whose most famous figures, such as Newman and Gladstone, found them convincing. Standard formulations, often echoing Newton, were produced in the works of William Paley, William Whewell, and other authors. Unlike the eighteenth century, however, in which Hume found it necessary to mask his arguments by indirection and the dialogue form, the nineteenth century witnessed an open and insurgent skeptical movement. The main arguments used by this skeptical movement, often echoing Hume, are discussed and analyzed.

Finally, a search is made into contemporary philosophy and theology in order to discover if the design argument and natural theology survived the battering religion had received at the hands of nineteenth-century skeptics. Modernism, humanism, neo-orthodoxy, theistic existentialism, positivism, and modern linguistic philosophy are examined. It is contended that the search is unsuccessful—that no vital philosophical or theological school makes use of the design argument, scientific theism, or even natural theology, in any of their traditional senses. No modern theology or philosophy breaches the logical wall, erected by Hume, which divides science and theology, reason and religion.

PART ONE

Newtonianism

Science and Theology in the Eighteenth Century

Whence is it that nature does nothing in vain, and whence
arises all that order and beauty which we see in the world?
—NEWTON, *Optics*, Query 28

CHAPTER 1

Newton's Scientific Theism

If Isaac Newton saw his science as a panacea, as a path to that "heavenly city" of progress on this planet, as did Voltaire and the *philosophes*, there is little evidence of it. Cool, seclusive, and quiet, he nevertheless pursued science and theology with the dedication of a consuming passion. Shut in his apartment, "nice to deal with" (in Locke's words), often not aware of his supper on the table, the only extrascientific application of his work in which he showed more than passing interest lay in a direction opposite to that of relieving man's practical problems. This interest was in the existence and glory of God.

He was not, therefore, an indifferent observer. True, he saw science as a quest for pure knowledge. But he also saw it as a means for resolving the ultimate questions of God's existence and character. Unlike Bacon, who saw science as man's main ally in the battle with nature, Newton, when not peering through a prism or telescope, or cogitating a mathematical problem, was gazing resolutely upwards towards the divine. Nature, of course, was fundamental to him, and his overwhelming interest lay in understanding it; but for Newton, nature is under the all-pervading eye of the cosmic-plumber-mechanic, ever watchful for the leaky valve and the burned-out bearing, and, incidentally, for the sinful soul.

Newton's position as one of the giants in the history of thought is unimpeachable, and therefore interest in his scientific work has almost completely overshadowed interest in his work in theology. Yet it is clear that he regarded this theological work to be of great importance, and that he was elated to find that his scientific conclusions seemed to support the main ideas of Christian theology. In his letter to Richard Bentley, chaplain to the Bishop of Worcester, he says, "When I wrote my Treatise about our system, I had an eye upon such principles as might work with considering men, for the belief of a Deity; and nothing can rejoice me more than to find it useful for that purpose." [1] The ways in which this support

---

[1] Isaac Newton, *Opera Quae Exstant Omnia*, ed. Horsely (London, 1782), IV, 429. Hereafter cited as *Opera Omnia*.

was worked out, the cross-fertilization of science and theology in the work of Newton, is the subject of this chapter.

Newton's was the first fully developed scientific synthesis after that of Aristotle, and the first great modern scientific synthesis. Galileo had applied mathematical techniques to the problems of motion in ways distinct from the somewhat mystical phantasies which characterized much of the work of Kepler and Copernicus, but his work was, nevertheless, far short of that of Newton. True, the scholastic notion of science, conceived in terms of categories such as substance and final causes, was rapidly being replaced by the modern conceptions of time, space, and force; but before Newton, mathematical demonstrations of those concepts of celestial and terrestrial phenomena reached in Copernicus, Kepler, and Galileo were not as yet unified into any systematic treatment for all bodies in motion. True again, Galileo had shown that no impressed force was necessary in order to keep a body in motion, and his work hinted at the inverse squares law of Newton; but as yet the implications of his discoveries were neither clearly understood nor developed. Galileo excepted, many thinkers were, like Kepler and Copernicus, still under the influence of mystical notions of mathematical realities. Even the clearest of thinkers were puzzled about what keeps planets in motion, and they relied upon the ancient notion of an ether, which was still mixed up with another ancient idea—that of animal spirits, psychic forces, and souls. Astrology was as yet confounded with astronomy, and alchemy with chemistry.

It can be said, then, that only with Newton was the world finally comprehended under one unified, dynamic mechanical system wherein the entire complex of movements of the solar system as well as the bodies of the earth were mathematically related to the postulate that each particle of matter behaved as though it attracted every other particle with a force proportional to the product of the masses and inversely proportional to the square of the distance between them, with the laws following from this postulate founded securely in observation. The laws of the universe were shown by Newton to exemplify one gigantic mathematical harmony, moving to the music of the dynamical principles established by the terrestrial experiments and inductions of Galileo and himself. The great laws of nature involved the laws of falling bodies, the law of inertia, the conception of mass, the parallelogram of forces, and the equivalence of work and energy. With Newton, the world was not only thought of as a machine, but was exhibited in detail as a function of mechanical laws—a system of the world. All matters of celestial and terrestrial mechanics, scattered and disconnected in Kepler, Copernicus, Huygens, Halley, Wren, Hook, and Galileo, were unified into a grand system of mathematical-mechanical laws.

An analysis of the development of Newton's theology shows that it appeared rather late in his life, and at widely separate intervals. In the order of production, as in the order of future fame, Newton's science came first. In the first editions of his scientific works no mention is made of theology. His first publication, a paper concerning a new and revolutionary theory of optics, which he sent to the Royal Society in 1672,[2] is strictly scientific. The first edition of *Mathematical Principles of Natural Philosophy* (1687), in which Newton submits to the law of gravity all celestial and earthly bodies, tides, and comets, does not refer to theology. His first published statements concerning theology came in 1692–1693 in a series of letters to Richard Bentley. Therein he outlined his theory that the frame of the world, its structure and processes, cannot be reduced to mechanical causes, and that the world order implies a divine agent.[3] In 1704, however, he published his *Optics*, and again theology is not mentioned. In the second edition, the *Optice*, a translation of the English text of the *Optics* into Latin by Samuel Clarke, seven Queries are added to the sixteen of the first edition; and two of them, twenty and twenty-three, treat of theology.[4]

It can be speculated from the above that Newton would rather have kept his science and his theology separate. Such a wish, however, would have been dashed for the simple reason that his opponents did not wish to do so, and as a consequence they attacked him on theological grounds. Leibniz called the *Principia* a Godless book, and Berkeley criticized Newton's conceptions of absolute space and absolute time as being atheistical notions.[5] Newton's response was to add to the second edition of the *Principia*, produced in 1713, the famous *General Scholium* to Book III, an addition in which he presented some of his basic ideas on theology.

[2] Sir David Brewster, *Memoirs of the Life, Writings, and Discoveries of Sir Isaac Newton* (Edinburgh, 1855), I, 77 ff. For the paper see *The Philosophical Transactions of the Royal Society of London*, abstr. John Lowthorpe (London, 1749), I, 134 ff.
[3] *Opera Omnia*, IV, 429–442.
[4] E. W. Strong, "Newton and God," *Journal of the History of Ideas*, XIII, No. 2 (April, 1952), 147–167.
[5] George Berkeley, "A Treatise Concerning the Principles of Human Knowledge," in *Essays, Principles, Dialogues*, ed. Mary Whiton Calkins (Scribner's Selections; New York: Charles Scribner's Sons, 1929), pp. 178–192.

Bentley, Roger Cotes, and Samuel Clarke were instrumental in getting Newton to make these additions. In the third edition of the *Optics*, 1718, Queries seventeen to twenty-three are renumbered twenty-five to thirty-one in order to make room for eight new Queries devoted to an etherial medium, which are numbered sixteen to twenty-four; and thus in Queries twenty-eight and thirty-one of this edition we have in English the theology given in numbers twenty and twenty-three of the second edition, the *Optice*.[6]

To return to the Bentley letters. Robert Boyle, the great chemist, provided in his last testament for a series of eight lectures dealing with the evidences of Christianity, to be given annually beginning in 1692. The first lecturer to be chosen was young Richard Bentley.[7] Newton's great fame had brought him to Bentley's attention, and Bentley, interested in the evidential possibilities of science in connection with theology, wrote to Newton and asked about his views on the subject. Thus was initiated the famous exchange of ideas in which Newton answers Bentley's questions by dressing the design argument in scientific clothing. There were four letters, the first three written in 1692, the last in February, 1693.[8]

In the first letter Newton's concern is to show that natural causes, those discovered by scientific investigation, do not sufficiently explain the world order.[9] Take, for example, the principle of gravity and the existence of matter. If it is assumed that matter is lucent, then gravity might work to form the sun and the fixed stars. But, Newton maintained, this still does not provide a satisfactory explanation of how matter is divided into two sorts: part into shining stuff fit to make a great sun, and the rest coalesced into many little opaque bodies. Or, if all were in the beginning opaque, why is it that only the sun became lucent? There are other, similar examples. Throughout the letters Newton points up those characteristics of the world process which are inexplicable in terms of mechanical laws—differences in orbs, planes of motion, the "just" degrees of velocity, the distances of the planets Jupiter and Saturn from the Sun. In one sense, then, Newton founds his theology upon the limitations of his science, and such attempts have proved, in the light of the continual progress of science throughout history, to be somewhat abortive. There is another important implication of these thoughts: Newton appears to have recognized the extent to which he could push his science. That is, he knew which statements were scientific and which were not. As we shall see later on, when

---

[6] Strong, "Newton and God," p. 156.
[7] J. H. Monk, *The Life of Richard Bentley* (Cambridge, 1833), I, 37–38.
[8] *Opera Omnia*, IV, 429–442.   [9] *Ibid.*, pp. 429–430.

he dealt with ideas not subject to scientific explanation, he labeled the statements "hypotheses," and followed them with discussions of the scope of experimental science which make clear his belief that they are not to be considered a part of scientifically established knowledge. Since his religious and theological beliefs do go beyond such knowledge, it is clear that, for Newton, science was not enough. To the theory of the ancient Epicureans he gave, in scientific terminology and conception, the answer of Plato and the Stoics, that fate, matter, and motion are incapable of producing the world as we know it. Strictly speaking, he did not yet produce the design argument; he merely alluded to it and set the stage for it. But we find it a little further on in the same letter:

> To make this system, therefore, with all its motions, required a cause which understood, and compared together, the quantities of matter in the several bodies of the sun and planets, and the gravitating powers resulting from thence; the several distances of the primary planets from the sun, and of the secondary ones from *Saturn, Jupiter*, and the Earth; and the velocities, with which these planets could revolve about those quantities of matter in the central bodies; and to compare and adjust all these things together in so great and variety of bodies, argues that cause to be not blind and fortuitous, but very well skilled in mechanicks and geometry.[10]

Thus Newton not only believed that one cannot reduce the world to mechanical causes, with regard either to its origin or its structure, but also that the geometrical and mechanical order evident in world processes implies an intelligent creator or designer. And God is a creator in the sense, quite explicit in the above passage, of a mechanic. He "compares and adjusts," is "skilled in mechanics and geometry." Newton made theological use of his scientific discoveries, then, in two ways, positive and negative. In the first place, he stated the limitations of his mechanical science; it is not sufficient to explain the origin and ultimate order of the world. Second, he stated that the very motions, positions, velocities, etc., which his science so successfully described, are evidence for the belief in the existence of a creator-mechanic. This is the venerable design argument, with a scientific basis. It is argued that God is not merely a designer, but a designer with certain specific skills, i.e., geometry and mechanics. These abilities, of course, are held to characterize intelligence. For Newton, "The hypothesis of deriving the frame of the world, by mechanical principles, from matter evenly spread through the heavens [is] inconsistent with my system. . . ."[11]

---

[10] *Ibid.*, pp. 431–432.   [11] *Ibid.*, p. 441.

The most significant contentions are the following: First, scientific mechanics gives no explanation for certain characteristics of the processes of the universe. Second, scientific mechanics does give us evidence, in mathematical-physical laws describing the geometrical and mechanical order of the natural objects of the universe, from which we may infer the existence and the intelligence of a creator. The argument is a posteriori, since it proceeds from a scientific description of observed sequences of events in nature. The argument is also analogical, in that the mechanical and geometrical character of the world order, since it is similar to the mechanical and geometrical productions of man, implies, as do such productions of man, an intelligent creator or producer. Put in another way, since orderly arrangements are always in man's experience the product of a creating mind, and since the world exhibits a geometrical and mechanical order analogous to the works of man, then the two have in common the other element—a creator. The argument, as are all design arguments, is teleological in that it takes purposive relationships as evidence. But the teleology or "purpose" emphasized in the Newtonian argument is not in nature itself, although there are purposes in nature which are cited by Newton later on. In this particular form of the design argument the purpose or intention is in the mind of the creator or mechanic, and he transcends nature. The order which is of significance here is *in* nature— geometrical and mechanical order—and would constitute order even were it not purposive in character. "Design" in the context of this argument meant the orderly, harmonious arrangements of elements in systems or a system. We shall refer to this sort of argument as the "argument *from* design."

In the *Optics*, Newton presented his theological notions in Queries twenty-eight and thirty-one.[12] Like the other Queries, which have to do with speculations concerning an etherial medium, etc., these are expressly described by Newton as theories not yet susceptible to empirical verification. (Again we see the distinction between science and theology.) Query twenty-eight begins with a consideration of light and its propagation in a fluid medium. After a lengthy discussion of the resistance of such a medium to the motion of bodies in it, noting that the "oldest and most celebrated

[12] All quotations from the *Optics* come from the third edition, published in 1718. The consideration of the *Optics* is placed before that of the *General Scholium* of the *Principia* because the theology involved is the same as that in the Latin edition *Optice*, which was published in 1706, before the second edition of the *Principia*, in which the *General Scholium* first appeared. The only change in the material of the two editions is a rewritten account of the method of analysis in Query 31 of the 1718 edition, which was Query 23 of the *Optice*. See Strong, "Newton and God," pp. 156–157.

philosophers of Greece and Phoenicia" had rejected such a medium, Newton turns to a discussion of hypotheses and natural philosophy. It is the business of natural philosophy, without appeal to hypotheses (metaphysical assumptions) to deduce causes from effects until we arrive at a first, nonmechanical cause.

Thus again Newton treats the problem of the first cause as a theological question which is beyond mechanical principles and hence beyond the explanation of physical science, and again his evidence is drawn from the characteristics of the world as conceived in terms of physical science. We find, however, that he adds some significant ideas to those presented in the Bentley letters.

Whereas the main business of natural philosophy is to argue from the phaenomena without feigning hypotheses, and to deduce causes from effects, till we come to the very first cause; which certainly is not mechanical: and not only to unfold the mechanism of the world, but chiefly to resolve these and such like Questions. What is there in places almost empty of matter, and whence is it that the sun and planets gravitate towards one another, without dense matter between them? To what end are comets; and whence is it that planets move all in one the same way in orbs concentrick, while comets move all manner of ways in orbs very excentrick; and what hinders the fixed stars from falling upon one another? How came the bodies of animals to be contrived with so much art, and for what ends were their several Parts? Was the eye contrived without skill in Optics, and the ear without knowledge of sounds? How do the motions of the body follow from the will: and whence is the instinct in animals? Is not the sensory of animals that place, to which the sensitive substance is present; and into which the sensible species of things are carried through the nerves and brain, that there they may be perceived by their immediate presence to that substance? And these things being rightly dispatched, Does it not appear from phaenomena, that there is a Being incopereal [sic], living, intelligent, omnipresent, who, in infinite space, as it were in his sensory, sees the things themselves intimately, and throughly [sic] perceives them, and comprehends them wholly by their immediate presence to himself: of which things the images only, carried through the organs of sense into our little sensoriums, are seen and beheld by that which in us perceives and thinks. And though every true step made in this philosophy brings us not immediately to the knowledge of the First cause, yet it brings us nearer to it, and on that account is to be highly valued.[13]

Like Socrates in the *Phaedo*, Newton asks those questions which he feels cannot be answered by the physical sciences and, again like Socrates, he appeals to purpose and intention. Nevertheless, in no uncertain terms he

[13] *Opera Omnia*, IV, 237–238.

affirms the use of science in theology. He repeats the point made in the
Bentley letters that the ultimate source of the origin and order of the
planetary bodies, the constitution of the world, is not mechanical. Any
ultimate explanation must be in terms of an intelligent agent responsible
for this order, an agent who had some intentions or purposes in mind for
its construction. This is a repetition of the argument *from* design that we
found in the Bentley letters. Yet another type of design argument is
present and emphasized: for with the discussion of contrivance in the
bodies of animals, Newton brings into the picture the element of purpose
in and among the objects in nature. Not only is the mechanical and
geometrical order of things in the world to be considered, but also the
purposive relationships of the parts of organisms within the world. Since
bodies and their organs show an amazing degree of contrivance for certain
goals and uses, then it must be that there was a contriver who constructed
them in such ways; for they cannot themselves have been responsible for
these relationships. The whole section in effect asks the question "why"
concerning these arrangements of things. This kind of analysis of the world
was not developed in the Bentley letters, where Newton dealt mainly with
the order and harmony of the parts of the whole universe and neglected the
purposive relationships among them. Here, however, Newton maintains
that the purposive relationships among the parts of organisms, their
means-ends character, imply a contriver-designer. Such purposive elements
within and between organisms could not have developed as a matter of
choice on the part of the organisms themselves. Here, then, we have the
argument *to* design, where the term "design" means intention.

There are other important points. First, Newton reinforces his belief
that God is necessary to keep the world in order. This is the purport of his
Query as to whether a contriver is necessary in order to keep the fixed stars
from falling upon one another. (Not being in motion, they seemed not
subject to the centripetal forces which would keep them in position.)
Second, he compares the divine intelligence to the human mind or
sensorium. They are unlike in that the divine mind perceives things
immediately, whereas the human intellect perceives only through the
mediation of images.[14] Infinite space is, "as it were," God's visual field,
and the things in this space are known by him in their complete inner
nature and complexity. Newton did not, however, in this particular passage,
completely identify infinite space with the Deity, as did More and other
Cambridge Platonists (excepting Cudworth). There is considerable

[14] This point is repeated in Query 31.

evidence that Newton was influenced by these thinkers, and we will consider this problem later. It is of interest to note at this place, however, that the passage under consideration was first published in the *Optice*, under the editorship of Samuel Clarke, who agreed with the Platonists. Newton was friendly, through Locke, with Lady Masham, Cudworth's daughter, and he knew Henry More.[15] One of Newton's teachers, Barrow, was a Platonist.

Among the most significant statements in the passage is that which proceeds "does it not appear from phenomena, that there is a Being . . . ," for it points up the a posteriori and empirical stamp of his version of the design argument. And while Newton did not place extensive emphasis upon this particular aspect of the design argument, it takes on more and more importance in the development of natural theology during this period. The reason is quite simple. Enamored of the new science, most writers upon theology were at pains to exemplify any analogies between science and theology. Newton's view was that we are able to get evidence for the existence and attributes of God by inference from the phenomena of the world, and "phenomena" meant the data of observation and experiment.

Query thirty-one begins with a consideration of the attractive powers in nature, and after a discussion of the possible extent of such powers, it proceeds to another discussion of God. Newton begins with the belief that the amount and variety of motion in the world is always decreasing, and he feels that this implies a need for its conservation and recruitment by active principles. We see in this contention the ancient metaphysical principle that motion is not intrinsic to matter: Matter is inert and passive, and therefore its initial inertia or motion must have been produced by something active. God not only puts things *in* order; he set things in motion in the beginning.

These considerations lead Newton to additional speculations about the origin and constitution of the world. In a tone or mood of musing contemplation he writes that the world *seems probably* to have come about by the action of God, who formed in the beginning matter in solid, massy, hard, impenetrable, movable particles; "most conduced to the end for which he formed them. . . ."[16] For the vortices of Democritus, Newton substitutes the artificer of Plato, but he keeps the atoms of the former

---

[15] L. T. More, *Sir Isaac Newton: A Biography* (New York: Charles Scribner's Sons, 1934), pp. 552, 629–630, 640–647.

[16] *Opera Omnia*, IV, 260–262.

philosopher. God is the original active principle, and the world is telic—
again we see the teleological principle of Plato substituted for the prob-
abilistic determinism of Democritus. With the help of the principle of
gravity, *vis inertia*, the laws of motion, etc., "all material things seem to
have been composed of the hard and solid particles above-mentioned;
variously associated, in the first creation, by the counsel of an intelligent
agent." Exhibiting that peculiar blindness of those who pay unconscious
homage to the idols of the tribe, Newton here uses both the order and
disorder of the celestial bodies in his argument. (This is a point which
Hume used with devastating effect later on.) If they are in order, then such
order implies an architect; if they are in disorder, then it is necessary that
there be a mechanic to put them back into order again. "Such a wonderful
uniformity in the planetary system must be allowed the effect of choice.
And so must the uniformity in the bodies of animals, they having generally
a right and a left side shaped alike, etc."

No significant change from Query twenty-eight is involved in this
passage. Again Newton works the principles of his science into his theology,
basing in them the concept of the order and harmony of the world system.
He does add symmetry with respect to animal bodies to the argument from
order, but the argument does not concern the purposive relation among
the parts of such bodies. Along with the appeal to the nonmechanical
nature of the ultimate origin and the order of nature, and the view that the
irregularities in nature imply the existence of a cosmic repairman, there is
still the emphasis upon the argument *from* design. The probable and
uncertain character of these speculations is explicitly recognized.

The sentence quoted above no sooner is completed, however, than we
have presented to us the teleological factor.

> Also the first contrivance of those very artificial parts of animals, the eyes,
> ears, brain, muscles, heart, lungs, midriff, glands, larynx, hands, wings,
> swimming bladders, natural spectacles, and other organs of sense and
> motion; and the instinct of brutes and insects, can be the effects of nothing
> else than the wisdom and skill of a powerful ever-living Agent; who,
> being in all places, is more able by his will to move the bodies within his
> boundless uniform sensorium, and thereby to form and reform the parts
> of the universe, than we are by our will to move the parts of our own
> bodies.[17]

The import of these lines is that the function of the organs of animal
bodies, their purposes, implies an intelligent contriver. And the analogy is

[17] *Ibid.*

to human purposive acts. The fact that the organs of animals are inter-related so as to function for the ends of seeing, hearing, thinking, working, pumping, breathing, flying, swimming, etc., none of which functions any creature could contrive for itself, implies that there exists some original creator who had these purposes in mind, and had in addition those skills of optics and mechanics which were necessary in order to effect the construction of organs for such purposes. Newton repeats his view that this creation takes place within the boundless sensorium of the creator. (Had he not quickly stated, "And yet we are not to consider the world as the body of God, or the several parts thereof as the parts of God," it might be concluded that Newton has fallen into some sort of pantheism.) God moves things at will within his divine sensorium, contriving and con-structing organisms with parts and organs which serve certain purposes. The *ultimate* purposes of things are, of course, unclear, as is usual in this kind of argument, and lie within God's will. The "first contrivance" of these "artificial parts" of animals implies the wisdom and skill of an ever living agent.

This is the argument *to* design. In it Newton draws upon the data of optics, sound, and medicine. He reaffirms his position that there are aspects of the universal processes of nature which are inexplicable in terms of mechanical science, and infers that certain irregularities in the orderly and mechanical processes of the celestial bodies necessitate a cosmic repairman who, from time to time, reorders the system. He explicitly asserts that the discoveries of natural philosophy and science present fundamental evidence for beliefs concerning the Deity: indeed, one may conclude the existence of an intelligent agent from these discoveries. Furthermore, we find repeated in the statement Newton's belief that this argument is a posteriori, that we know the Deity "from the appearances of phenomena." The double impact of early modern science upon theology—both with respect to its empirical methods and its body of knowledge about nature—is again evident. It should be kept in mind that Newton wrote much of his theology in the form of Queries (in the *Optics*), and that he did not therefore include such speculations in the body of scientifically established knowledge.

The fact that he kept separate his science and his theology—that is, that he did not confuse them—is an important and touchy area of concern. In the introduction to this section I suggested that Newton probably made the addition of the theology of the *General Scholium* of the *Principia* in order to counteract the criticisms of Leibniz, Berkeley, and others. Otherwise, I think, he would not have included his theological notions in the body of his scientific publications. Not that he was untruthful about his religion, for other sources of his views show that he was a firm believer. Charges of irreligion—"infidelity"—were in Newton's time quite serious.[18] The laws concerning irreligion were still in force, and they were reinforced by public opinion, denunciations from the pulpit on the part of preachers, and by the vituperations of such writers as Warburton. We know that Newton was aware of Leibniz' opposition, for in 1713 when the second edition of the *Principia* was in preparation for the press, Cotes, the editor, wrote Newton and asked him to make some additions to it in order to clear himself of the charge of atheism. Cotes refers to a letter from Leibniz to Hartsoeker in which Leibniz had charged Newton with atheism because his book on the system of the world said nothing about God.[19] It was noted above that the first edition of the *Principia* contained no theological statements.

It seems likely, therefore, that in the second edition in 1713 Newton sought, by adding the theology of the *General Scholium*, to allay the suspicion of atheism. It begins with an argument against the hypothesis of vortices which was the major component of the mechanical theory of the Cartesians. He discusses in general the fact that vortices form an unsatisfactory explanation of the motions of the planets and reaffirms his position that the celestial bodies move according to the law of gravity. He then proceeds to make certain observations which his system of the world seems to him to imply.

He first points out that while mechanical laws sufficiently explain the orbits of the planets, "yet they could by no means have at first derived the regular position of the orbits themselves from these laws."[20] Thus the ideas presented in this passage remain consistent with those in the Bentley letters and the *Optics*. After stating that there are certain characteristics of the motions and order of the world system that cannot be reduced to natural causes, he goes on to present the design argument. The primary planets revolve around the sun in concentric circles; the systematic directions, planes, orbits, of the celestial bodies, the regular motions, "this most beautiful system of the sun, planets, and comets, could only proceed from the counsel and dominion of an intelligent and powerful Being."

[18] One should be reminded of Hume's distressful cry to Eliot concerning the publication of his Dialogues. See page 133, below.

[19] Brewster, *Memoirs of Sir Isaac Newton*, II, 219–222.

[20] This and the next five passages are from *Sir Isaac Newton's Mathematical Principles*, ed. Florian Cajori (Berkeley: University of California Press, 1934), pp. 543–546. Hereafter cited as *Mathematical Principles*.

There is no mention of purposive order in the world. The design, order, harmony of planetary motion, as formulated in scientific laws of motion and gravity, imply an intelligent creator. The passage includes a reference to the beauty of the system, closely related to the notion of benevolence mentioned above, and this is an esthetic concept often used by the writers of the age; but it is not emphasized and it does not change the form or central purport of the argument. The remainder of the passage is devoted to putting these theological statements into traditional religious form, to expressing the view that speculative hypotheses not derived from observation and experiment are not a part of experimental science, and to a brief discussion of the possibility of an ethereal medium. Newton states that the "being" known through the order and harmony of the world is called Lord God, that he is a living, intelligent, and powerful Being; and, from his other perfections, that he is supreme, or most perfect. He is eternal and infinite, omnipotent and omniscient . . . he is not eternity and infinity, but eternal and infinite; he is not duration or space, but he endures and is present.

It is apparent that these statements involve much more than the design argument per se. The situation might perhaps be explained in the following way. The passage indicates the manner in which the Newtonian "System of the World" supports the Christian conception of God and shows how scientific ideas can be used in a proof of God's existence and intelligence. It is clear that the design argument, however, will serve only as a method of arriving at God's existence and intelligence (and perhaps in addition his goodness), if a good many of the problems of theological ethics are slurred over. The other elements which Newton introduces here are in no way logically connected with this proof. Like most of his contemporaries, Newton, after having made the initial step of inferring an intelligent cause by analogy, makes an unsupported leap to other traditional characteristics of the Deity. Not that he is completely unaware of the leap. He does recognize the somewhat mystical character of these other characteristics. "Whence also he is all similar, all eye, all ear, all brain, all arm, all power to perceive, to understand, and to act; but in a manner not at all human, in a manner not at all corporeal, in a manner utterly unknown to us." Since the kernel of the design argument is the analogy between the human intelligence as creating orderly mechanisms and is thus completely anthropomorphic, it seems rather peculiar to find Newton withdrawing the analogy almost as soon as he has produced it. But, one might speculate, he does not want to put himself in the position of confusing man and God.

"We know him only by his most wise and excellent contrivances of things, and final causes. . . ."

We see, then, that in the *General Scholium* Newton repeats all his former arguments for the existence of God, except that he spends little time on the teleological or purposive nature of things. He does not completely neglect the telic aspect of nature—the argument *to* design; but his only mention of it in the *Scholium* is in the quotation just cited concerning final causes, which for Newton meant the purposes, aims, or ends for which things are made. The fact that Newton subordinated the teleological element in his arguments is no accident, for the most important use of his scientific discoveries in theology is in support of the argument from the design exemplified in the motions of celestial bodies. And this argument would be complete without reference to purposes. Therefore, this is the argument he favored. Finally, he again asserts that the design argument is a posteriori, and, further, that it is analogical and probable. ". . . all our notions of God are taken from the ways of mankind by a certain similitude, which, though not perfect, has some likeness, however. And this much concerning God; to discourse of whom from the appearances of things does certainly belong to Natural Philosophy."

We have seen that Newton from time to time in the presentation of his theological ideas went beyond the conclusions which follow logically from the design arguments. Thus, we find him speaking of the omnipotence, omniscience, eternity, duration, etc., of God, none of which is demonstrated by means of the design argument as he used it, even if we grant its validity. These traditional Christian tenets, despite the almost universal eighteenth-century opinion to the contrary, have no special claim upon the design argument. One is reminded of Pascal's statement that Nature proves God only to those who believe in him on other grounds.

There is, however, no doubt that Newton accepted these more traditional tenets of Christianity. In the following pages I shall deal briefly with some of his other religious and theological notions, particularly those concerning biblical history, chronology, church government or ecclesiastical authority, the doctrine of the trinity, and miracles. And of course I shall note those aspects of his beliefs which appear to have been a result of his scientific beliefs.

During the Age of Reason many thinkers labored at chronology—the study of the temporal sequence of human events—mainly in terms of Old

Testament history. Newton was regarded as one of the important chronologists by his contemporaries who shared his interests, including John Locke, Hook, Boyle, Leibniz, the Cambridge Platonists, and others. He seems to have developed his chronological ideas concerning the Old Testament in connection with the discussions of the group of theologians and philosophers who surrounded Queen Caroline. She asked him for a copy of his *A Short Chronicle from the First Memory of Things in Europe to the Conquest of Persia by Alexander the Great.*[21] This work represented a personal copy, unfinished and not fit for publication, which Newton did not consider completely thought out. Despite the forbidding length of the title, the work seems to have attracted some attention in and around the Royal Circle. Abbe Conti made a copy, after promising Newton it would not be published. It was loaned, however, to a French chronologist named Freret, who translated it into the French language, and although Newton refused his consent, it was published. The resulting contention with other writers on chronology caused the great scientist, although now old and ill (1722), to amend it for publication. He was not, however, to see it published, for it came out in 1728, after his death, under the title *The Chronology of Ancient Kingdoms Amended.*[22] Beginning with the genealogy of the Old Testament, the essay seeks to establish the date of the creation and in turn discusses the early history of Greece, Egypt, Assyria, Babylonia, and Persia. By calculations based upon the data given in the Old Testament and also upon various classical sources, Newton's contemporaries had established two main dates: the deluge as in 2348 B.C. and the creation as in 4004 B.C. Accepting these dates, Newton attempts to give the temporal sequence of the history of every nation, squaring this chronology with "nature, with astronomy, with sacred history, with Herodotus the father of History, and with itself."[23] There is not much to occupy us here, other than to point out that he makes some use of his scientific capacities in the discussions of ancient astronomy (pages 55–75) and in his use of the calculations of the equinox in order to establish certain dates (page 64).

The same may be said of his interpretation of the Apocalypse and the prophecies of Daniel. He had a wide correspondence with other thinkers, including John Locke,[24] concerning these subjects. Bentley and More

[21] More, *Sir Isaac Newton: A Biography*, p. 612. See also Frank E. Manuel, *The Eighteenth Century Confronts the Gods* (Cambridge: Harvard University Press, 1959), Chap. III.

[22] *Opera Omnia*, Vol. V.

[23] *Ibid.*, p. 7.

[24] Peter King, *Life of Locke* (London, 1830), I, 402–404.

contended that his mathematizing of them had led Newton astray.[25] His specific interpretations are of little importance to us except in that they exhibit his views on ecclesiastical matters. "The authority of emperors, kings, and princes, is human. The authority of councils, synods, bishops, and presbyters, is human."[26] It is obvious from all of this that Newton was a Protestant and that he held no brief for the doctrine of the divine right of kings or clergy. His most important reason for producing these works is consistent with such views: he wished to show that the little horn of the fourth beast in Daniel was prophetic of the Roman Church and the Catholic downfall, and this manifests Newton's anti-papist leanings.

Newton's latitudinarian views are also evident in his attitude towards the doctrine of the Trinity. William Whiston, trying also to prove concordance of science with scripture, said that Newton was an Arian, that is, that he denied the Son's coeternality with the Father;[27] and in the essay *Two Notable Corruptions of Scripture*, Newton seems to bear out this judgment. Both Horsley, the editor of his works, and Sir David Brewster, his biographer, were so worried about his heterodoxy that they went out of their way to withhold, whenever possible, those of Newton's personal papers which appeared to them to express any such taint. Horsley did, however, include the above tract in the *Opera Omnia* under the title *An Historical Account of Two Notable Corruptions of Scripture*. Newton sent it to Locke in 1690 with the purpose of having it translated abroad anonymously, but later he asked that publication be prevented. This request was respected and it was not published until the 1750's, long after his death.

In its major purpose of casting doubt upon the doctrine of the Trinity, as well as upon several of the particular concepts usually offered in support of it,[28] the work is quite obviously Arian and rationalistic in tenor. It exhibits Newton's protestantism; indeed, it is vigorously anti-papal, anti-Catholic, and anti-Trinitarian. He is careful to state that he will not believe what he cannot understand, a standard which causes him to reject the mystical elements in the Trinitarian notion, mainly on grounds of inconsistency. In the light of these writings, it appears that Newton was not the credulous conservative that some have made him out to be.[29] Leslie

[25] More, *Sir Isaac Newton: A Biography*, pp. 622, 630.

[26] *Opera Omnia*, V, 305.

[27] William Whiston, *Mescellanis: Historical Memoirs of the Life and Writings of Dr. Samuel Clarke* (London, 1748), p. 8.

[28] *Opera Omnia*, V, 508.

[29] See J. H. Randall, Jr., *The Making of the Modern Mind* (Cambridge, 1926), p. 263. E. A. Burtt, *The Metaphysical Foundations of Modern Physical Science*

Stephen says that Newton illustrates the truth that a man may be an eminent mathematician and a childish theologian. I am not certain that I follow this sort of criticism. In the first place, as we have seen, this essay reflected an interest shared by many very intelligent and liberal men, including Locke and Leibniz. Newton used what knowledge he had at his disposal, submitted chronology and text to historical study, placed authority in the Bible and in reason, and attempted in a number of ways to square his religion with his science. This all seems quite reasonable to me, and to criticize him for it smacks of the retrospective fallacy. My point is this: Newton was quite as abreast of his time in his theology, including the notions concerning the prophecies and Daniel and the Trinity, etc., as he was in his science. The fact that many writers of the present day consider his scientific work more important than his theological work is a normative judgment liberally sprinkled with hindsight.

In truth he was quite modernistic in his interpretation of miracles. In a *Portsmouth Paper* note he states, "For miracles are so called not because they are the works of God, but because they happen seldom and for that reason excite wonder." [30] In other papers he supports Arius; holds the papists to have usurped Christian authority; and says that "homoiousios," the font of the doctrine of the Trinity, is unimportant to Christianity. Further, he constantly rejected consubstantiality. [31] Any modern writer can, of course, depending upon his religious tastes, pick out those of Newton's ideas which he does not personally approve and damn him for silliness, [32] but this seems to me to be rather like saying that he was silly for believing in an ethereal medium and in absolute space and time, for the reason that these concepts are no longer accepted. It would be good to remember that Newton did not claim that his religious and theological notions were subject to experimental verification.

In summary, Newton's theology reveals that his scientific materials are marshalled in support of the belief in an intelligent and all-powerful God. Simply stated, the argument amounts to the following: (a) certain conditions with respect to the origin and order of the universe are inexplicable in terms of rational mechanics; (b) the basic constituents of the world of

(London: Routledge and Kegan Paul, 1949), p. 203. Leslie Stephen, *A History of English Thought in the 18th Century* (London: John Murray, 1902), I, 212.

[30] More, *Sir Isaac Newton: A Biography*, p. 623. See also *Sir Isaac Newton: Theological Manuscripts*, ed. H. McLachlan (Liverpool: University of Liverpool Press, 1950), p. 17.

[31] Brewster, *Memoirs of Sir Isaac Newton*, II, 342, 532. More, *Sir Isaac Newton: A Biography*, pp. 640–644.

[32] Stephen, *loc. cit.*

nature, the atomic particles of matter, are passive and incapable of originally ordering themselves or of putting themselves into motion; (c) from the order and harmony of the celestial bodies in the cosmic system, the symmetrical character of the parts of organisms, the purposive structuring of animals and plants and their interrelationships, and the purposive relationships of their parts and organs, we are able to infer by analogy the existence and intelligence of a first cause—God; (d) knowledge of God's existence is known a posteriori; (e) since the variety of motion is decreasing, and there are various other eccentricities evident in cosmic processes, God must comprehend the world of things in space and time in order to insure its preservation; (f) absolute space is the sensorium, or perceptual field, of God, in which he immediately apprehends all that occurs in the universe.

There are, in addition, the ecclesiastical and Arian notions dealt with above. They are not, however, connected particularly with the design argument which properly has only to do with elements (c) and (d). The first two propositions constitute a rejection of the materialistic explanation of the world order. On the levels of cosmology (his system of the world), and epistemology (his empiricism), the effect of Newton's science upon his theology is marked. The latter part of the argument stands alone, however, and is not necessitated by the other parts. Elements (a), (b), and (e) are also explicated in scientific terms. Only (f) is disconnected from science.

It is clear, therefore, that Newton's science was intrinsic to practically all of his considerations on theology. The materials are not always drawn from mechanics or physics; much is taken from biology and optics and psychology. I should like to expand on this scientific influence, to review the ways in which Newton's science, as a body of knowledge or system of the world, and as a method, influenced his theology. Since I should like to show in some detail the fact that succeeding theologians were heavily influenced by his thinking, a full review will be most useful. First consideration will be devoted to his system of the world, and after that I shall proceed to a consideration of his methodology.

Our division of his scientific ideas into cosmology and methodology is not at all artificial. Newton's age, from Bacon through Locke, even to modern times, was preoccupied with methodological considerations for the reason that the scientific revolution instituted by Galileo and Newton was even more of a revolution in methodology than of systems and conclusions. Newton's natural philosophy reflects this division and is two-sided, one part concerned with methodology and the other concerned with a system of the world. Both make up what was in his day called "natural philosophy," and their use in religious thinking produced what was called "natural theology." Both were preoccupations of most of the educated people of his time, in the sense that these people were interested not only in the new notions of gravity, laws of motion, *vis inertia* and other elements which made up the "system of the world" developed by science, but also in the kinds of methods and techniques that lead to scientific discoveries.

First the system of the world. As we have seen, Newton's *Principia* presented a conception of the world as a system of numberless bodies, masses, moving within the framework of absolute space and time, in accordance with the natural laws of motion. These laws were called "mechanical principles," and the physical world of nature, functioning according to these laws at the behest of the Deity, is a mechanical world. Natural bodies are constructed of solid, massy, impenetrable, movable particles or atoms,[33] and the process of nature, which is "very conformable to itself, and simple," results from the association and separation and motions of these indestructible atoms.[34] The invention of more powerful microscopes, Newton (and Locke and others) believed, might make possible the observation of these atoms. The world of *physical* nature is, then, a machine. But matter, originally, is dead, inert, passive; and therefore it must be given its original impetus and order by some active agent. This original agent is God, and without this wise and powerful creator the system of the world could not have existed. It is evident, then, that Newton did not conceive of the cause of the world as ultimately mechanical—that is, as completely reducible to matter in motion. He was a dualist.

Unlike God, human beings are not able to know the "inward nature" of the objects in the world.[35] Newton accepted the distinction between primary and secondary qualities which implies that since we perceive only sensations of things, we are restricted from any immediate contact with the outside world. In common with the empiricists of the day, he believed that the motions and characteristics of bodies are transmitted to the human mind through nerves or "animal spirits." In this belief, and that of atomism, Newton was in agreement with Locke, Boyle, and the Cambridge Platonists. It is the conception of the world machine, first born with Democritus, and come of age with Galileo, Copernicus, and Newton.

[33] *Opera Omnia*, IV, 260. *Mathematical Principles*, p. 399.
[34] *Opera Omnia*, IV, 258.   [35] *Ibid.*, pp. 238, 262–263.

It is this mechanical conception of the "system of the world," of course, that is fundamental to Newton's theology. It forms the basic analogy by means of which he is able to infer a mechanic-geometrician-contriver, for, like human artifacts and machines, the world machine must have a contriver. The world machine, a machine because it functions in processes embodying forces which are geometrically describable in terms of the mechanical principles of causality and the laws of motion, demands a machinist. It is no different with regard to living organisms, for the study of optics and medicine and anatomy exhibit the wonderful contrivance and purposive arrangement of parts and organs for seeing, hearing, speaking, etc., and by analogy to human purposive activities, always initiated by a mind, there must be a contriver who created this arrangement for such purposes.

Methodological considerations are also of fundamental importance. Most of the natural theologians of this period thought that the analogical argument to God's existence was scientific—a posteriori—based upon observation and experiment. We have seen that Newton believed his theology to be a posteriori. Basically, "a posteriori" at this time meant argument from effects, the effects being something in the observed world order. Also, the argument is held to be probable or conjectural in conclusion —that is, it does not afford certainty. I am sure that few if any of the thinkers up to Hume, with the possible exceptions of Berkeley and Butler, understood the ramifications of this problem. Be that as it may, Newton's theology involves inference from perceptual appearances, from phenomena, and this was a basic mode of influence of science upon theology. Indeed, "natural" as distinct from "revealed" theology means essentially that natural theology tends to exclude the mystical aspects of Christian belief, that religion is to be based upon the deductive and empirical avenues to knowledge, that in this way theology is analogous to science, and therefore is rationally respectable. The modern tendency to make observation and experiment fundamental to the acquisition of knowledge had begun with Francis Bacon, but it is in Newton that there came to be the complete fruition of what we have come to call the experimental method: the conscious use of controlled observation in combination with precise measurement. It is certainly not unusual that the followers of Newton, and other educated people of the day who were at pains to keep up with advances in science, should seek to apply such methodological ideas to such other fields as theology. Therefore, it is of interest to understand in what sense Newton considered his methods to be empirical, and how such methods were related to theology. Another reason for a full understanding of these methodological considerations lies in the fact that it is on the level of their logic that Hume directs his most conclusive attack against the design arguments.

In Newton's conception of methodology, sensory observation played an important role, not to be confused with naive gaping. First, he believed that our ideas concerning nature must be derived from observation—*controlled* observation of phenomena. Formulated in terms of measurement, and stated as descriptive propositions or hypotheses, they must in turn be verified by experiment and observation. In the case of contradiction between two such propositions, or when the validity of one is doubted, an *experimentum crucis* is effected. Further, and still on an empirical plane, such scientific statements are held to be probable and continuously subject to change or modification when such is warranted by the development of new experimental evidence. These views are clearly expressed in the *Principia*, at the beginning of Book Three. The rule of parsimony, the rule that the same causes have the same effects (the principle of the uniformity of nature), the rule that we can generalize from samples, the rule that we must in experimental philosophy accept what induction tells us until experimental evidence shows otherwise, hypotheses notwithstanding; all these are important methodological considerations and show the significance of observation and experiment in Newton's method. Propositions about nature must be derived from observation and experiment, and verified by observation and experiment. "We no other way know the extention of bodies than by our senses," and similarly with hardness, impenetrability, and inertia (Rule IV, explanation). This experimental source of our knowledge of nature is the fundamental tenet of Newton's scientific method, and he returns to the subject often.[36]

It is clear that he thought the results of scientific procedures to be probable. Such is the contention in Rule IV, just mentioned, and in the *Optics* he argues that inference from experiments and observations by induction is not demonstration of general conclusions—that it does not afford certainty. "And although the arguing from experiments and observations by induction be no demonstration of general conclusions; yet it is the best way of arguing which the nature of things admits. . . ."[37]

This summary of Newton's beliefs concerning the nature of scientific method makes evident, I think, that in his science he was a thorough

[36] *Ibid.*, pp. 263–264.
[37] *Ibid.*, p. 263.

empiricist. Some writers, such as Burtt,[38] have held that Newton's rejection of what he called "hypotheses" constitutes an anti-empirical element in his thought. This interpretation simply represents a verbal confusion. The term "hypothesis" in the *General Scholium* and in the *Optics* refers not to scientific theories derived from observation and subject to empirical verification.[39] It refers to metaphysical explanations and assumptions not subject to empirical verification or empirical source. Newton's quarrels with Hook and Pardies and others whose criticisms of his ideas were based upon metaphysical assumptions invited Newton's comment that such assumptions were "dreams and vain fictions of our own divining."[40] Thus his polemic was not directed at empirical hypotheses which serve as guides to experiments, but at a priori speculations. It would bear noting, I think, that we are here dealing with Newton's scientific ideas, not his theological ideas. "Theory," "query," "explanation," are the terms Newton uses for hypotheses in the methodological sense of explanatory ideas drawn from observation of phenomena. At one place he uses the term "hypothesis" in its modern context—that is, for working explanations of the relationships among events in nature. "For hypotheses should be subservient only in explaining the properties, but not assumed in determining them, unless so far as they may furnish experiments."[41]

We have so far in our discussion slighted the mathematical element in Newton's science, an element of singular importance. Newton was extraordinarily adept at both ingenuity of experiment and observation and at mathematical invention and demonstration. With respect to the latter, he would undoubtedly deserve a great place in the history of thought on the basis of his mathematical discoveries alone, which include a version of the infinitesimal calculus. His view of nature is that its structure and processes are amenable to mathematical treatment.[42] This belief was behind his rules for reasoning in philosophy, where the assumptions of periodicity and simplicity and uniformity of nature denote properties of the world which make it amenable to mathematical treatment. For Newton mathematics is the art of measuring.[43] The measurements of natural events (quantity and properties), stated in terms of mathematical formulae,

[38] Burtt, *The Metaphysical Foundations of Modern Physical Science*, pp. 222–225.
[39] E. W. Strong, "Newton's 'Mathematical Way,'" *Journal of the History of Ideas*, XII (January, 1951), 90–110.
[40] *Mathematical Principles*, pp. 398–400.
[41] *Philosophical Transactions*, III, 740.
[42] Strong, "Newton's 'Mathematical Way,'" *passim*.
[43] *Mathematical Principles*, p. xvii.

make up what he and his followers called "mechanical principles," and from these mathematical-mechanical statements one may deduce other occurrences in nature. Such deductions are often of the nature of predictions.[44] In summary, Newton was concerned with construing the processes in mathematical terms, and these constructions constitute what he called mechanical principles such as the law of gravity and its constituent laws of motion, which, as we have seen, in turn form the basis of his theological ideas. Thus, "mechanical principles" are propositions describing nature, formulated in mathematical terms.[45]

We may summarize Newton's methodological ideas in the following way. Scientific endeavor begins with sensory observations, and from them certain propositions are rendered general by induction. This is his referent when he speaks of "deducing" or "inferring" from phenomena. Second, these propositions are further generalized and made into universal statements by the principle of induction. Such are the laws of motion and the theorems of his *Optics*. When such inductive propositions are formulated in mathematical terms, they become "mechanical principles." By means of these principles, it is possible to deduce other phenomena, such as the motions of the planets, and if such demonstrations are verified by observation and experiment, then they are held to be true. If such verifications are not forthcoming, then the principles must either be discarded or modified. No mechanical or physical principles—that is, principles purporting to describe the world of nature—are deducible from purely mathematical principles. It should be mentioned that Newton was, of course, interested in mathematics for its own sake.[46]

Newton's mathematical ideas were of considerable importance to his theology. As we have seen, he stated that God must be a geometer.[47] If the physical phenomena of the world are characterized by mathematical-physical principles, and God instituted these principles, then God must be a geometer-mathematician. Further, the mathematical formulations of the orbits and motions of celestial bodies with respect to their mechanical system express basic characteristics of the world order which enabled Newton to argue to an orderer—that is, enabled him to characterize the

---

[44] Strong, "Newton's 'Mathematical Way,'" pp. 94 ff.

[45] *Mathematical Principles*, p. xvii.

[46] Strong, "Newton's 'Mathematical Way,'" p. 96.

[47] For the problem of the separation of science and theology in Newton's theories see the following articles by E. W. Strong: "Newton and God" and "Hypotheses Non Fingo," in *Men and Moments in the History of Science*, ed. Herbert M. Evans (Seattle: University of Washington Press, 1959), pp. 162–176.

world as a machine. It is this factor which, more than any other, distinguishes Newton's contribution to the design argument from those of earlier thinkers, and it is this factor that led Newton to say that God is a geometer. As we take up the thinkers who followed Newton, we will discover that some of them, notably Clarke, Craige, and Cheyne, attempted to employ the mathematical method in order to found an a priori theology. For the most part, however, they followed the new science and attempted to incorporate a posteriori principles into their reflections. The latter, as we have seen, was Newton's way.

It appears to me that Newton's theological efforts were essentially logical in intent. Although he often expressed himself in terms which exhibit considerable emotional involvement, a property scarcely ever absent from religious disquisitions, particularly in that awareness of the "most beautiful system" and its awesome immensity and complexity, nevertheless Newton belongs to those theologians who are concerned with formulating a logical argument, with the logical and evidential possibilities of the design argument. The style of the logical clothing is, of course, the style of the Age of Reason—scientific style. The coat is mathematical and the pants empirical. The underwear is religious and old-fashioned. That Newton was the fashion designer and leader is a point at which we shall now labor. His lead, that of the greatest scientist of the age, perhaps of any age, was followed by most of the educated people of the day, not only in England but across the Channel and throughout the continent of Europe. They rejoiced that science, far from being the source of atheism it often appeared to be in some quarters, was a positive source of arguments in support of religion.

Two directions of interest appear to follow this analysis of Newton's beliefs. One is the influence which Newton exerted upon his colleagues and contemporaries, a development which leads finally to a sustained attack by the arch-skeptic, Hume. Another is the historical development of design theology, a process culminating in Newtonian theism. In this I assume, hypothetically, of course, that the general notion of the design argument did not originate in Newton but was found by him after a long and ancient tradition to which he was exposed. The first problem is to analyze Newton's influence upon his contemporaries and their formulations of the design argument. Ancient and medieval formulations will be explored in Part Two.

CHAPTER 2

Other Contemporary Scientists

Newton's distinguished work will be the safest protection
against the attacks of atheists, and nowhere more surely
than from this quiver can one draw forth missiles against
the band of godless men.
—ROGER COTES, Preface, *Principia*, Second Edition

Some of the men whose ideas we will now consider were Newton's
disciples, some were not; some produced their theology before Newton
produced his, and it will be of interest to note how they disagree with him.
In our discussion we shall deal with scientists of almost every sort and
persuasion. Boyle, for instance, was a chemist. Barrow, Newton's teacher,
was a mathematician. Keill, Cotes, Whiston, Pemberton, and Craige were
mathematicians. Ray was a distinguished botanist. Derham was an able
astronomer. Halley, of course, is as famous in the history of thought as the
comet which bears his name. Clarke, while known primarily as a meta-
physician, was also a mathematician, and his editorship of Newton's *Optics*
and of Rohault's work on physics exhibit his scientific activities. The
extrascientific works of these men and of numerous others like them present
a sort of intellectual theme with variations, the theme being science and
theology, with variations upon the subject relative to the differences in the
capacities and interests of the performers. In their books these thinkers
constantly refer to one another as suggesters of ideas, as friends, and of
course they quibble among themselves over their manifold theories. A
reading of the first fifty years of the *Philosophical Transactions* of the Royal
Society of London indicates that these men were of considerable importance in the development of the new astronomical, mechanical,
biological, and mathematical sciences. The fact that they are practically
unknown today except to treatises of this sort is no argument to the contrary, for our knowledge of past thinkers is clouded by time, bringing with
it different interests and different perspectives. We know the great ones—
the Newtons and the Galileos—and we know them in terms of our own

age. We understand those whose ideas are most like ours. When the ideas are not like ours, we tend not only to misunderstand their authors but to show them undeserved disrespect also. Thus, the lesser figures of an age are often ignored, even when their work is of contributory significance. This can be likened to viewing only the major peaks of a mountain range. Here we will investigate the lesser outcroppings.

As a result of their theological ideas, the works of many of these men have often been cast onto the scrap heap of intellectual history, and discussed only as productions of intellectual oddity by fools who prove only the fact that scientists can be childish in other respects. Leslie Stephen and others have criticized Newton's works in chronology, in textual criticism, and in theology. They have snickered at Ray and Derham because of their attempts to give a rational interpretation of Genesis. While comprehending the importance of early modern science because of its obvious place in the chain of scientific development, they have ridiculed the attempts on the part of scientists responsible for this progress to apply these ideas in the field of theology. As a consequence, the thought of an important group of men—affording excellent examples of the ways new ideas influence and modify earlier ideas—has been neglected. If such writers were merely showing the development of our accepted and valued ideas, such interpretations would be permissible. But if they are meaning to give an objective and undistorted view of the history of thought (and they seldom declare that they are not), then they are in error. And the error, once we approach the materials with less bias, is evident. It is the reverse side of the retrospective fallacy. These writers have gone into the study of the seventeenth and eighteenth centuries armed with the mighty sword of truth, sense, and significance and have resolutely sliced away as stupid any ideas not acceptable to modern thought. Paradoxically enough, to some extent this is what the theologians they criticize were doing! All of these men represent, for their time, a radical attempt at the modernization of religious thought.

To be sure, the activities of Whiston, Ray, Derham, Cheyne, and others, in attempting a scientific explanation of the world based upon the history and chronology of the Old Testament, appear to us to be absurd. It is easily forgotten that we go to the materials of history with a background of paleontology and anthropology, philology, comparative religion, and philosophy that these men had not at their disposal. If we condemn Newton, Boyle, and other scientists for their use of the design argument, we must also condemn practically every other major thinker of the day. If we condemn Newton, Boyle, and others for doing chronology, we must also condemn Locke and the Cambridge Platonists. If we condemn Ray, Whiston, Derham, and Cheyne for discussing the scientific explanation of the origin of the world in the light of prevailing science, we must on the same grounds condemn Leibniz and most modern physicists. Leibniz was in the vanguard of those who damned Newton's *scientific* treatises for not comprehending God.

No discussion of the Age of Reason, of course, can omit a contemporary of Newton, Robert Boyle, who reflects the general influence of science before Newton's great synthesis. Closely aligned with the Baconian school of experimentalists, he came, after some hesitation,[1] to accept the corpuscular and mechanistic theories of nature. He was learned in alchemy and medicine, penned light literary essays,[2] and wrote voluminously on theology. He is of particular interest to us because his work yields an interpretation which might be called a "pre-Newtonian" scientific attitude toward theology. In other words, Boyle provides an excellent foil for displaying some of the developments in theology brought about by Newton and his followers.

Pursuing the lead of the experimentalists, Boyle rejected the scholastic notion of substantial forms and based his scientific theories, in particular those concerning chemistry, on the theory that the properties and qualities of bodies can be explained in terms of matter, motion, and rest. He accepted, then, the mechanistic-materialistic hypothesis of Newton and Galileo—nature is explainable in terms of "mechanical principles" and the "corpuscular hypothesis." Like Newton, however, he rejected a complete materialism. He refused, for example, to give up the category of final causes, or purpose, in the investigation of nature, and this refusal was at least partially dictated by nonscientific considerations, i.e., theology. It is his contention that purposes form the best source of arguments for belief in the existence and attributes of God. Science, of course, furnishes such arguments. It goes without saying that Boyle was extremely religious. It is said that he always solemnly hesitated before pronouncing the word "God." Further, he clearly believed theology to be a subject superior to that of science.[3]

[1] Herbert Butterfield, *The Origins of Modern Science: 1300–1800* (New York: Macmillan Company, 1951), p. 99.

[2] Robert Boyle, *Occasional Reflections upon Several Subjects* (London, 1865).

[3] Robert Boyle, *The Excellency of Theology, Compar'd with Natural Philosophy, and, Some Occasional Thoughts about the Excellency and Grounds of the Mechanical Hypothesis* (London, 1764), Preface.

It is, therefore, through final causes that Boyle makes his basic theological appeal. He inquires into the uses of things in order not only to benefit from the increased knowledge they afford but also in order to thank their creator.[4] It should be remembered, I think, that although he disagreed with Gassendi, Descartes, and other scientists about final causation as a scientific category, he did not neglect efficient causes. But to return to teleology, he differentiated four classes of purposes. There are those of a universal order—God's purposes. There are cosmic purposes—those which relate things according to mechanical laws; there are the means-ends relations within and among animals and plants; and, lastly, there are human purposes.[5] It is clear that Boyle looked upon cosmic, plant, and animal purposes as subsidiary purposes of God. Man, apparently, exhibits both sorts in that his body is made up of parts and organs which are connected so as to perform certain kinds of operations and in that, like other organisms, he has instincts. Insofar as he consciously wills to act in one way or another, and thus *intends* certain ends or goals, he may or may not be acting in accordance with God's purposes (God's intentions). Be that as it may, Boyle tends to follow the times in interpreting all of these sorts of purposes except those of God's intentions in mechanical terms. Therefore, the universe, the planets and their motions, the earth, animals, men, and the parts and organs thereof, are all *engines* functioning in accordance with certain purposes.[6] Mechanical causes are God's ways of making the world go 'round; but, and this is a very important exception, the initial cause of things, God himself, is neither mechanical nor material. Descartes' problem of the material and the mental is here repeated, of course, but to my knowledge neither Newton nor Boyle believed them to come together in God's pineal gland.

And so we see the major difference between Newton and Boyle in matters theological. The importance of Newton's world-synthesis, his mathematical formulation of mechanical principles (Boyle was no mathematician), makes the difference. Therefore, while Boyle had much in common with Newton, and we should mention that he agreed with Newton in the Platonistic idea that space and time constitute the "sensorium of God,"[7] he nevertheless represents in the. main a pre-Newtonian theology little different from that of the Stoics. He accepted early modern mechanical science, and he accepted in the main its corpuscular metaphysics. But he

[4] Robert Boyle, *A Disquisition about the Final Causes of Natural Things* (London, 1688), Preface, and p. 157.

[5] *Ibid.*, pp. 6–9, *passim.*

[6] *Ibid.*, p. 17.

[7] *Ibid.*, p. 91.

missed its most striking application to the theology he so loved. And why is this? Because it is difficult to discover the "uses" of the planets and stars![8]

Just as Boyle did not place the same emphasis upon the mechanical-mathematical aspects of order as did Newton, other thinkers deviated, consciously or unconsciously, from Newton's views as to the a posteriori and probable character of the design argument. It is no wonder, for if the conclusion of this argument shows that it is merely probable that an intelligent, beneficent, all-powerful God exists, then the argument affords much less in the way of support for religion than most theologians and preachers would desire. However, this does not appear to be the main cause for these differences of opinion. It is particularly in those who were impressed with the mathematical element in Newton's philosophy that we see a priorism develop. As in the instance of Descartes, these men find inspiration in the apparent certainty of mathematical thought. The inspiration is still very much that of the new science, and is still Newtonian in source, but there is a shift in emphasis. We have seen that Newton himself never wavered in his belief in the need for empirical grounding and verification of his mathematical-mechanical principles of nature. But the fact that his great progress in science was in part, indeed in great part, made possible by discoveries in mathematics, and the further fact that he developed his scientific treatises in mathematical form, were not without consequences. The well-balanced methodology of Newton, which gave mathematics and experiment their due importance, was not consistently understood by some of his followers, hence they were led to frame theories which placed an exclusive emphasis upon either one or the other facet of his thought. Two such thinkers were Samuel Clarke and George Cheyne.

Samuel Clarke, regarded by his contemporaries as the greatest British philosopher after the death of John Locke, was a mathematical rationalist. Nevertheless, he was, in his own consideration, a Newtonian. He was a leader in the circle of intellectuals around Queen Caroline;[9] he was involved in the famous correspondence with Butler,[10] who rejected his a priori methods in philosophy. He was acquainted with the turbulent Whiston,[11] friend of Newton. He translated Newton's *Optics*, which so delighted the old scientist that he gave Clarke a gift of five hundred pounds, one hundred

[8] *Ibid.*, pp. 33–34, 77–78.

[9] E. C. Mossner, *Bishop Butler and the Age of Reason* (New York: Macmillan Company, 1936), p. 4.

[10] *Ibid.*, p. 1.

[11] Whiston, *Mescellanis: Historical Memoirs*, pp. 12–13.

for each of Clarke's children. Clarke was also in part responsible for bringing Newton's science into Cambridge,[12] and he defended Newton's thought against the criticisms of Leibniz.[13]

His metaphysics, based upon a universal mathematics, divided reality into two areas—the material and the spiritual. There is a hierarchy of spirits from the divine to the human, and all other properties of the world are modifications of spirit resulting from the interactions of matter and spirit. Reason is the method of knowing the invariable relations between these ultimate elements,[14] and sense experience is relegated to a secondary position, as it was in Plato, because it presents only variable and transient unrealities.[15] In *A Discourse Concerning the Being and Attributes of God* (Boyle Lectures, 1704-1705) he states in the preface that his method is to be as close to the mathematical as possible; hence it is no surprise to discover that his criterion of truth is a priori—the principle of non-contradiction. When Whiston criticized him for holding a rigid and nonscientific view, Clarke replied that he was only using in favor of religion the method that Hobbes and Spinoza had used against it.[16]

Now although it seems clear to the modern philosopher that this kind of thought is dissimilar to that of Newton, Clarke did not think so. At least he thought it grounded in Newton's theories, believing that religion and theology had their most important support and source in the new science.[17] Clarke did not altogether ignore the a posteriori form of the design argument; indeed, he used it and characterized it as a posteriori.[18] Nevertheless, he was convinced that the a priori method is a superior method for proofs of God's existence, and he therefore limited the design argument to the proof of God's intelligence. Further, he dwelt upon the purposive nature of the world order, and thus placed most force upon the argument *to* design. Finally, he believed that theology provides the basis of science.[19] For the rest he agreed with Newton, making the point that a sheer mechanical materialism provides no explanation of the order and symmetry

[12] Brewster, *Memoirs of Sir Isaac Newton*, p. 333.

[13] Samuel Clarke, *Collection of Papers Which Passed Between the Late Learned Mr. Leibniz and Dr. Clarke* (London, 1717).

[14] Stephen, *A History of English Thought in the 18th Century*, II, 5-6.

[15] *Ibid.*

[16] Whiston, *Mescellanis: Historical Memoirs*, pp. 6-7.

[17] Clarke, *Collection of Papers*, p. v.

[18] *Ibid.*, p. 51.

[19] Samuel Clarke, *A Discourse Concerning the Being and Attributes of God* (Boyle Lectures, 1704-1705) (8th ed.; London, 1732), pp. 11 ff.

of the universe; and he infered that, since matter is dead, its present order can only be explained in terms of an intelligent agent.

Cheyne's theories are a conglomeration of all the sciences of the age. Constantly referring to Newton, Keill, Halley and other astronomers and mathematicians, to Derham, Ray and other biologists, botanists, and geologists, and to Boyle the chemist, he runs the gamut of their ideas in order to glean from them material for theological purposes. He was something of a mathematician, although professionally he was a physician of the "iatrophysicist" school of medicine, which was quite popular in his day. His argument is a prioristic, though in a manner somewhat different from that of Clarke.

By nature, I understand this vast, if not infinite Machin [sic] of the universe, the perfect and wise production of almighty God, consisting of an infinite number of lesser Machins, every one of which is adjusted by weight and measure. By the laws of nature, I mean, those Laws of Motion, by which natural bodies are commonly govern'd in all their Actions upon one another, and which they inviolably observe in all the changes that happen in the natural state of things.[20]

This is the analogy of the world machine in explicit form; and Cheyne marks, on pages five and six of this same work, it as analogical argument— "The noble art of just analogy" is the most important kind of metaphysical thought. "Thus this great Machin of the Universe has a Resemblance to the lesser one of a human creature, for, as in the last, the vital functions are performed by general and constant laws." Holding to the view that mechanical principles are not sufficient for the explanation of the world order, in particular because matter is dead, he follows Newton in the thought that God is needed in order to keep the world from getting into disrepair and for putting it back into shape when it does. Note the explicit use of legislative terms such as "govern'd" and "inviolably observe," which shows how most of these thinkers confused prescriptive moral and legal law with descriptive scientific law. It is almost as if natural objects choose. These opinions, as should be clear by now, are common to almost all seventeenth- and eighteenth-century theists. It is almost as if one pushed a button and they clicked away, each saying very much the same thing, a habit which, unfortunately, did not end with the Enlightenment.

From here on, however, Cheyne plunges more deeply into metaphysics

[20] George Cheyne, *Philosophical Principles of Religion: Natural and Revealed* (London, 1715), p. 2.

of a highly speculative order. He maintains that principles of attraction and repulsion explain all reality; he contends that analogical argument gives mathematical certitude; he believes in a microcosm-macrocosm theory of eternal forms and exemplars (again the pervasive Cambridge Platonism); and he accepts the view that space and time are the sensorium of God.[21] His thought is a mathematical logomachy largely foreign to the ideas of Newton.

In the work of John Craige, a mathematician, we find an attempt to reduce the probabilities of the external evidences of Christianity (prophecy and miracles) to geometrical form. His *Theologiciae Christinae Principia Mathematica* applies Newton's law of inverse squares to the analysis of textual evidence, and proclaims that by the year 3150 all evidence of Christ will have disappeared.[22] Such computative activities were extremely common in this period. Other men were writing political, geographic, and economic arithmetics.[23] This is simply the normal procedure of milking methodological principles and techniques for all they are worth and a good deal more.

Only a few of Newton's followers, however, went in the extreme a priori direction. Whiston, Ray, Derham, Keill, Maclaurin, Desagauliers, 's Gravesande, Pemberton, all considered theology to be based upon a posteriori arguments. Moreover, not all of their theological efforts were directed towards proofs for the existence and attributes of God, for, as mentioned earlier, some of them dealt extensively with scientific interpretations of the scriptures. Some attempted to explain the origin as well as the destruction of the world according to Genesis in terms of scientific principles. These attempts, with all the attendant problems, such as the creation of the world in seven days, the deluge, the nature of the construction of the world, resulted in a set of theories which reflect the remarkable degree to which scientific discoveries can spread throughout the texture of thought. Cosmological speculations of this type began to attract attention in the 1690's, and retained their popularity for half a century or more.

Two important men in this tradition were Thomas Burnet and John Ray. Burnet was a physician and mathematician, and Ray was an eminent

[21] *Ibid.*, Pt. 2, p. 45.

[22] Mossner, *Bishop Butler and the Age of Reason*, pp. 66–67.

[23] G. N. Clarke, *Science and Social Welfare in the Age of Reason* (2d ed.; Oxford: Clarendon Press, 1949), pp. 131–135. See also Butterfield, *The Origins of Science*, pp. 48, 57–58, 64–67, 80–81, 87, 134.

botanist. Ray was a close friend of Isaac Barrow, Newton's teacher. Both were well versed in all the new sciences of the day. Ray's *Three Physico-Theological Discourses* was published in 1693.[24] Therein, in addition to theories concerning the "primitive chaos," the "deluge," and the "creation," as well as the "dissolution of the world and future conflagration," he makes extensive use of the design argument. In this connection he supports his opinions with the principle of gravity and the idea of mechanical principles in general. He does not, to my knowledge, mention Newton; but, since he was a member of the Royal Society of London and refers repeatedly to its *Transactions*, it is likely that he knew of Newton's work and that of other natural philosophers. The primary sources of his thought lay in geology, biology, and botany, and since these interests dictated the kind of design argument in which he was interested, it is to be expected that the argument *to* design would predominate in his work. Other writers, such as Woodward, Hakewell, Robinson, to say nothing of Boyle and the Stoics, had worked this kind of argument over in detail. In his book *The Wisdom of God Manifested in the Works of the Creation* (1701), Ray follows this tradition, presenting the teleological argument to design in multifarious ways in which celestial and terrestrial means-ends relationships are emphasized. He begins by acknowledging his debt to More and Cudworth, and quotes from Cicero's *De Natura Deorum*. Philosophically and theologically he adds little to the views of the Cambridge Platonists. He accepts their logos doctrine and their notion of an immaterial plastic nature. Final causes, purposes, contrivances, often explicated in mechanical terms, are his forte. Even the world machine is treated in this fashion. Every man to his last, and Ray's biological last directed his attention to purposive relationships.

Burnet was one of the most famous writers of the period. In his *Archaeologiae Philosophicae* (1692) he asked some embarrassing questions concerning the Bible: what language Adam spoke, whence came the needles for making aprons, etc.[25] But it was in his *Sacred Theory of the Earth* (1689) that he produced his cosmology. Accepting the machine analogy,[26] he formed his detailed view of the world in terms of it. The world is like a clock, a "great machine of the world, or of the earth," and the animals and other biological species which inhabit it are also placed in the mechanical category. It has to be kept in mind, however, that these

[24] John Ray, *Three Physico-Theological Discourses* (4th ed.; London, 1721), pp. 1–9.

[25] Mossner, *Bishop Butler and the Age of Reason*, pp. 57–58.

[26] Thomas Burnet, *Sacred Theory of the Earth* (Glasgow, 1735), I, 35–36.

men were not complete mechanists; hence, although animals and plants are viewed mechanically, they are not *mere* automata, as they were with the Cartesians.

In terms of this mechanical frame of reference, Burnet sought to explain the origin, the deluge, and the final conflagration of the world, a world which is formed by the divine art of geometry. His use of the design argument is expressly a posteriori—argument from observed effects.[27] Along with Newton he holds that the laws of motion and other natural laws do not sufficiently explain the origin and form of the world. One must go "upon supposition of an author of nature . . . an intelligent being. . . ."[28] His design arguments are almost identical with those later given by Bentley, upon the advice of Newton, and with those of Newton. It is likely that Newton had read Burnet's work. Both his *Telluris Theoria Sacra* and *Archaeologia Philosophica* appear in the de Villamil catalogue of Newton's library,[29] and it is known that they corresponded concerning the origin of the world.[30] Again, like Newton, Burnet produced the argument *to* design, but either emphasized the argument *from* design, or reduced the purposive element to the mechanical. Thus we see that Burnet's view is quite similar to that of Newton, both with respect to the system of the world and to the a posteriori character of the inference to God's existence. In the latter vein he carefully called his theories hypotheses. Whenever, in his theological works, Burnet found that scientific ideas conflicted with those of religion or theology, he usually chose the scientific alternative. He went far beyond Newton in his speculations concerning the cause of gravity and the origin and end of the world, but for all that, he realized the empirical basis of natural science and the hypothetical nature of his theology.

This is also true of William Whiston. He agreed with Burnet and Newton concerning the hypothetical nature of his theological and cosmological speculations, and at one place noted that this is because no scientific verification is possible in such inferences. Whiston's point of departure is mechanical science, particularly astronomy. It was his contention that the earth originated in the atmosphere of a comet;[31] its end, in turn, would come about through a collision with a comet. All natural philosophy, in his opinion, is empirical and a posteriori.[32]

---

[27] *Ibid.*, p. 312.   [28] *Ibid.*, p. 288.

[29] Robert de Villimil, *Newton: the Man* (London: G. D. Knox, 1931), p. 69.

[30] H. S. Thayer, *Newton's Philosophy of Nature* (New York: Hafner Publishing Company, 1953), p. 58.

[31] William Whiston, *A New Theory of the Earth* (London, 1696), pp. 73–78, 95, 185.

[32] *Ibid.*, p. 184.

A rather interesting character in his own right, Whiston spent his life, and was disgraced, in the attempt to propagate unreceived religious and theological ideas. On Newton's recommendation he was in 1701 elected to the Lucasian professorship of mathematics at Cambridge.[33] Together with Roger Cotes, he was instrumental in the development of Trinity College into a prominent school of science, and in bringing to Cambridge the most advanced scientific thought of the times.[34] Bentley approved of him as a scientist, as did Newton. Collins, a Deist,[35] believed Whiston to be a man of extraordinary mental parts in mathematics, philosophy, and theology.[36] In 1710, Whiston was dismissed from his professorship because of his unorthodox religious belief—Arianism[37]—which, in his opinion, was also held by Newton and Locke.[38] He was correct in this opinion.

In the *Astronomical Principles of Religion*[39] he spends the first part in a restatement of the scientific discoveries of Newton, his main object being to set up the necessity for a cause of gravity which is other than mechanical.[40] With Newton, he refused to consider the cause of gravity to be inherent in or essential to bodies. If the cause of motion and order could be imputed to gravity as its essence, or as one of the primary qualities of bodies, then of course the whole case for an unmechanical cause of the order and motion in the world would fall. Therefore, it was of extreme importance for his theology, as for that of all of these design theologians, to make clear the point that gravity is not an essential property of bodies. If it is so considered, then Occam's razor slices away any need for God! Gravity, then, is the power of a superior, intelligent being or agent.[41]

Whiston joins with Newton and the other writers we have considered in the view that science is incapable of explaining all the order and motion in the universe. The almost inevitable correlate of this view is the belief that matter is passive or dead. Since the world does exhibit order and motion, the inference is that the world process implies an active agent as its cause. Whiston stresses this argument with respect to anything not explained by science,[42] and expands the theological passages in the *Principia* and the *Optics* of Newton, including the argument that God's

[33] More, *Sir Isaac Newton: A Biography*, p. 488.
[34] Monk, *The Life of Richard Bentley*, I, 203.   [35] *Ibid.*, p. 32.
[36] Anthony Collins, *A Discourse of the Grounds and Reasons of the Christian Religion* (London, 1737), p. 237.
[37] Monk, *The Life of Richard Bentley*, I, 250.
[38] Whiston, *Mescellanis: Historical Memoirs*, pp. 7–8.
[39] London, 1717.   [40] *Ibid.*, pp. 45–46.   [41] *Ibid.*, p. 46.
[42] *Ibid.*, pp. 82–83.

providence is necessary for the repair of the failures in the workings of the world machine.[43] He presents the design argument in both its forms and separates them, spending one whole section on the "uses" of things, primarily in order to prove God's providential goodness.

I have already noted the explicit hypothetical and a posteriori character which he assigns to his theology. As an empiricist he contends that science is based upon observation and experiment,[44] and, like Burnet, maintains that religious and theological ideas must bear scientific analysis and criticism—they must in the end conform to scientific knowledge.[45] I take this to mean, not that they must be directly verifiable or proved with certainty, but that they must be consistent with scientific knowledge. It is plain that Whiston based his theology upon knowledge of nature, and that he considered scientific knowledge of nature to be the best kind. Here, then, we see that Whiston applied his scientific ideas to theology in the same two ways we found in Newton—as knowledge describing the order and system of the world and as a posteriori inference based upon observation.

He has come in for derision, like most of the other thinkers being discussed, for these theological speculations. J. M. Robertson holds that he "clogged the path of science."[46] Similar adverse comments come from Leslie Stephen and David Mossner. I have already said that I find these criticisms puzzling. In effect, the claim is that these men thought that they were doing science when they were doing theology, and that this in some sense interfered with the advance of science. In the first place, I think that I have shown that Whiston and Newton and some of the others did not confuse science and theology, either as to methodology or as to results. In the second place, it seems rather clear to me that the view that the new science could be put to use for theological purposes, for the furtherance of traditional religious beliefs, may well have made it much easier to get support for science and to introduce it into the universities. The opposition which kept Newtonian physics out of the universities came mainly from those who maintained Cartesianism, and not from theologians. Further, it is a matter of record that Whiston, for instance, was one of the men to first introduce, and to labor for, the new science. Finally, Whiston was disgraced exactly because *he did attempt* to modernize religious beliefs so

[43] *Ibid.*, p. 89.

[44] *Ibid.*, p. 100.

[45] *Ibid.*, p. 133.

[46] J. M. Robertson, *A History of Freethought* (London: Watts and Company, 1936), II, 753–754.

as to make them square with science. Writers who would scoff at any criticism of seventeenth-century generals based upon the fact that they did not use machine guns nevertheless level a similar charge against these early scientists. The assumption, apparently, is that they should have developed a completely modern sophistication in all areas of thought at the time that they were just beginning to develop sophistication in physics.

John Keill was an excellent mathematician, and, as a friend of Newton and other scientists of the day, took an active part in scientific developments. Among the men discussed, he stands almost alone in one respect. He noted that naturalistic and scientific explanations of miracles and other biblical events reduce the religious efficacy of such events. To show that miracles, the creation of the universe, and other events such as the deluge, are a result of natural causes is, in his view, to lessen the credibility of religion and the Bible.[47] For this reason Keill was critical of all those semi-scientific cosmologies treated above.[48] Herein lies a good example of the pathos of any age—the fact that new discoveries and techniques always make inroads upon established and cherished beliefs. Of course, most of the men being discussed were more than willing to give up those religious ideas which were mystical and traditional, so long as they were able to keep the kernel of Christian belief, the "natural" religion which tended more and more to lose its traditional Christian character and turn into ethics. I shall return to this subject in detail later.

There is no real dissension between Keill and the other thinkers discussed concerning the world order. They all agree, on the basis of the limitations of science as they understood it: that mechanical laws will not explain certain aspects of the world order. In this they were correct in the main. Following Newton and Whiston, and the Baconian tradition, Keill is quite explicit as to the experimental and observational ground of natural philosophy.[49] Keill supports the Newtonian claim that the most forceful theological arguments are those based on a posteriori inference from the world design made apparent by the discoveries of science.[50] Many others agreed. Roger Cotes, editor of the second edition of the *Principia*, and Henry Pemberton, editor of the third edition, emphasize the a posteriori

[47] John Keill, *An Examination of Dr. Burnet's Theology* (2d ed.; London, 1734), p. 108.
[48] *Ibid.*, pp. 18, 26.
[49] *Ibid.*, p. 18.
[50] John Keill, *An Introduction to the True Astronomy* (6th ed.; London, 1769), Preface.

character of the argument from design and its basis in the scientific system of the world.[51] Halley, the noted astronomer and the man who nagged Newton into publishing the *Principia*, held similar views.[52]

Colin Maclaurin is of special interest. Holding ideas on natural theology similar to those of other Newtonians, his wording of the design argument reappears in Hume's *Dialogues*. He was born in Scotland in 1698, and in 1709 he matriculated at the University of Glasgow. There he exhibited high proficiency in mathematics, and at the age of fifteen took his M.A. degree with a thesis on the power of gravity.[53] In 1717 he began teaching mathematics at the College of Aberdeen, and during the vacations of 1719 and 1721 he went to London, met Clarke and Newton, and became a member of the Royal Society. A little later Newton assisted him in obtaining the chair of mathematics at Edinburgh after the death of James Gregory, its famous occupant. Maclaurin was eminently successful as both teacher and scientist, and after Newton's death he was probably England's greatest mathematician.

In 1748, two years after Maclaurin's death, his *An Account of Sir Isaac Newton's Philosophical Discoveries* was published, a book which expounds and defends the theories of Newton.[54] In both the scientific and theological parts of it we find expressed the empirical point of view. Theology must be a posteriori, and the Newtonian design argument, with its basis in scientific knowledge and methods, fulfils this criterion.

> His existence and his attributes are, in a sensible manner, displayed to us in his works: but his essence is unfathomable. From our existence and that of other contingent beings around us, we conclude that there is a first cause, whose existence must be necessary, and independent of any other being; but it is only *a posteriori* that we thus infer the necessity of his existence, and not in the same manner that we ... deduce truth in geometry.[55]

Notice the connection of a posteriori and necessity in this statement. Whether he feels that certainty comes only with "deduced" argument is not clear. This poses a problem of interpretation to which we will return later, but a few remarks at this point would not, I think, be out of order.

---

[51] Henry Pemberton, *A View of Sir Isaac Newton's Philosophy* (London, 1728).

[52] Edmund Halley, *Miscellanea Curiosa* (3d ed.; London, 1726), I, 54.

[53] Colin Maclaurin, *An Account of Sir Isaac Newton's Philosophical Discoveries* (3d ed.; London, 1775), Preface.

[54] One has only to look at Robert Spearman's *An Enquiry After Philosophy and Theology* (Edinburgh, 1755), to see that Newton and his followers were under attack.

[55] Maclaurin, *An Account of Sir Isaac Newton's Philosophical Discoveries*, p. 405.

The one obvious meaning of "a posteriori" in this period, as in the Middle Ages, was "argument from effects to causes." The cosmological argument, which infers a first cause, identified with God, from some observed events or objects in experienced nature, is thus a posteriori. The argument postulates the principle of causality, and this principle is held to be *self-evidently true*. It was not until Hume that there is a serious questioning of this principle. (Although the Pyrrhonistic skeptics of ancient and early modern times, as we shall see, antedated Hume's arguments.) Now the combination of elements in this sort of argument is interesting. First, it proceeds from *experienced effects* and infers a *cause*; and in this sense it appears to be similar to scientific induction. Second, it makes use of a self-evident postulate, the principle of causality, and thus its conclusion is held to be *certain*. Such a way of looking at a posteriori arguments is now out of fashion since modern logicians and philosophers tend to regard the conclusions of any a posteriori argument as contingent and probable. Thus when a modern writer comes upon a statement such as that of Maclaurin above, where God's existence is held to be necessary and yet the argument proving his existence is held to be a posteriori, he tends to find the whole thing rather paradoxical. The only response to this feeling of paradox is that seventeenth- and eighteenth-century thinkers did not find it paradoxical. The conclusion therefore seems to be this: early modern thinkers divided a posteriori arguments into two poorly distinguished and somewhat confused classes—the first class being those arguments such as the cosmological argument for God's existence, which attain certainty although moving from effects to causes by self-evident steps. The second class covers those much less general inferences by induction which characterize the physical sciences, which are held to be hypothetical. Now two things should be remembered at this point. One, that many of the Newtonians held the design argument to be probable and hypothetical—Whiston and Keill, for instance. Two, that the design argument, since it infers from experienced effects in the world (order and design) to a designer-cause, is a species of the cosmological argument. Therefore, the ambivalent view of a posteriori arguments with respect to their probability or certainty characterizes a good deal of the theological argument of the times. The kind of argument excluded is a priori argument characterized by deductive truth in geometry, which is referred to in the above statement from Maclaurin. This sort of argument, remember, was used by Descartes, referred to in John Locke, used by Clarke, and harks back to Anselm.

It is therefore unclear, to me at least, whether or not Maclaurin thinks that the design argument is probable or certain. By *necessity* he may be referring merely to the belief that God, being the first cause, was not himself an *effect*—that is, that he was self-caused. One thing is quite clear, however, and that is the fact that Maclaurin thinks the design argument is based upon scientific discoveries which show the exquisite order and structure of the world.[56] Wisdom and intelligence are seen, according to Maclaurin, in "the motion of the greatest and subtlest parts." The main argument comes in the following:

> The plain argument for the existence of the Deity, obvious to all and carrying irresistible conviction with it, is from the evident contrivance and fitness of things for one-another, which we find throughout the universe. There is no need of nice or subtle reasonings in the matter; a manifest contrivance suggests a contriver. It strikes us like a sensation; and artful reasonings against it may puzzle us, but it is without shaking our belief. No person, for example, that knows the principles of optics and the structure of the eye, can believe that it was formed without skill in that science; or that male and female in animals were not formed without skill in that science; or that male and female in animals were not formed for each other, and for continuing the species.[57]

This argument follows closely the Newtonian development of the teleological argument *to* design, and yet it is couched in mechanistic terms: "contrivance" and "optics." Actually, since the purposive relationships are interpreted in mechanical terms, we have the argument *from* design. With Newton, Maclaurin utilizes science for the design argument in reasoning from the order and contrivance displayed in scientific laws of nature, and in reliance upon a posteriori inference. It is this argument that Cleanthes enunciates in Hume's *Dialogues*. I shall return to this point in Part Three.

[56] *Ibid.*, p. 4.
[57] *Ibid.*, p. 400.

CHAPTER 3

Philosophers and Theologians

That there is a God, and what that God is, nothing can
discover to us, nor judge in us, but natural reason.
—LOCKE, quoted in King, *Life of Locke*

So far it has been shown that the design argument was accepted by
Newton's scientist contemporaries and followers. I should like now to
show the extent to which other thinkers, who were not scientists but
philosophers and theologians, exemplify these as well as other interests.
Of course, their emphases vary with their occupations. Yet even these
nonscientists agree with Newton in the use of design theology. I have
divided the study into two parts. The first deals with the philosophers
proper, i.e., thinkers such as Bacon and Locke, who treated theological
considerations as part of a general philosophy. The second considers
theologians, i.e., thinkers such as Browne and Bentley, whose principal re-
flective activity was theological. These divisions are somewhat arbitrary and
heuristic because in the seventeenth and eighteenth centuries the relatively
clear-cut separation of occupations which we find today did not exist.

On the threshold of modern science and philosophy Francis Bacon
believed that even those things that are new must be understood by
comparison with the old, and thus analogy comes into play whenever we
seek to explain and understand some heretofore unknown event.[1] Among
his "prerogative instances" he lists in Number Six a view which reverts
to the Stoic concept of analogy, and beyond this to Aristotle's "example."
It is what he called "conformable or proportionate instances," "which we
are also wont to call physical parallels, or resemblances."[2] In this kind of
thinking, according to Bacon, inferences from object to object are based
upon likeness. Such inference lends itself to the formulation of new
hypotheses, a process which leads on to new discoveries, and is therefore

[1] Francis Bacon, *Novum Organum*, tr. G. W. Kitchin (Oxford, 1855), Book I,
Aphorism 34; Book II, Aphorisms 27, 42.
[2] *Ibid.*

quite useful. Bacon gets somewhat near to Hume in his insistence upon verification of hypotheses suggested by analogy. Such reasonings, thus, do not give us the surety in the form of "axioms," which for Bacon meant general scientific laws of nature verified by experiment. "Prerogative instances" are for Bacon methods or supports for induction, and those based upon analogy must in his opinion be carefully considered.[3] Analogies must, he cautions, relate to real and substantial resemblances, and not those which are casual and superficial, or superstitious and curious. He also mentioned analogy as a means of inferences where our senses fail us entirely.[4] We will see this function of analogy cited in almost all of our subjects, ancient and modern.

In Bacon's conception of analogy, therefore, we draw near to the modern view. Basing his ideas mainly on those of the Stoics, he broke away from Scholastic logic with its view that all reasoning is syllogistic. Despite a number of limitations and confusions, he was extremely influential in propagandizing inductive thinking with its appeal to observation and experiment. Insofar as he believed in and wrote about analogy in terms of its methodological usefulness, he probably furthered its acceptance by later thinkers, who looked upon him as a sort of scientific godfather.

Although Bacon was not preoccupied with the design argument, he accepted it, along with natural theology. In *Advancement of Learning* he makes clear such a commitment:

> For as the power and skill of a workman are seen in his work, but not his person, so the works of God express the wisdom and omnipotence of the creator. . . .[5]

Bacon seems not to have linked analogy with the design argument. But he does believe that science exhibits, in its comprehension of nature, the wisdom and intelligence of God. Carefully separating sacred from natural theology, Bacon did not link science with the former.

There is no need to spend space enumerating John Locke's theories and extolling their significance in the history of thought. Here I am interested in his theology and how science affected it. I am also interested in his use of certain terms which I take as the basis for a discussion of the ambiguity and vagueness of certain religious and theological concepts in the eighteenth century. Pursuant to these purposes, I shall begin with his theological beliefs.

---

[3] *Ibid.*   [4] *Ibid.*, Book II, Aphorism 21.
[5] Francis Bacon, *Advancement of Learning* (New York: American Home Library Company, 1902), p. 142.

In treatments of Locke's theology it is sometimes not realized that he used the design argument. In the *First Treatise on Civil Government*, however, we find him appealing to the mechanical structure of the eye: ". . . the structure of that one part is sufficient to convince us of an all-wise contriver, and he has so visible a claim to us in His workmanship that one of the ordinary appellations of God in Scripture is 'God our maker'. . . ." [6] This, of course, is an elementary statement of the argument from design, wherein the order and functional means-ends relations of the parts of an organism are looked upon as mechanical properties. A similar view is expounded in the *Essay*, where Locke says, "For the visible marks of extraordinary wisdom and power appear in all the works of creation, that a rational creature, who will but reflect on them, cannot miss the discovery of a Deity." [7] Locke, then, is substantially in agreement with Newton and other design theologians, and, as we shall see, with the Cambridge Platonists. This is of interest for two reasons, one of them not at all obvious. First, there is the fact that Locke's main theological argument in the *Essay* is cosmological in character, and is held to be a posteriori but *certain*. It is a posteriori because it deduces its conclusion from premises, one of which is an effect—the intuition of self-existence; and it is certain because the intuitive knowledge of the self, and the other premise, the principle of causality, are held to be certain. (The reader will recall the discussion of the a posteriori in the section dealing with Maclaurin.) This sort of argument exhibits no utilization of scientific ideas or scientific methods. And so we see that Locke's main theological argument for God's existence differs somewhat from that of Newton and the bulk of his followers on two grounds: he regards his conclusions as certain and he does not make use of the laws of motion, etc., as exhibiting mechanical order. The reason that Locke spent so little time on the formulation of the design argument is likely to be that he believed its validity so very obvious. We shall return to this point in connection with other thinkers, such as Butler and Hume, but, all in all, it is apparent that Locke makes little use of science in his theological reasonings, and in this sense his theology is pre-Newtonian. Both the *Treatise* and the *Essay* were written before the *Principia*.

From the work of Locke and other thinkers covered above, it is manifest that ideas of natural religion and natural theology were widespread before

[6] John Locke, *Two Treatises of Government*, ed. T. I. Cook (New York: Hafner Publishing Company, 1947), First Treatise, Sec. 53.

[7] John Locke, *An Essay Concerning Human Understanding*, ed. E. C. Frazer (Oxford, 1894), Vol. I, Book I, Chap. 4, Sec. 9.

Newton's work appeared. For purposes of contrast, I should like to dwell
upon some of the general religious and theological notions prevalent in the
late seventeenth and early eighteenth centuries. I have argued and will
continue to argue that scientific influence upon theology was solidified
only after the appearance of Newton's work. In addition, it will be claimed
that it is quite easy to overwork the idea that there is a great deal of unity of
belief in the seventeenth century "climate of opinion," and that there is a
good deal of confusion due to the ambiguous nature of certain terms, such
as "reason," "law of nature," and "mechanical hypothesis," which were
commonly used in science proper and also in a variety of philosophic
points of view. Hobbes, Bacon, Locke, the Cambridge Platonists, Continental natural law theorists such as Grotius and Pufendorf, and Descartes
all used terms such as "natural law," "natural religion," "right reason,"
and "reason"; but these terms and phrases do not, in my opinion, appear
to bear much unity of meaning. It would be more appropriate, I think,
to say that the period exemplifies considerable unity of attitude, and I
shall spell out the details of this point later.

Now I have said that Locke spent little time on the design argument,
probably because he thought it so obviously acceptable and also because
he was not primarily interested in natural theology or physico-theology.
He was interested in *natural religion*. These terms are quite often lumped
together in the secondary literature of the age, but there are important
variations in their use. The difference between "natural" and "physico"
theology, and "natural" religion, is exhibited in this quotation from Locke:

> But natural religion, in its full extent, was nowhere, that I know, taken
> care of, by the force of natural reason. It should seem, by the little that
> has hitherto been done in it, that it is too hard a task for unassisted reason
> to establish morality in all its parts, upon its true foundation, with a clear
> and convincing light.[8]

This is an interesting passage for a number of reasons. First, it exhibits the
vagueness of the term "reason" in the period under discussion. Locke
includes under the heading of "reason" intuition, demonstration, sensation,
and, paradoxically enough for empiricists, probability. And the Cartesian
phrase "clear and convincing light," used in the passage, shows well
enough that here he is taking natural reason to mean some sort of intuition.
Furthermore, he clearly connects natural religion and morality; and,
finally, he limits the applicability of even "natural reason." "Natural

---

[8] John Locke, *The Works of John Locke* (9th ed.; London, 1794), VI, *The
Reasonableness of Christianity*, 139.

religion," then, can for Locke involve several possible conceptions. First, it is a species of morality or ethics. Second, it is based upon an intuitive "clear and convincing light"—upon self-evident conviction. Third, reason is defined in terms of this self-evidence. Here we have the skeleton of Locke's rationalistic ethics, which appears to be related to religion.

What could this sort of "natural reason" have to do with the highly specific mathematical and inductive and experimental techniques of Newton? It does not even clearly exhibit the *empirical* character of scientific thought so emphasized by Newton and his followers, nor by Locke's epistemology either, for that matter. But this leads to another seeming paradox.

What kind of knowledge does one get from such an intuitional source? The answer comes with another of Locke's fundamental notions—that of the law of nature.[9] "But such a body of Ethics, proved to be the law of nature, from principles of reason, and teaching all the duties of life; I think nobody will say the world had before our Savior's time.[10] Even good and evil, defined by Locke in terms of the hedonistic criterion of pleasure and pain, are *morally* good or evil only if they result from the obedience or disobedience of a law of nature.[11] And, further, such laws of nature are rules instituted by God, or some other lawmaker. The world is, for Locke, telic.[12] It seems evident, therefore, that what Locke meant by "natural religion" was such a system of rationally grounded moral ideas wherein "rational" has a meaning which is not comparable to inductive techniques, and is only partially comparable to deductive techniques. That is, it will involve "demonstration," or inference by self-evident steps, which is common to science, but it also involves a sort of self-evident intuition of the truth of its ultimate premises, a notion foreign to Newtonian science. Further, it seems to be perfectly clear that he meant by "laws of nature" intuitively certain or self-evident moral principles, which are eternal and unchanging.

> He, that anyone will pretend to set up in this kind, and have his rules pass for authentic directions, must show, that either he builds his doctrine upon principles of reason, self-evident in themselves; and that he deduces all parts of it from thence, by clear and evident demonstration; or he must show his commission from heaven.[13]

[9] *Ibid.*, p. 144. [10] *Ibid.*, p. 141.
[11] Locke, *Essay*, Book II, Chap. 28, Sec. 5.
[12] *Ibid.*, Book I, Chap. 3, Sec. 12.
[13] Locke, *The Reasonableness of Christianity*, p. 142.

Now one conclusion is clear. Locke's conception of laws of nature as self-evident moral rules is not to be confused with the scientific conception of natural laws we found in Newton's thought. Newton's laws are descriptive—the laws of motion and the laws of optics, for instance. Locke's laws are prescriptive. Locke did not, by the way, attempt to deduce an "ought" from an "is," as he often has been accused of doing with regard to his moral theory. For reasons we have just seen, such an accusation could result only from the confusion of his "prescriptive" laws of nature with Newton's "descriptive" ones. Since Locke's laws of nature are prescriptive and have nothing to do with scientific laws of nature, his laws are "oughts" from the beginning. Furthermore, it is quite clear that the Lockian notion of "reason" is only in part comparable to the conception of inductive and deductive reason, analysis, and synthesis, which dominates Newton's ideas of "reason"; and, in particular, it is not to be confused with the carefully detailed conception of experimental verification in science which is found in Newton's work, and which forms the proof of Newtonian laws of nature.

It seems to me, therefore, that the following kind of statement can be extremely misleading. "Locke stands at the end of the Seventeenth century and at the beginning of the Eighteenth; his work is at once a summing up of Seventeenth century conclusions and the starting point for Eighteenth century enquiries."[14] If this statement is taken to mean that Locke in some sense summed up seventeenth-century thought, it is in part correct, to be sure, for his epistemological empiricism (sans, for obvious reasons, his Cartesian rationalism) was a seminal idea among Deists and philosophers. But if it is taken to mean that Locke's theories concerning reason and natural law were a philosophical interpretation of Newton's conceptions of scientific methods and laws of nature, then it is simply and clearly false. The development of experimental methods, their relationships to mathematical principles, as well as the scientifically unified view of the system of the world according to mechanical and mathematical principles, is fulfilled only in Newton; and the future directions which these concepts took and were applied are due to Newton. Locke was not in this sense the philosophical interpreter of Early Modern physical science.

We see a broad distinction developed here between the natural theology of Newton and the scientist theologians and what Locke called "natural religion." The essential agreement between the two is that both are based

[14] Basil Willey, *Seventeenth Century Background* (Garden City: Doubleday Anchor Books, 1955), p. 263.

in some way on man's rational capacities ("reason," as we have already discovered, is quite ambiguous), and are thus opposed, as "rational" religion, to the kind of religious thought that is based on revelations. However, and keep in mind Locke's notion of intuition, Locke often referred to the "light of reason" as "natural revelation"; and it is amusing to see, therefore, how very close this "reason" is to "revelation," after all. There is a repetition of this in Cambridge Platonism. The distinction between the natural and the revealed is found throughout the Age of Reason; and quite often the Deists use "reason" in much the same way that Newton used it. The Deists also quite often put Newton's idea of natural law over against claims based upon miracle and revelation. When miracle or revelation is offered as proof of a belief, the Deists refuse to accept the claim as true if it is inconsistent with natural law in the *Newtonian* sense. One thing that can be said, then, is that "natural religion" often means at this time the kind of ethico-moral theory, reinforced or not reinforced by Christ's message, that we find in the quotations adduced above. In one sense it is not theology at all, i.e., it does not deal with arguments for the existence and attributes of the Deity. These vaguenesses in the meanings of "natural religion" and "law of nature" are, I think, important to keep in mind.

One further point: I have argued that Locke's conception of natural law is not to be confused with the Newtonian scientific conception of it. The question then becomes, what is its source? It is my feeling that Locke's concept of natural law as self-evident moral rules is rooted in Cambridge Platonism and in Stoicism. The doctrines of intuitionism, natural law, light of reason, propositional truth, assent, all can be found quite clearly in Stoicism, as can, in addition, the concepts of *tabula rasa*, sense-knowledge, and probability.[15] Locke, in common with the Stoics, believed in ethics as based in self-evident knowledge of natural law. Both made natural law a concomitant of divinity, although Locke did not conceive God's reason in pantheistic fashion as the Stoics often did. He came close, however, by his identification of space with the visual field of God. In this he agreed with Newton, and their common source is Cambridge Platonism. Both Locke and the Stoics used the design argument.[16] Both considered reason to be the essential nature of man.

[15] Sextus Empiricus, *Sextus Empiricus*, tr. R. G. Bury (London: Wm. Heinemann, Ltd., 1933-49), Vol. II, *Against the Logicians*, i, 93; ii, 88 ff.; ii, 10; ii, 397, 476; i, 236-239; i, 60; i, 27. Cicero, *De Natura Deorum*, tr. F. Brooks (London, 1896), ii, 12, 13, 17; ii, 30.

[16] Cicero, *De Natura Deorum* ii, 4, 5, 34.

Both make reason a "spark" of divine reason in man.[17] Both classify actions as good, bad, and indifferent according to the law. Both made self-preservation important. All of these ideas were readily available to Locke in the writings of Cicero, Seneca, Stobaeus, Sextus Empiricus, and Diogenes Laertius. Locke found them a part of his reading in the University, and he found them in the Cambridge Platonists. Many of these ideas were also held by Hooker, Grotius, Pufendorf, as well as other thinkers of the age.[18] Incidentally, the Platonist Henry More was one of the few men of importance other than Locke and Spinoza who attempted a mathematical ethics.

Locke was a latitudinarian in other religious matters. His Christianity was a simple and undogmatic kind, and he demanded that it be consonant with reason. Belief in the Messiah was his only obvious dogma.[19] He was anti-Catholic, anti-clerical,[20] and had little patience with the endless sectarian squabbles that seemed to him to come to no resolution and to serve no practical or theoretical purpose.[21] He accepted with qualification revelation and miracles and the divinity of Christ,[22] so he was not, in any basic sense, a Deist. (The Deists, however, used his epistemology with devastating effect.) Metaphysically, Locke agreed in general with Newton in that he was a dualist who believed that the material world is a machine which God constructed out of material, atomic particles; and he accepted the primary-secondary quality distinction.

There is a wide divergence, however, between the Newtonians and Locke on matters theological, in interest as well as in emphasis. As we have seen, the rather common contention that Locke's philosophy was heavily influenced by Newtonian science is likely to be overstated. There is much in his theories that is found in Stoicism, Cartesianism, and in Cambridge Platonism, as well as in the ideas common to continental rationalists such as Grotius and Pufendorf. Of course, Locke accepted the mechanical and materialistic conception of the *physical* world which was an important aspect of early modern science, but this was a view shared by

[17] Locke, *The Reasonableness of Christianity*, pp. 133–141.

[18] Sterling Lamprecht, *The Moral and Political Philosophy of John Locke* (New York: Columbia University Press, 1918), p. 9. Henry More, *Enchiridion Ethicum* (New York: The Facsimile Text Society, 1930), pp. 40, 54, 81 ff., 204. J. A. Passmore, *Ralph Cudworth* (Cambridge: Cambridge University Press, 1951), pp. 91 ff. R. I. Aaron, *John Locke* (London: Oxford University Press, 1937), pp. 29, 258.

[19] Locke, *The Reasonableness of Christianity*, pp. 17, 32, 51.

[20] *Ibid.*, p. 135.

[21] Locke, *Works*, VI, *A Vindication of the Reasonableness of Christianity*, 296.

[22] Locke, *The Reasonableness of Christianity*, pp. 132, 139.

almost everyone outside the sectarian religions of the period, and even by some of them. This mechanistic metaphysics was not new, for it went back, in almost unchanged form, to Lucretius and Democritus.

Throughout our discussion we have consistently encountered the imprint of Cambridge Platonism. We have seen the ideas of Cudworth, More, Smith, and Whichcote crop up in the work of Newton, Locke, and Boyle; and we shall discover them frequently in our perusal of other early modern thinkers. With Newton, it will be recalled, there were personal as well as intellectual ties with these neo-Platonists. This was true of many other important thinkers. Locke, for instance, spent his last days in the home of Lady Masham, Cudworth's daughter, and even before this he was often in the company of Platonists.[23] His friend Limborch was attached to the group. Locke once remarked that all preachers should read Cudworth's *The True Intellectual System of the Universe.*[24] Whichcote, who made, as did most of these interesting men, much of the law of nature, was Locke's favorite preacher. All this exemplifies the wide personal, as well as philosophical, connections between the Cambridge Platonists and other thinkers of their era. Thus, a somewhat detailed examination of the philosophy of Cambridge Platonism is warranted, particularly since many modern historians of thought view their kind of theory as an unproductive blind alley leading away from the advance of modern science. While our treatment will not be complete, it should go far towards exhibiting the manner in which these men effected a significant and profound influence upon the Age of Reason, and in particular upon our design theologians.

Their thought is an attempt to protect and insure the existence of key religious elements against the encroachment of Hobbesian materialism. But this, while important, was not the only problem they faced. In addition, they were concerned with the problem of removing religion from the arena of sectarian dispute. It was their belief that a great deal of the political and spiritual chaos of the times was due to the underlying factiousness of Puritan and Catholic religious disagreement, a factiousness which had helped to produce a century or more of bloody religious wars and threatened to split Christianity asunder. We might remind ourselves

[23] H. E. Fox-Bourne, *The Life of John Locke* (London, 1876), I, 476–477. E. M. Austin, *The Ethics of the Cambridge Platonists* (Philadelphia: University of Pennsylvania Press, 1935), pp. 78–79.

[24] Austin, *The Ethics of the Cambridge Platonists*, pp. 78–79. Lamprecht, *The Moral and Political Philosophy of John Locke*, p. 10. Phyllis Allen, "Scientific Studies in the English Universities of the 17th Century," *Journal of the History of Ideas*, X (April, 1949), pp. 218–253.

that discussions of intellectual currents, with their preoccupation with arid metaphysical and epistemological distinctions, tend to neglect the fact that philosophical and theological matters often develop in a context of bloody strife. The fabric of seventeenth- and eighteenth-century culture was rent constantly by troubles which had at least part of their source in religious disagreement. Recognizing that peace and progress were dependent upon more rapprochement between factions, the Cambridge Platonists, along with the Deists, Locke, and many others, sought to work their way behind the façade of religious beliefs to what they considered to be the sound central core of Christianity, "Christianity as old as the creation." These fundamental religious touchstones, they felt, had been buried by priestly and other cultural accretions which had destroyed religion's simplicity and its power to help men find the good life.

I shall not work the ground of this latter subject, mainly because it has been discussed in connection with Locke and because I will return to it in later chapters. It might well be pointed out, however, that Newtonian theism, along with most early modern appeals to the design argument, shares in this common effort to establish a few basic religious beliefs, rational in support, which are acceptable to all Christians. In this effort the Cambridge Platonists are squarely within the tradition of natural religion if not among its most powerful purveyors.

To return to the basic problem—the attempt of the Cambridge Platonists to protect theology and religion from the dread materialism—we see that they developed a set of metaphysical and epistemological conceptions that were of lasting influence. The first two of the following quotations exemplifying their thought should suffice to show their appeal to reason and their Platonistic metaphysics.

> For Right Reason, which is in man, is a sort of copy or transcript of that reason or law eternal which is registered in the mind divine.[25]
>
> The truth is, all men do agree, that the supreme law is right reason.[26]

Evident here is an emphasis upon reason, in effect little different from revelation, and the expression of a Platonic view of the world. In addition to this "candle of the Lord," a system of divine archetypes and a dualistic view of reality form the ramparts of this defense of religion. Welcoming the new science, More and company agreed that the material world is to a large extent explainable in terms of material and mechanical laws of nature and that it can be known by scientific methods. (Their conception of

---

[25] More, *Enchiridion Ethicum*, p. 15.   [26] *Ibid.*, p. 114.

scientific method was largely Cartesian.) Such methods, however, and their attendant explanatory categories are not satisfactory or adequate for the comprehension of the spiritual aspects of reality, or even for certain ultimate and fundamental aspects of the material world. The physical or material world reflects a divine mind, a divine order, to which there is a spiritual key. This key of eternal and changeless forms, exemplars, archetypes, all elements of the divine mind of God, forms the ultimate cause and organization of the universe. As More put it,

> The phenomena of the world cannot be solved merely mechanically, but there is the necessity of the assistance of a substance distinct from matter, that is, of a spirit, or being incorporeal.[27]

These statements have the appearance of old friends. Here again is the common denominator of all the design theology discussed above. Like our theologians, these "saints" of Emmanuel College reject a complete materialism, reject a complete mechanism, and reject the claim that scientific principles give a complete explication of the world order. They unite in facing Hobbes from an entrenched position of Platonic dualism in which none of the ultimates such as the cause of motion, magnetism, cohesion, gravity, etc., are reducible to mechanical causes.[28] More is quite correct in his appraisal that materialism has difficulty with these notions. All of them appear to involve action at a distance, a conundrum which drove Newton and others to accept an aetherial medium, another idea which was knocking around the Cambridge camp. We have also noted before, a consistent reference to the fact that the dead and inert particles posited by early modern physical science demanded a first-mover as well as a designer in order to explain the motion in which the scientists found them. Platonistic metaphysics maintained that a full comprehension of reality demands an incorporeal or spiritual world in addition to the material one. Indeed, there is a "spirit" of nature, a universal "soul," an "*anima mundi*," which squires the physical elements of the universe around.[29] It is an active principle, an agent by means of which God orders and administers the estate of the world, material as well as spiritual.

[27] Robert Boyle, *Works*, ed. T. Birch (London, 1772), VI, 513 ff.
[28] Henry More, "Enchiridion Metaphysicum," *The Philosophical Writings of Henry More*, ed. F. I. Mackinnon (New York: Oxford University Press, 1925), Chaps. 9–15.
[29] Henry More, "Immortality of the Soul," *A Collection of Several Philosophical Writings of Henry More* (London, 1712), Chaps. 12 and 13. See the chapter on Cambridge Platonism in Burtt, *The Metaphysical Foundations of Modern Physical Science*.

Acting uniformly, it is analogous to the "animal spirits" or nervous system of the human organism. It is extended, penetrable, and able to penetrate, as well as impart motion to matter.[30] In More's view it has "essential spissitude," a capacity to contract and expand, a sort of spiritual "massiness." Finally, and of considerable importance, infinite space is identified with the sensorium, or more precisely, divinity as omnipresence extends through all space and time, filling the universe and all of its parts. Space is characterized by the attributes of God—"one, eternal, complete, all-pervasive"; it is a "representation of the essential divine presence."[31] Thus we find in Cambridge Platonism at least two levels of spiritual reality: a world soul, and God.

It has already been claimed that Newton took a number of these Platonistic ideas for his own. I should like to reinforce this contention by citing two quotations from Newton which particularly indicate his Platonic heritage. In turn, I will show that the Platonic formulation of the design argument is also very similar to that of Newton.

In a letter to Oldenburg (January 25, 1675, and December 7, 1677), Newton reports that the world was:

> ... after condensation wrought into various forms at first by the immediate hand of the Creator, and ever since by the power of nature, who by the command Increase and Multiply became a complete immatator of the copies set her by the Protoplast.[32]

This statement is so obviously Platonic in content that little more need be said about it. Here are the notions of imitations, copies, protoplasts, forms, a creator or demiurge, and a Christian connection in the reference to "increase and multiply"—all characteristic notions of Cambridge Platonism. Another example provides more in the way of indicating Newton's debt to Platonism. In formulating the last queries of the *Optics*, Newton carried them to Gregory, the editor. Gregory's comment upon them is as follows:

> His doubt was whether he should put the last Quaere thus. *What the space that is empty of body is filled with.* The plain truth is, that he believes God to be omnipresent in the literal sense; and that as we are sensible of objects when their images are brought home within the brain, so God must be sensible of everything, being intimately present with everything: for he

---

[30] More, "Immortality of the Soul," Chap. 12, Paragraph 1.

[31] More, "Enchiridion Metaphysicum," Chap. 8.

[32] *Newton's Correspondence*, ed. H. W. Turnbull (Cambridge: University of Cambridge Press, 1959), I, 364, 414.

supposes that as God is present in space where there is not body, he is present in space where body is also present. But if this way of proposing this his notion be too bold, he thinks of doing it thus. *What cause did the ancients* assign of gravity? He believes that they reckoned God the cause of it, nothing else, that is no body being the cause; since every body is heavy.[33]

Here is the famous notion of the divine presence of God throughout space, so important to More. And if Newton does not exactly identify space with God, it is clear that he comes very near to such an identity. In our treatment of Newton it was seen that he talks of space as the sensorium of God, a position very near to that of the Platonists. It is no surprise to find that among the books in Newton's library there were many by More, one of which bears, in his handwriting, the inscription *Ex dono Reverendi Autori.*

A further similarity between Newton's ideas and those of the Platonists lies in their common use of the design argument. Although the Cambridge men held that there is self-evident and innate knowledge of God, nevertheless they ran the design argument in order to prove the existence of a spiritual reality identified with God. Again it will be noted that the formulation is very much like those of Newton, Boyle, and company.

Wherefore the whole creation and every part thereof being so ordered as if the most exquisite reason and knowledge had contrived them, it is natural to conclude that all this is the work of a wise God. . . .[34]

"Exquisite reason," "contrived," words so often found in Newton's theology and that of his followers—this statement from More could easily have graced the pages of any of them. Cudworth produces the design argument as it appears in Cicero's *De Natura Deorum,* and refers to God as the "divine architect and geometer."[35] He comments that the argument came from Balbus the Stoic. Again from More:

That be the matter moved how it will, the appearance of things are such as do manifestly intimate that they are either appointed all of them, or at least approved, by a universal principle of wisdom and counsel.[36]

[33] David Gregory, *Isaac Newton and Their Circle*, ed. W. G. Hiscock, in B. I. Cohen, *Franklin and Newton* (Philadelphia: University of Pennsylvania Press, 1956), p. 193.

[34] Henry More, "Antidote to Atheism," *A Collection of Several Philosophical Writings of Henry More*, Book II, Chap. 12.

[35] Ralph Cudworth, *The True Intellectual System of the Universe* (New York, 1838), II, 90 ff.

[36] More, "Antidote to Atheism," Book II, Chap. 1, p. 6.

Instances could be multiplied. Fortunately, it is unnecessary to do so, for it is clear that, except for the reformulation of design in terms of scientific laws of nature, and the emphasis upon the a posteriori character of the analogical inference involved, both of which are important in Newtonian theology, this argument is very much like Newton's.

We may say, I think, that one of the main sources of Newton's theology and that of his followers, as well as that of Locke and of most other thinkers of the late seventeenth and the eighteenth centuries, lies in the efforts of the Cambridge Platonists. There is, first, the dualistic view of reality, material and spiritual. There are the varying notions of Platonism which were connected with this dualism. There is the consequent rejection of mechanistic and materialistic monism. There is the attempt to reformulate religious beliefs in terms of basic, commonly accepted theological principles, excluding sectarian trappings. Specifically, with respect to Newton, Boyle, and Locke, there is the identification of absolute space in some way with the divine presence of God. Finally, there is the view that the design argument bespeaks God's actual presence, his contact, so to speak, with man; and there is general use of the design argument as a fundamental proof of God and spiritual reality.

In the light of these obvious ways in which Cambridge formed a fertile source of later thought, it is difficult to understand the following statement from Cassirer:

> ... the Cambridge School had, so to speak, sealed its literary fate; it had shut itself up in the scholar's study. Its influence in the immediate future—disregarding its very limited and indirect, and for the most part negative effect on Locke—did not carry beyond the walls of English universities.[37]

Cassirer is, I think, simply mistaken.

We have dwelt upon the ways in which the philosophic ideas of Cambridge Platonism influenced future philosophy and theology. Now we should point out those ways in which their views differed from Newton's theories and those of many of his followers. First, the Cambridge notion of reason is clearly a muddled combination of mysticism, intuition, Cartesian "clear and distinct ideas," self-evidence, and innate truth. In their acceptance of the doctrines of innate ideas and common consent as the basis for certain truths, the Platonists harbored notions that were rapidly outmoded, a fate which is clearly seen when these epistemological concepts are compared with the developing methods of physical science epitomized in

[37] Ernst Cassirer, *The Platonic Renaissance in England*, tr. J. P. Pettigrew (Austin: University of Texas Press, 1953), p. 159.

Newton's work. Closely associated with these problems, their conception of "reason" in natural theology and in natural religion is not, therefore, to be confused with Newton's empiricism, or with the particular techniques of induction and deduction plus mathematical definition and formulation characteristic of Newtonian physics. Neither Locke nor Newton were likely to accept the Platonistic view that natural laws are known by means of general consent.

The mention of natural law brings us to another point of disagreement. Newton did not appear to accept the Lockean and Platonistic conception of natural law. For Newton, as we have seen, laws of nature are descriptions of the processes of the world of physical nature, discovered by observation and experiment, and, when possible, mathematically organized and formulated. The Platonistic view of natural law is quite different, and is similar to that of Locke and the Continental Rationalists.

Finally, Newton and most of his followers emphasized the a posteriori, quasi-scientific character of the design argument, and did not claim that its conclusions partake of certitude. The Platonists, with their doctrines of innate ideas, of self-evidence, and of general consent, are far afield of Newtonian experimentalism. The rationalistic Cartesian type of science they accepted was rapidly outdistanced, and the team to which the Platonists belonged lost the scientific race.

There are, undoubtedly, other similarities, other differences, between the philosophies and theologies of the Newtonians and the Platonists. But I believe that enough has been said to make clear the relationships between Cambridge Platonism and the main currents of theology in the Age of Reason.

We turn next to several theologians: Richard Bentley, Peter Browne, Archbishop King, Bishop Butler, and Bishop Berkeley. Not all of them occupied themselves with science and its uses in theology. Butler and Berkeley and Bentley did, it is clear, but Browne and King did not. I want to treat the ideas of the last two men, however, because they were concerned with the analogical character of theological knowledge and argument. This analogical character of the logic of the design argument forms the main target of Hume's critique in his *Dialogues*. It will be seen that Hume does not deny the order of nature as it is exhibited by science, but he does deny that it constitutes any sort of conclusive evidence for God's existence.

Little needs be said about Bentley. He is important at least in being the instigator of Newton's first published statements about theology. Since he, for the most part, took Newton's opinions point for point,[38] there is small use in repeating all of them, although, as the first Boyle lecturer and the first to make a great public ado about scientific support for theology, his talks made him famous. They also made the Newtonian form of the design argument famous. Bentley had, however, ample grounds for fame. As one of the most important classical scholars of the age,[39] he seems to have got into innumerable controversies As Master of Trinity, he was instrumental in introducing the new science into the curriculum, and it was he who engaged Roger Cotes and William Whiston for this purpose,[40] selecting them because they were Newtonians rather than Cartesians. Bentley seems also to have helped to persuade Newton to include the theological *General Scholium* in the second edition of the *Principia*.[41] He went beyond Newton, however, in matters theological. That is, he used all of Newton's ideas and a good many in addition that were not Newton's. Newton did not, for instance, make gravity inherent in matter.[42] The appropriation of scientific ideas comes predominantly in the Seventh and Eighth Lectures and involves mainly very detailed arguments about what can and what cannot be explained by mechanical laws. Much, in Bentley's opinion, cannot; and the order depicted by science implies an intelligent God.[43] Again, unlike Newton, Bentley went into fantastic detail regarding the uses of things and their final causes,[44] with even the velocities of the planets considered in terms of their uses to man.

As for his view of the formal character of the argument, Bentley calls it a "reflex argument." This appears to be another name for argument by analogy.[45] However, it is not clear whether or not he thinks of his conclusions as probable or certain, a priori or a posteriori. He does reject innate ideas and is a Lockean empiricist, for whatever that is worth.

Bentley was, in short, utilitarian about science. He emphasized the argument to design, using science mainly in order to show not the order of the world but, in negative fashion, to show what science cannot explain. He went to great lengths to fit scientific concepts, such as velocity, gravity, etc., into the terminology of final causes. Everything was *made* for the use of man—everything that could possibly be construed as of utility to the

---

[38] *Opera Omnia*, IV, 427–443.

[39] J. E. Sandys, *A History of Classical Scholarship* (Cambridge: Cambridge University Press, 1903), Vol. II, Section on English Scholars.

[40] Monk, *The Life of Richard Bentley*, I, 202–203.

[41] *Ibid.*, p. 228.   [42] *Opera Omnia*, IV, 437.

[43] Richard Bentley, *Works*, ed. A. Dyce (London, 1838), III, 119.

[44] *Ibid.*, pp. 174–177.   [45] See Johnson's *Dictionary*, under "analogy."

human species was made the basis of a teleological argument *to* design; and the argument is then given a scientific veneer.

Browne, in a pamphlet entitled *A Letter in Answer to A Book Entitled Christianity Not Mysterious* (1697), directed against John Toland, held that all of our knowledge of God is indirect, as distinguished from complete and proper sensory experience.[46] Later, in another book (1726), he detailed his contentions. His view is that such mediate or indirect knowledge is analogical. In other words, it conceives all supernatural things in analogical terms since such objects are not reducible to sensed ideas.[47] In 1709 Archbishop King, following the ideas of Browne's earlier letter, argued for the analogical notion therein, and he was immediately attacked by Anthony Collins. In 1733, Browne published another work on the subject: *Things Divine Conceived by Analogy with Things Natural and Human.* The word "conceived" is a keynote in all these works, for none of them argues for the existence and attributes of God. They are discussions and arguments about how we are able to conceive of God's attributes, accepting the fact that God is already known to exist. They are not, then, arguments or inferences at all—they are metaphors. Browne remarked that such "analogical" procedures are as old as the oldest Fathers of the Church, which is quite true. His work seems to be an attempt to refute the Deists and Fundamentalists, who between them held that the Bible must be translated either literally or figuratively. Browne held to a third way, analogy.

He claimed that knowledge gained by analogy is certain,[48] and in this claim disagreed with most of the men we have discussed, including Locke, who stated that analogical methods give only probability. Browne, in fact, confused two quite different modes of thought: first, metaphorical conception, a sort of imaginal construct, and, second, analogical inference as a type of induction. His view is based upon the Thomist concept of analogy, which does not involve analogy in the scientific sense or in the sense necessitated by the design argument. Newton is not mentioned and no interest is shown in marshaling the laws of science into the service of theology.

Now this material may seem afield of our topic. But I wish to make clear that there were at least two notions of analogical reasoning which were in general use during the Age of Reason, and they should not be

[46] Peter Browne, *The Procedure, Extent and Limits of Human Understanding* (London, 1729), Pt. 2.
[47] *Ibid.*, p. 2.   [48] *Ibid.*, p. 270.

confused. In Hume's *Dialogues* we will find that the logical character of analogy becomes perhaps the most important aspect of his criticism of the design argument. In addition, it is important to note the fact that the whole topic of analogy was a quite common and controversial subject.

The controversy over analogy did not escape the keen eye of Berkeley. The *Alciphron*, his "American" work, was written in opposition to Browne and others holding to the above views concerning analogy. He proposed that we do have that "direct and proper" knowledge of God which Browne had denied to human beings. Berkeley used the design argument in several of his works in several ways; and he connected it with the conception of analogy, evidencing a historical knowledge of analogy that is unusual in the writers with whom we have dealt. His major principle "esse est percipi" necessitates, since it denies a world of substantial material objects in nature, some spiritual explanation of the "series" of ideas we sense in experience. Since these ideas and their order are asserted to be merely passive, they cannot have produced either their own existence or their own orderly relationships. Since they also are not dependent upon our wills, an external source for their occurrence must be sought.[49] No material cause is possible, and therefore some other will or spirit must produce the ideas. If we closely attend our sensory experience, Berkeley believed, we can make out such a spiritual substance. Once we take this conception out of the jargon of Berkeleyan metaphysics, it is evident that he is talking about the order of ideas called natural laws or scientific laws. It is amusing to note that Berkeley was a mechanist but not a materialist. After much metaphysical thrashing about, he substituted a spiritual machine for the Newtonian material machine. It is in this context, then, that we get Berkeley's main argument for God's existence. It is the argument *from* design and it is in mechanistic form.

> But if we attentively consider the constant regularity, order and con-catenation of natural things, the surprizing magnificence, beauty, and perfection of the larger, and the exquisite contrivance of the smaller parts of creation, together with the exact harmony and correspondence of the whole, but above all the never enough admired laws of pain and pleasure, and the instincts or natural inclinations, appetites, and passions of animals; I say if we consider all these things, and at the same time attend to the meaning and import of the attributes, One, Eternal, Infinitely Wise, Good, and Perfect, we shall already perceive that they belong to the aforesaid spirit, "who works all in all," "and by whom all things consist."[50]

[49] Berkeley, "Principles," Pt. I, Paragraph 29.   [50] *Ibid.*, I, 146.

Quite similar to the Newtonian statement in the *Optics*, this passage involves elements of both the arguments to and from design. It is not unimportant that Berkeley mentions the constant order, regularity, and concatenation of natural things (see paras. 30, 34, 60, 107 in the same work) for few writers have more emphasized the view that it is the uniformity of ideas which provides the basis for scientific laws of nature. Berkeley is in agreement with Newton and the scientists that these ideas, called laws of nature, these conjunctions and series of events, are not connected by necessity but are matters of fact based on observation.

Nevertheless, he was not ready to view his arguments for the existence and attributes of God as hypothetical or probable. His view is somewhat confused and contradictory. He wished to maintain that the conclusions of his theological reasonings are certain; yet, since he also states that the scientific laws of nature which he uses as premises in the design argument are probable and conjectural, and since in addition he admits that inferences from such premises are probable, it is difficult to see how he can avoid the conclusion that the inference to God's attributes and existence is also probable. In the *Alciphron* he sometimes seems to accept the idea of probability in religious questions. Aside from his claims to theological certitude in the *Principles*,[51] there are passages in the *Alciphron* (Dialogue IV) directed at Browne's contention that our idea of God is not "proper," where he claims that our knowledge of God is as certain as our knowledge of other selves. But he does not make clear how certain our knowledge of other selves is.

In the *Alciphron* he explicitly rejects the cosmological and ontological arguments, and produces the design argument based upon the machine analogy in a form that is like that of the Newtonians.

The soul of man actuates but a small body, an insignificant partical, in respect of the great masses of nature, the elements, the heavenly bodies, and the system of the world. . . . A man with his hand can make no machines so admirable as the hand itself. Does it not follow, then, that from natural motions, independent of man's will, may be inferred both power and wisdom incomparably greater than that of the human soul ? . . . Further, is there not in natural productions and effects a visible unity of counsel and design ? Are not the rules fixed and immovable ? Do not the same laws of motion obtain throughout ?[52]

[51] *Ibid.*, I, 149.
[52] Berkeley, "Alciphron Dialogues," *Essays, Principles, Dialogues*, Dialogue IV, Paragraph 5.

For all his idealism, then, Berkeley had a great deal in common with Newton. Sans efficient causes (except, peculiarly enough, between God and man's sensed ideas), sans matter, sans dualism, no matter how one turns it, Berkeley pictures the world order in mechanical terms. This is the Newtonian argument from design. A few sentences later he puts it into other terms—a sort of divine sign language. This element is a Berkeleyan variety of the Cambridge Platonic "inner sense" of God, a direct awareness of God which is so often linked to the contemplation of the order and unity of the world system. In Berkeley it is a rather puzzling view, for it is not clear whether or not he still means us to believe that knowledge of God is mediate and inferential.

Finally, again in the *Alciphron*, Berkeley comes to the question of analogy as it was involved in the "hugger-mugger" between Browne, King, and company. We have, according to this doctrine, no adequate and correct (universal) knowledge of God. To say that our terms "intelligence" and "goodness" apply univocally to God would be to fall into the anthropomorphic heresy. Nevertheless, the terms are not held to apply equivocally. They apply analogically. God's intelligence, goodness, etc., are analogous to, but far greater than and different from, man's intelligence and goodness. The degree or content is relative to the degree of perfection: God's goodness and knowledge are to God's being as man's goodness and knowledge are to his being. Thus we see Berkeley accepting in the main the Thomistic doctrine of analogy in addition to the Newtonian.[53] Unlike Thomas, however, Berkeley continues to regard analogy as an argument or inference.

Another outstanding thinker was Butler. Born in 1692, a merchant's son, at the time of his death he was a bishop of the Anglican Church.[54] He studied, unhappily it seems, at Oriel College, Oxford, where he took his B.A. in 1718, B.C.L. in 1721, and D.C.L. in 1733. His youthful exchange of letters with Samuel Clarke early demonstrated an uncommon ability in philosophical matters, and marks well the a posteriori stamp that characterized his later thought. His spiritual father was John Locke and not the mathematical, a prioristic Samuel Clarke; and in his ethical thought, at least, he had some uncles among the Cambridge Platonists. In 1719 he was chosen preacher at Rolls Chapel in London,[55] and in 1725 he was chosen for the preferment at Stanhópe where he published his *Fifteen Sermons at Rolls Chapel*,[56] a definitive set of ethical writings. After

[53] *Ibid.*, Dialogue IV, Paragraphs 19, 20, 21.
[54] Mossner, *Bishop Butler and the Age of Reason*, p. 1.
[55] *Ibid.*, p. 3.   [56] *Ibid.*, pp. 3–4.

other preferments, culminating in the appointment to the bishopric of Durham in 1750, Butler, now one of the most dignified and respected men in the church, died at Bath in 1752.

Although Butler's most important contribution to philosophy lies in his ethical work, our interest centers upon his theological and religious views. In particular, we are interested in his *Analogy of Religion,* which was published in 1736 shortly after Butler was made Clerk of the Closet of Queen Caroline. (He was a member of the Royal Circle mentioned above in connection with Clarke.) The *Analogy* is basically a defense of religion against the Deist criticism, and there is little in it that is original.[57] It is, however, ingenious in its consistent development of the method of analogy. Butler's conception of analogy, like that of Bacon, is based upon empirical doctrines which state in general that like causes have *like* effects—"For when we determine a thing to be probably true, suppose that an event has or will come to pass, 'tis from the mind's remarking in it a likeness to some other event, which we have observed to come to pass."[58] His notion of analogy, then, is empirical and quite different from the ideas of King and Browne. Butler believed that the method of analogy, based upon observation and induction, is similar to that of science. He does not always consistently apply this method, but one use of it that is consistent lies in his conception of the design argument, which he rightly offers as an example of the method of analogy (page 65). Actually, insofar as the main intent of the book is concerned, Butler assumes the existence of God (page viii) and spends little time developing arguments for it. Like Locke, he was interested in something else. There is no doubt, however, that he accepted both the arguments to and from design.

What, then, does he do with analogy? One famous example is his argument that the distribution of pleasures and pains among humans comprises rewards and punishments dealt out by God. They are distributed in payments for actions; and this distribution of justice implies a distributor just as a design implies a designer. So we have the theory that the moral government of the world is rendered probable by analogy. And in this argument we see the specific purpose of *The Analogy of Religion*—to provide a probable basis for belief in the afterlife. In support of his contention he calls to his aid the observed continuities of change in the processes of life and nature. All creatures, he states, exhibit development

---

[57] *Ibid.*, p. 79.
[58] Joseph Butler, *The Analogy of Religion, Natural and Revealed, to the Constitution and Course of Nature* (4th ed.; London, 1750), p. viii.

from one differing phase into another. This is a general law of nature.[59] Therefore, since human beings have in their lives and processes this chain of development, and other existing creatures have it also, it is probable by analogy that there is a continuity of existence in some other phase, some new form, after death.

This is Butler's use of analogy. It is reasoning from the known to the unknown. But Butler forgets that with the Newtonian design argument the cause and effect of the object or situation from which we take the analogy are both experienced; that is, both the watch and the watchmaker, the machine and the mechanic, are experienced. Hence, if one can show the world to be analogous to the machine, he can argue to a mechanic. There is, theoretically at least, only one unknown object reached by inference— the world mechanic. Such an analogical inference is as valid as are the similarities between machines and the world order. Unfortunately, in neither of the cases mentioned above—the moral government of the world and the future life—does Butler have such an analogy at his disposal. There seems to be no analogy of this type at all in the latter, and in the former he depends upon an identification of pleasure and pain with retribution or reward which at best begs the question. Hume was quick to see these problems.[60]

Our conclusions, then, are as follows: first, Butler agreed with Newton and others who make such a posteriori argument probable or conjectural. He did not claim certitude. Moreover, he agreed that the design argument is analogical in form and considered such methods to be similar to those of science. Finally, he accepted the design argument in both its forms and made it the basis of his belief in the existence of God. In the *Analogy* he frequently refers to Newtonian science. Such interests were not, however, his basic ones. These lay elsewhere, primarily in dogmas such as immortality and God's providence; and though he thought his method with respect to these subjects to be the same as that of the design argument, he was mistaken.

[59] *Ibid.*, p. 18.
[60] Mossner, *Bishop Butler and the Age of Reason*, pp. 120 ff. See Hume, "Of a Particular Providence and a Future State," in David Hume, *An Enquiry Concerning the Human Understanding* (La Salle: Open Court Publishing Company, 1952), Sec. XI.

CHAPTER 4

Deists

I understand by natural religion the principles of morality
common to the human race.

—VOLTAIRE, *Œuvres*, XXII

The interest aroused in morally oriented "natural religion," it is becoming clear, was no isolated phenomenon. Those "principles of morality common to the human race," which we have seen emerging in our study of Locke and the Cambridge Platonists, became the focal point of interest for many theorists. In a sense this line of development was finally epitomized in Butler's work. It was also the fundamental quest of the Deists. Analysis of their beliefs will again display the two closely related clusters of ideas which have come into view in our study. To review them briefly: one involves a group of beliefs relating to an ultimate and common set of simple moral and religious beliefs, unencumbered by sectarian dogmas, based upon some sort of reason and tied to some notion of nature. This type of religious point of view is usually called "natural religion." The other cluster of ideas relates to a somewhat variant group of arguments for the existence and attributes of God, with the premises of such arguments in some sense derived from nature. This sort of theological activity is typically called either "natural theology" or "physico-theology." The differences in interest and in attitude which are exemplified by laborers in the theological garden can be expressed and described in terms of these two clusters of ideas, although it is patent that the terms "natural religion" and "natural theology" are often used interchangeably. The division of labor will be evident in the productions of the Deists, to whom we now turn.

Deism represents, in England, the somewhat varied thought of a number of men during a temporal span of over a century and a half. On the positive side Deistic views exhibit throughout their development a tendency to reduce religion to rational ethics, and, if one might so speak, to rationally simplify religious beliefs. On the negative side Deism tends more and more to reject the mystical aspects of religion, such as miracles, revelation, verbal inspiration, etc. Another negative element is their tendency to deny the historical veracity of the scriptures. These tendencies did not develop all at the same time, of course, or in the same men; but the negative element did tend to become more and more prominent.

With Lord Herbert of Cherbury, usually taken to be one of the earliest Deists, we have a largely positive kind of theory. But his was most certainly not the first Deism.[1] If we credit Paul Viret, a Swiss theologian who in 1563 wrote of persons who called themselves Deists, the strain of thought reaches at least to the early sixteenth century.[2] In addition, there is reason to believe that the Deists were influenced by many ancient religious ideas. Among them are Gnosticism, the allegorical methods of interpretation found in Origen and other members of the Alexandrine school and the Trinitarian, Chronological, Pelagian, and Arminian controversies. They seem also to have been acquainted with the "natural" religions of the Stoics, Cicero, Seneca, and the Epicureans; and there appears to be a familiarity with the anti-Christian writings of Celsus, Porphyry, and Philostratus. Last, there was a connection between their thinking and that of Renaissance thought in Italy and France.[3] Despite the interesting character of these matters, our purpose is to discover what relationships, if any, hold between Deism, science, and natural theology, and not to follow out these fascinating historical details.

I think that probably the most enlightening perspective on the Deists is the one mentioned above—a review of the positive and negative aspects of their doctrines. Since the negative element was and still is the most controversial one, it is, as is usual in such cases, the more famous. On the positive side the Deists are usually interpreted as conceiving the world as a machine, and God as a machinist, with the functions of the world process being understood in terms of general mechanical laws. It is a natural or rational religion that the Deists supported. In the use of the machine analogy, and in particular the notion of general mechanical laws of nature, they reflect over a time span both the burgeoning and the mature influence of science, depending on which end of the Deistic period we attend. In addition, they emphasized a Lockean type of rational ethics or moral theology, the theory that religion should be simple and reasonable, and that it should provide rules for human behavior. Their positive thought, then, is essentially ethical in tenor. The negative element, on the other

[1] John Orr, *English Deism: Its Roots and Fruits* (Grand Rapids: William Erdmans Publishing Company, 1934), pp. 32–40.

[2] Robertson, *A History of Freethought*, II, 265.

[3] Orr, *English Deism*, Chap. II, *passim*.

hand, was essentially anti-miracle, anti-scriptural, anti-prophesy, anti-revelation, anti-verbal inspiration; and these negative elements were receiving increasing attention as Deism matured. In this connection Deism in England had an archaic as well as a mature period.

Moving from Herbert to Charles Blount, and influenced by Thomas Brown, Hobbes, Tillotson, and Locke, Deism became more and more negative as it moved through the end of the seventeenth and the first half of the eighteenth centuries. It was under the influence of Locke that Deism moved into the mature, deadly, critical period of Matthew Tindal, John Toland, Anthony Collins, Thomas Woolston, Thomas Chubb, etc.[4] Woolston was somewhat different, and dominantly a positive thinker. We will sample the theories of these men so that we may better see their relation to theology and to each other during the Enlightenment.

The Deistic thinkers mentioned by Viret in the *Instruction Chrétienne* (Geneva, 1546) were apparently opposed to atheism, but deeply involved in what we have called natural religion and natural theology. There had for some time been an active discussion of these naturalistic principles, and, as the English Ambassador to the French Court, Lord Herbert probably came into contact with some such discussion and speculation. His natural religion, wherein "natural" means "rational," links both to reason in man because reason is taken to be man's essential nature. His most important treatise, *De Veritate*, was published in Paris in 1624, and was translated into French in 1639. Its contents were developed in subsequent works, particularly in the *De Religione Gentilium* published posthumously at Amsterdam in 1663.[5]

The long epistemological discussions which characterize his work can be abstracted into rather simple form. The main theory is similar to that of Descartes, and as with Descartes there is an emphasis upon reason. For Herbert there were two kinds of truth. The first is of reason; the second is innate. Natural religion is universally based upon the latter, and expounded in terms of the former.[6] There are five basic innate principles of all religions: (1) that there is one supreme God, (2) that he ought to be worshipped, (3) that virtue and piety are the chief part of divine worship, (4) that we ought to be sorry for our sins and repent of them, and (5) that divine goodness dispenses rewards and punishments both in this life and after it.[7] As innate, these principles are also universal and certain. Note

[4] Mossner, *Bishop Butler and the Age of Reason*, pp. 46, 52.
[5] *Ibid.*, p. 47. Orr, *English Deism*, p. 61.
[6] Orr, *English Deism*, pp. 61–69.
[7] Herbert Cherbury, *The Ancient Religion of the Gentiles* (London, 1705), pp. 3–4.

that he did not pay much attention to developing arguments for God's existence. For Herbert, the idea of the existence of God is innate, and the subject is left at that. He did not state that the Christian idea of God is the best or the only one possible; but he did think Christianity to be the least corrupted religion.

As the "Father of Deism," Herbert left some important legacies. First, he put little emphasis upon sectarian trappings and dogmas—one religion is about as good as another. Second, the source of religion and religious belief should be reason; revelation and miracles are not needed. Third, the major historical religions are corruptions of this basic rational religion, and along with this idea comes another dominant note in future Deism, the view that the major cause of such corruptions is the priesthood. Of fundamental significance for Deism was the third innate principle, that virtue and piety are the chief parts of divine worship. Not only does this point up the anti-sacrifice, anti-sacerdotal character of Deistic natural religion; even more important, it exhibits that basic moral and ethical character [8] which was remarked in the theory of Locke and the Cambridge Platonists and becomes so characteristic of natural religion.

Therefore, although when taken in isolation Herbert appears rather innocuous, still, viewed in context, he is a source of much of what came after him. He planted the seeds of the negative attitude of later Deism, even though the notion of reason and nature shifted radically from his rationalistic doctrine of innate ideas. He carefully avoided a direct attack upon the Bible or upon Christianity, specifically criticizing heathen books, miracles, revelations—ideas analogous, of course, to those of Christianity— as corruptions of the religion of nature. Yet he scarcely touched upon the design argument. He held that the belief in the existence of God is innate— is a priori in its truth, and no other arguments for his existence or attributes are necessary. Further, it is questionable whether any scientific influence was operating upon Herbert except perhaps in the vague general sense that Descartes' rationalism characterizes the view of nature and truth of some of the early modern scientists. The conception of the innate idea of God's existence, and of general consent as a criterion of truth, were common among the Stoics. These same a priori principles were among the first to fall by the wayside upon the birth of the new science. Of course the new science, in the work of Galileo, Kepler, and Copernicus, was in germination at this time, but it came to fruition in the work of Newton, and Herbert does not show its effect.

[8] Orr, *English Deism*, p. 65.

Although Herbert was its father, it was some time before the Deist child began to grow. Meanwhile Hobbes and Spinoza put forth their labors, and while they are not properly to be called Deists—the scope of their philosophies being far more extensive than the narrow meaning of that term—nevertheless they exerted important and extensive influences upon the development of Deism.

Hobbes bitterly attacked the Bible and the Catholic religion in the *Leviathan*. He set no store on revelation, and had so little respect for miracles that he placed the decision with regard to their acceptance in the hands of the sovereign. We can know that God exists, but not what he is, and his existence can be known only by reason, and not by revelation.[9] One of the first thinkers to offer genuine comparison and criticism of biblical texts, Hobbes probably engendered similar activities on the part of Spinoza.[10]

Spinoza, in his *Tractatus Theologico-Politicus*, criticized certain biblical sources, and in so doing contributed to the rising science of textual criticism as did Hobbes. It is only in later times that he gained the title "God-intoxicated."[11] Carrying the Cartesian methodology of mathematics to its conclusion and reducing God to all being, Spinoza was hated in his own day and in the following century. The *Tractatus*, with its naturalistic interpretation of miracles, was translated into English in 1689 and was used by the Deists. He examined the Pentateuch and decided that it was written by Ezra, with its author being given the name of Moses simply because Moses was the name of its principal character. Both Hobbes and Spinoza, then, while not Deists, certainly offered grist for the Deist mill. Their influence was in the main what we have been referring to as a negative influence—that is, it was destructive in its effect upon received opinions concerning religion. Further, both Hobbes and Spinoza in their effects again exhibit a source of influence that was not scientific in any significant sense, but philosophical.

It is with little surprise, then, that we find the next important Deist, Charles Blount (1654–1693), making use of their materials. He collected, in fact, most of the strands supporting Deism and presented them ingeniously and clearly. Like Herbert, and for the same reasons, he carefully phrased his materials so as to avoid trouble, developing from pagan sources

[9] Thomas Hobbes, *The English Works of Thomas Hobbes*, ed. W. M. Molesworth (London, 1839), III, *Leviathan*, Chaps. 31 and 34.

[10] *Ibid.*, Chaps. 33–34, 44–47. See Orr, *English Deism*, p. 79, and Mossner, *Bishop Butler and the Age of Reason*, p. 39.

[11] Stephen, *A History of English Thought in the 18th Century*, I, 31–32.

⁄ his ideas concerning disbelief in immortality. He collected Hobbes' statements favoring Deistic notions, and translated Spinoza's *Tractatus* chapter
which gives a naturalistic interpretation of miracles. He gathered together,
in other words, all the Deist sources and all materials favorable to the
Deistic conception of religion, both positive and negative.[12] Showing an
excellent knowledge of sources, he quoted from many ancient writers;
hence, materials from Philostratus, Porphyry, Celsus, Lucian, Seneca,
Cicero, Averroes, Pompanatius, and Erasmus, as well as Montaigne,
Bacon, Spinoza, Hobbes, and Locke, fill his pages.[13] In his positive beliefs
—set forth in seven articles—he only subdivided a couple of Herbert's
ideas, and with respect to morality he agreed with the good man that
morality is the most important factor in religion.[14] With respect to epistemology (page 134) he could not decide between reason and innate ideas.
More negative than Herbert of Cherbury, and bitterly anti-clerical, he
rejected miracles, particularly with regard to the birth of Christ,[15] and
treated many leading biblical characters simply as imposters.

The tendency begun in Herbert and developed in Blount, as may be
seen, presses towards a generally negative attitude toward all aspects of
Christian revelation, with Blount expressing a more naturalistic sort of
attitude. On one side is found natural religion, based epistemologically
either on the rationalist conceptions of Herbert and Blount, although the
latter was tending towards empiricism, or the empiricist ideas of Locke;
and on the other side is the doctrinal Christian religion, based on revelation
and textual materials. Although scientific materials are forever hovering in
the background, and form the evidence for rejecting miracles and revealed
truths, there is no particular influence from this quarter in the degree and
emphasis found in Newton and his followers. Such Deistic charges of
irrationality against religious claims would ordinarily be directed toward
the inconsistency of some religious belief (for instance the virgin birth)
with scientific knowledge of such natural processes.

With John Toland, Deism began to turn to empirical epistemology and
to reject the innate ideas of Descartes. Born in 1670, he began life as a
Roman Catholic. Later, rejecting Catholicism, he passed through the stage
of Deism, and, finally, if we take the ideas in his *Pantheisticon* to represent

[12] Mossner, *Bishop Butler and the Age of Reason*, pp. 49–50.
[13] Orr, *English Deism*, p. 109.
[14] Charles Blount, "Oracles of Reason," in *Miscellaneous Works of Charles
Blount* (London, 1695), p. 91.
[15] Charles Blount, *The Life of Apolonius Tyaneus*, p. 13; noted in Orr, *English
Deism*, p. 111.

his beliefs, died a pantheist.[16] Sensed ideas are the sole foundation of all reasonings; knowledge is the result of the perception of the agreement and disagreement of our sensed ideas;[17] and the truth of this knowledge, if not self-evident or demonstrative, is probable.[18] Note the moderate character of the empiricism involved and recall that such a view, little different in fact from that of Descartes in that real knowledge is intuitive or demonstrative, was also found in John Locke. Nevertheless, Toland's position differs from that of Herbert and Blount. His criteria are observation and induction or self-evidence, and not the innate ideas of Cherbury. Rational or natural religion flows from these two founts, and any belief that is non-rational in these senses is classified as mysterious. In this light he attacked revelation, faith, miracles, priests,[19] and tradition in general.[20] In one of his most telling works, the *Amyntor* (1690),[21] he punctures the historical and textual authenticity of the scriptures, contending (on pages 193, 199) that the books of the canon were uncollected until the time of Trajan and Hadrian, and that they represent a limited selection with no clear criterion. In the *Nazerenus* (1718) he considered biblical and textual problems anew, again criticizing those aspects of Christianity and religion that are not natural and rational.

I should like to weigh a point for a moment. Quite often the Deists are presented and interpreted as being merely a critical, negative, tatter-demalion crew, who made no positive contribution to the development of thought. Aside from the fact that good criticism, in destroying nonsense, is almost always healthy and positive, and the fact that almost all their conclusions have been accepted by modern biblical scholarship in one way or another, I believe this represents a superficial view. The Deists, for one thing, were influential in the development of toleration and in the resultant lessening of bigotry. But I am mainly interested in another point, although I shall not be able to dwell upon it: the methodological aspect of their historical-textual activities. Probably the greatest single intellectual advance of the nineteenth century was in historical methodology. The Deists, through their critical scholarship, must be given at least some credit for it, and to this extent the roots of modern history lie in some degree with

[16] Orr, *English Deism*, pp. 116–117.

[17] John Toland, *Christianity Not Mysterious* (London, 1696), pp. 11–12.

[18] *Ibid.*, pp. 13–14.   [19] *Ibid.*, Preface, and pp. 1–17.

[20] See *Hypatia and Tetrydamus: Miscellaneous Works*, II. There he describes the priestly murder of a fair female philosopher.

[21] John Toland, "Amyntor," in *The Life of John Milton, with Amyntor* (London, 1761), pp. 176–179, 186.

them. It is their concern with what could have happened with respect to
reasonable possibilities (possibilities defined in terms of observable
sequences in nature), concern with concrete and actual events, with the
real, which made the Deistic criticism so effective. To have helped to
develop this historical methodology is a valuable and positive contribution.

The whole range of Deistic criticism, then, becomes clear in Toland.
I have already noted that he based his view upon Lockean epistemology.
". . . ideas . . . are the sole matter and foundation of all our reasoning. . . .
Knowledge is, in effect, nothing else but the perception of the agreement
and disagreement of our ideas. . . ." [22] For Toland, as for Locke, the
immediate objects of the mind in thinking and reflection are ideas. The
power of forming ideas, of affirming and denying upon the basis of agreement and disagreement of ideas, is evident upon introspection. How did
he use these tenets in an attack upon traditional Christianity? The answer
is simple: his criterion of knowledge and probability form the standard of
reason in religion; rational religion is natural religion; and rational religion
is based on either knowledge or probability. Whatever belief is not self-
evident or based upon probability, and the latter is in turn based upon the
observation of the sequences of nature, is nonrational and mysterious. In
this light he attacked revelation. It cannot be above reason, even aside
from the possibility of being contradictory to reason. "Could that person
justly value himself upon being wiser than his neighbors, who having
infallible assurance that something called Blictri had a being in nature, in
the meantime know not what this Blictri was?" [23] Anything repugnant to
clear and distinct ideas, and untraceable to sensory observation, is against
reason and unacceptable. Here is the empiricist epistemology so clear in
Newton's thinking—anything not derived from or verifiable by sense is a
vain hypothesis. The relationship of this to "clear and distinct ideas,"
however, and to common sense, is no clearer than it was in John Locke.
But the "mysterious," which is interpreted quite properly to mean the
unknowable, is quite clearly outside the limits of any sort of knowledge
which is clear and distinct in any way. Faith, for instance, must be assent
based upon knowledge according to Toland; and therefore faith based
upon anything mysterious is rejected. Miracles are subjected to the same
treatment—actions "exceeding all human power, and which the laws of
nature cannot perform by their ordinary operations." Nevertheless, they
are "produced according to the laws of nature, though above its ordinary

[22] Toland, *Christianity Not Mysterious*, pp. 10–12.
[23] *Ibid.*, p. 133.

operations." [24] In this quotation there is a clear reference to laws of nature as the orderly sequences of nature, i.e., laws of nature in the Newtonian sense.

We have seen that the literature of the seventeenth and eighteenth centuries exemplifies a rather general tendency among many such thinkers as Toland to reduce religion to simple moral injunctions. They apply common sense and scientific notions of natural law to religious beliefs, rejecting those which do not square with them. A quite normal question occurs—just why did religion become so encumbered with mysterious elements ? And Toland, as well as most other Deists, has a stock answer: the cupidity of the priests, first pagan and then Christian,[25] both of which were later joined together.[26] Now, of course, this stock answer is no longer acceptable. It is a sort of "demon theory" of the development of ideas; and modern investigations of the development of religion make rather clear that the Deists got things rather turned around. It is extremely unlikely that there ever was an early period of "natural" religion—simple morality—which was complicated and corrupted by priests. But the somewhat romantic view of an original state of nature was common in politics, and it is not unusual to find it here in the religious ideas of the period. "Rational" religion should, in Toland's view, however, eschew both mystery and ceremony.

The whole range of Deistic criticism, then, becomes clear in Toland. Like Locke, he believed in God and in his Goodness—this was his idea of religion; but all mystical and non-natural elements must be removed. In keeping with the other Deists considered, however, Toland was not interested in proofs for the existence of God or of His attributes. Toland determined by his work the Deism that came after him because he set the critical line (1) against external evidences—miracles and prophecy, (2) against the argument from tradition—the priestly line and the historical authenticity of texts and scriptures, and (3) against internal evidences—revelation. The thinkers who came after him, with few exceptions, reiterated and amplified his arguments. Anthony Collins, for example, in his *Essay Concerning the Use of Reason* (1707), takes Toland's position with regard to mystery and revelation.[27] In his *Discourse of Freethinking* he defended toleration and freedom of thought, particularly with regard to religion.

[24] *Ibid.*, pp. 6, 150–157.
[25] *Ibid.*, Preface.
[26] *Ibid.*, p. 154.
[27] Anthony Collins, *An Essay Concerning the Use of Reasoning in Propositions* (London, 1707), pp. 13, 15, 23.

It is only mental freedom, he believed, that will exorcise superstition and mystery. The reason, again, is that only with freedom is it possible to discover and propagate knowledge of nature and of man. The ethical interest of Deism in the positive sense—and here we should note again that this ethical element was based upon the observed sequences of nature, another variety of "natural law" than that cited above—is evident in Collins' deep concern in arguing that disbelief in mystery and superstition and revealed religion does not necessarily lead to immorality.[28] Locke liked Collins' work. Bentley and Swift criticized Collins, but since they simply ignored his arguments, their criticism reduces to the trivial point that he had made a few slips of scholarship and was an example of "whiggish danger to the church."[29] Therefore, there is no need to analyze their comments. Along with the common attack upon the "roguery and folly of bishops and churchmen," Collins gave to natural religion the usual ethical connotation.

These men had their theological opponents hung upon a dilemma. Using the notion of scientific law of nature in their criticism of mystical and miraculous aspects of religion, the Deists said in effect that if the miraculous events described contradict nature's processes, then they are false; if the events fit nature's processes, then they by definition are not miraculous. Either way, little remains to give churchmen joy. This sort of attack upon miracles and revelation was most brutally pressed home by Thomas Woolston (1670–1733), who lived his mature years during the great Newtonian synthesis which pictured the world as a vast machine. His point of departure was ridicule, which was particularly effective because he applied rational standards to some of the claims of revelation in such a way as to make them appear downright silly. Often called "mad,"[30] he was jestive and coarse, but this interpretation is suspect in that the very elements which underlie it in fact reveal his rather fiendish talents for getting his point home without suffering *odium theologicum*.[31] Using a Rabbi for his mouthpiece, he presented six discourses deriding miracles before he was stopped by the clergy. For example:

> But, however, I can't read the story [of Jesus' apparition after his death] without smiling, and there are two or three passages in it that put me in

[28] Anthony Collins, *A Discourse of Freethinking* (London, 1713), pp. 5, 12, 101, 177.

[29] Mossner, *Bishop Butler and the Age of Reason*, p. 56.

[30] Stephen, *A History of English Thought in the 18th Century*, I, 87.

[31] Mossner, *Bishop Butler and the Age of Reason*, p. 75.

mind of Robinson Crusoe's filling his pockets with biscuits when he had neither coat, waistcoat, nor breeches on.[32]

In 1730, Matthew Tindal published the "Deist Bible," *Christianity as Old as the Creation: Or, the Gospel, a Republication of the Religion of Nature.* The very title of this work indicates the view that there was an original, rational, and natural religion which had been corrupted. A fellow of All Souls College, he was perhaps the best educated of the Deists.[33] Combining a treatment of the conception of natural religion in the ethical sense, as did Clarke, Woolston, the Cambridge Platonists, and the rest of the Deists, with the empiricism of John Locke, he brought together a number of the arguments of his era that were critical of official Christianity. Basically, he contended that the anciently created religion of nature is Christianity. In its original and uncorrupted state Christianity was quite reasonable and natural. As moral law giver, God gave reason to man for the purpose of cognizing the eternal, perfect, and universal laws of nature. Since these laws are concerned with morality and God's relationship to man, to follow them constitutes natural religion.[34] Again we find the usual vague delineation of reason, nature, law, and other commonly used terms. In Tindal, therefore, we note a repetition of the predominantly moral character of the positive side of Deistic natural religion, and the express point that the goal of all religion, its essential property, is morality.[35]

Our treatment has not covered all of the Deists, but those with whom we have dealt display the basic elements of the movement. Annet, Chubb, Middleton, Shaftsbury, and Bolingbroke have not been discussed, but they continue the attitudes and arguments with which we have become familiar. The latter two thinkers, of course, did add other philosophical considerations, and I have not done them justice in their own right, but such considerations are peripheral to our main line of interest—the relationships of early modern science and theology.

In summary, there are a number of important facets of the Deist movement. In the first place, their interest was somewhat different, from the beginning, from that of Newton and his followers, and their use of scientific materials was rather limited in scope, although it was important. In the positive aspect of Deism, that is, its natural religion-rational morality, the point of view which dominates their work is philosophical in

[32] Thomas Woolston, *Woolston's Works* (London, 1753); noted in Mossner, *Bishop Butler and the Age of Reason*, p. 69.

[33] Mossner, *Bishop Butler and the Age of Reason*, p. 75.

[34] Matthew Tindal, *Christianity as Old as the Creation* (1730), pp. 13, 60–63.

[35] *Ibid.*, pp. 11–12, 13–16, 46, 54–56.

the wide sense rather than scientific. Beginning with Herbert of Cherbury and moving up through the eighteenth-century thinkers, there is evident a shift away from innate ideas, self-evident laws of nature, rationalism of the Cartesian variety, and appeal to common consent, towards empiricism. In general, following Locke as well as Descartes, they view the physical world in mechanical terms, a metaphysical presupposition common to both philosophy and science during the whole period, and one which grew in strength and acceptance. The rationalism of Herbert and Blount, however, changes to the empiricism of Locke, Toland, Collins, etc.

The Deistic theology, therefore, does not represent a mode of positive influence of science on theology of the order that was found in Newtonian theism. On the negative side, however, there is a constantly enlarging awareness of the discoveries concerning nature's processes arising out of the labors of the new scientists; and the Deists increasingly appealed to these scientifically discovered and described laws of nature as criteria to be used in the criticism of traditional Christian beliefs relating to miracles, prophecy, and the textual authenticity of the scriptures. The design argument was accepted by most of the Deists, but their works do not seem to display any real interest in the philosophical problem of the existence of God.

The development of Deistic thought, therefore, exhibits two main characteristics, one positive and one negative. For the Deists the basic element in religion, as it was for Locke and many other thinkers during the age, was human conduct. Natural religion is the simple, reasonable conception of God and goodness found in the Gospels and even in other religions. On the negative side, Deism represented the critical consideration of the main points justifying the supernatural character of religion. They attacked miracles, prophecy, the traditions of the priestly line, revelation, and the historical truth of the Bible, culling away those elements of religion which are in their view not simple and rational—are not a part of "natural religion." And scientific discovery, as we have seen, was of increasing significance in this critical Deism.

The Deists were simply disinterested in what we have called natural or physico-theology.[36] In line with this interpretation of their ideas, it might be of interest to add that English Deism is not characterized by the commonly accepted view of Deism as a belief in an absentee God. Hefelbower remarks:

[36] S. G. Hefelbower, *The Relation of John Locke to English Deism* (Chicago: University of Chicago Press, 1918), pp. 85–91.

... that the Deists as a class seldom touched the problem [of God's existence]. Although at first they emphasized innate principles of God's existence, as the group approached its most active and influential stage this gave way to the teleological proof, and also, they do not seem to have made a clear distinction between the last two arguments.[37]

Where the Newtonians dwelt on the uses of science in theology, the Deists scarcely dealt with the question at all. Where the Deists spent tomes in dealing with the ethical and moral ideas of religion, and the possibility of grounding them in reason, the natural theologians rarely touched upon the subject. Where the Deists criticized all the mystical and sacerdotal elements of traditional Christianity, the natural theologians seldom took up the issues, being more interested, even delighted, in the view that the discoveries of natural science could be used for the support of religion. Where the Deistical point of departure was primarily philosophical and historical on both the positive and negative sides, the Newtonians based their thinking in scientific ideas and discoveries, and tried insofar as is possible to have it accord with the observational methods and techniques so closely related to those discoveries.

There was, however, one real sense in which the scientific conception of laws of nature formed, so to speak, the background of Deistic criticism of miracles, revealed truths, and other religious ideas; and this tendency grew along with the growth of science. Generally speaking, the Deists rejected any so-called "miraculous" event, any assertion in religious discourse which is inconsistent with natural law as discovered and described by empirical and rational methods. Now, as we have seen, the terms "rational," and "natural," and "natural law" are ambiguous and vague in usage during this age. But as time passed, "natural law" as used in these critical ways came to mean the processes or sequences of events as discovered and described by the Newtonian type of science. In effect, this means that the Deists rejected as false or improbable any religious claim that conflicted with any scientific law or claim. And, of course, as science developed and produced more knowledge of natural processes, an increasing number of biblical and religious claims came to be disputed. Many of the opponents of the Deists sought to show that such miraculous events were explainable in terms of natural law, but as the Deists pointed out and as was later pointed out in detail by Hume, this is of no avail. For to exhibit the fact that a miraculous event *is* an instance of a law of nature is to show that it is not miraculous at all.

[37] *Ibid.*, p. 89.

This Deistic attack upon religion was in general successful, although some of their claims concerning an original "natural" religion, unencumbered by mystery, are obviously wide of the mark. The pathos of their position is no less than that of the Newtonians, however, in that the scientific point of view, which seemed so fine and desirable to both for the purpose of amending and supporting their particular brands of religion, was soon turned upon them. Hume, again, was one of the first to see clearly what Butler saw, and what most of the opponents of Deism were no doubt dimly aware of—that "natural religion," in removing miracles and revelation and the divine inspiration of the scriptures, begins a process which removes the supernatural. When Toland stated the ambiguous credo of the age—we have got reason enough if only we will take the trouble to be reasonable [38]—he held to a natural theology which views the world as the work of a creator. But it could not last. As Hume said, "Our most holy religion is founded on faith, not on reason; and it is a sure method of exposing it to put it to such a trial as it is by no means fitted to endure."[39] Those who attempt to found religion on reason and natural law, and reject in the process revelation and miracles, are "dangerous friends" or "disguised enemies" of religion.

[38] Toland, *Christianity Not Mysterious*, pp. 56–66.
[39] See Hume's essay "Of Miracles," in Hume, *Enquiry*, Sec. X.

CHAPTER 5

Conclusions to Part One

We have seen how the mechanical-geometrical conception of the world order provided Newton with the basis for his theological speculations. The law of gravity, the laws of optics, the laws of organisms, all exhibit order and system—an exquisite design—and a design implies a designer. But Newton's theology also exemplified the marriage of new ideas with old ones. From the time of Thales, as shall be seen, the world was thought of as orderly; but it was Newton who certified this conception. From the time of Thales onward, again, the order of the world was held to evidence an *orderer*, but with Newton the system of the world was held to be so beautifully displayed, its cognitive character so well determined, its mechanism so clearly formulated in terms of mathematical proportions, that the designer could be specified as an intelligent geometer. This use of scientific notions in theology provided theologians with a reinvigorated design argument which dominated religious thought for a century or more.

Yet Newton did not rest his case simply on the design argument. From his science again, as we have seen, he argued for the metaphysical necessity of a first cause. In common with most of the scientists of his time, and with most of the philosophers, Newton accepted a metaphysical dualism which divides the world into two sorts of substance—one spiritual, the other material. The material world is a machine, constructed of passive, corpuscular particles, related according to those laws of nature discussed above. Most of the objects and processes of the world of nature are explicable in terms of laws of nature. On the other hand, these laws and the objects and processes they determine are the creation of a spiritual being, God, who is present throughout space, whose providence carries Him to the innermost intimate aspects of all things, whose divine sensorium or visual field is space, and who ultimately governs the universe through the force of gravity. In addition, God formed first an original set of objects and processes, and by His providential power over the universe determined that these original objects and processes be the patterns in accordance with

79

which the universe functions. Here are final causes, forms, Platonism.
Nature's functions embody "copies" of the divine "protoplast," first
forms or patterns, originally conceived and constructed by God. Newton's
metaphysics is therefore eclectic and dualistic. It embodies a Platonic
spiritual world of forms created by a Platonic creator who is, however, less
of a Platonic artificer than a geometer demiurge.

In the Godhead, therefore, Newton locates both the final cause, the
ultimate purposes of the universe, the forms or patterns, and the efficient
cause—the beginning of motion. The fact that the material particles, atoms,
are passive and inert necessitates an active principle, which is intelligent
and good. A machine, being but a machine, has to have force applied to it,
some power, in order that it begin to function. In addition, Newton believed
that a number of properties of the world-system itself are inexplicable in
terms of mechanical principles. Examples are: the particular velocities of
celestial bodies, their lucent or opaque character, their particular orbits,
their distances from the sun, the number of celestial bodies, their planes of
motion. Seeing that the fixed stars do not appear to move, and thus seemed
not to be subject to the laws of motion that keep other bodies in their places,
Newton wondered why they did not fall out of place due to gravitational
attraction. Finally, he looked upon comets and other fortuitous conjunctions
of events as disfunctions in the system, and held that a constant control by
God over the system is necessary in order to keep it working. Of course,
there is pathos in these beliefs and arguments. Most of these problems are
resolved by modern-day science—a fact that exhibits the problematic
nature of founding one's theology or metaphysics upon the specific
conclusions of science as they stand at any one time.

And so we can view Newton's thought concerning the system of the
world as a conjunction of several ideas, new and old. His works are a
remarkable scientific achievement, one whose implications are even at
present not entirely worked out. Intertwined with his science, however, is
a materialistic metaphysical conception which arose in a mature form with
Democritus and Leucippus. The world is ultimately a product of atoms in
space whose permutations are described by causal laws of motion, and
whose basic elements, inert and passive atoms, demand an active principle
to put them into order and into motion. In addition, he believed in a
second type of stuff—a spiritual reality whose intelligence and active power
ultimately determine the character and processes of the universe through a
continual exercise of power through gravity and the laws of motion. Such
a view of the ultimate cause of the universe and its processes is Platonic,
with space conceived to be the divine visual field in which an intelligent

creator maintains a constant watch and control over the processes of nature. Capping the whole dualism is Newton's use of the conception of an orderly and systematic universe as described by scientific laws of nature in connection with the very ancient, venerable, and impressive design argument for the existence and attributes of God. Thus we see a cluster of ideas—theological, metaphysical, scientific—forming the basis of a world view wherein the charm and power of a new and successful mode of thought is used together with ancient and received ideas in order to formulate a position which supports much of traditional theology and religion.

But this is not the only way in which science was instrumental in supporting received religion. Intimately connected with the metaphysical and cosmological ideas detailed above was the methodological and epistemological aspect of the new science. It was claimed that the design argument is further reinforced by science because it applied scientific methods to the proof of God's existence. The design argument is held to be similar in character to scientific methods, to the exclusion of the traditional a priori proofs. Scientific method, beginning at least with Lord Verulam, and certainly with Galileo, was increasingly conceived as based upon observation and experiment. This idea involves epistemological, logical, and methodological facets. First, like science, the design argument is held to be a posteriori; that is, we have seen Newton and his followers constantly appeal to the fact that the argument from design moves from premises which describe nature or some aspect of it *as effects* to God as the *cause*. Furthermore, it is claimed that these effects are *observed*; the laws of nature and the other systematic and orderly patterns of phenomena are a matter of observation and experiment. Finally, the argument from *analogy*, based upon the principle of *like-causes-like-effects*, is held to be essential to empirical and scientific methods. The argument from design, since it is an instance of argument by analogy, is therefore viewed as scientific in character.

And so we see that design theology in Newton seeks to borrow another conception of science: empirical epistemology, which holds that all knowledge must (and this can be quite vague) originate in sensation and in perception. Newton, as we have seen, never ceased to reiterate the principle that scientific thought proceeds from observed sequences in nature, by induction, to more and more general laws. And these laws, in order to qualify as a legitimate part of the body of science, must be experimentally verified. To be sure, he did not claim that his Platonic theology or metaphysics is a part of science, or experimentally verified. These conceptions were formulated in terms of queries or hypotheses. Yet his theology was viewed by both him and his followers as basically analogous to science in that it involves inference from empirically and experimentally established ideas to the existence of a first cause who is proved intelligent by the very character of the empirically discovered and mathematically described laws which show the world to be an order or a design.

A further implication of the empirical and methodological character of design theology and metaphysics is that the resultant conceptions and beliefs are often viewed as *probable*. Newton, as we have noted several times above, never claimed certainty for either his science or his theology. A priorism is rejected. In addition, Newton did not conceive of his theological speculations as verified in the experimental sense, as did some of his followers. But nevertheless a good deal of the popularity of the design theology found in Newton and picked up by the age is due to the claim that the existence and goodness of God are founded on scientific methods, or at least on methods very much like those of science.

There is another cluster of ideas. As can easily be seen, the sort of theology under discussion is not particularly Christian in character. The existence of a God who is good is only one facet of a full theology, and most religions have involved a great deal more in the way of dogmas and beliefs about the character of the Godhead. Further, they have been concerned about the ways in which this Godhead is related to man in the moral and ceremonial senses. What relations did early modern science have to these more particular aspects of religious belief? As we have seen, with respect to the problem of the existence and goodness and intelligence of God, the influence of science was in the main positive. But we have also seen that it was by no means entirely positive. Indeed, in the work of the Deists and other theologians and philosophers, including Newton himself and many of his followers, it was quite often extremely negative in its treatment of some of the traditional tenets of Christianity. Further, it has been shown that many scientific notions were confused with nonscientific notions; and, as a result, the view of the manifold influences of science upon religion is apt to be confusing.

It is clear that, along with other thinkers of the age, Newton was interested in a wide range of religious subjects. He was interested in applying rational criticism to the analysis of biblical chronology, prophecies, miracles, ecclesiastical controls, the doctrine of the trinity, to textual criticism in general. These problems are not the general metaphysical-theological problems with which we have been primarily concerned. They are much more specific, more peculiar, more intrinsically Christian in character. In these matters Newton shows himself to be quite as liberal, even radical, as he was in his scientific productions.

He was, for instance, quite obviously an Arian or Unitarian. Biblical claims, with respect both to history and to nature, must be reasonable. This in effect means that if in the scriptures there is a claim that an event happened, it must square with what is known scientifically about the sort of event it is. Further, religious claims cannot be self-contradictory. Miracles are explicable in terms of established knowledge of natural happenings, in which case they cease to be miraculous; otherwise, they are mysterious and impossible. All of these negative considerations resulted from the application of scientific criteria to religious beliefs; and they whittled away at the traditionally supernatural character of Christianity.

This subject, then, is more peculiar than the general problem of the existence and attributes of God. The qualities usually included under the themes of inspiration and faith, the mystique, so to speak, of Christianity itself, came in for rude jolts from the same scientific sources that were taken to support the traditional doctrine of the Godhead. Newton followed Old Testament genealogy and chronology, attempting to square it with "nature" and with other historical sources. Some of his materials are drawn from his knowledge of astronomy and mathematics. He also applied mathematical analyses to the interpretation of the Apocalypse and the prophecies of Daniel, which, as we saw, led to the charge of mathematicizing the scriptures. The only significant import of this work lies in that it led him to reject the doctrine of the authority of councils, synods, bishops, etc. In the *Two Notable Corruptions of Scripture* he denies the traditional doctrine of the Trinity and rejects the Son's coeternality with God. He rejects "homoiousios" and consubstantiality. In addition to his claim that the sources of the trinitarian doctrine are spurious, Newton claims that the idea of the Trinity is contradictory and beyond understanding and thus to be rejected. Miracles, also, come under his attack, being, in his opinion, not exceptions to laws of nature but simply unusual occurrences which would excite wonder in the minds of ignorant people.

In effect, therefore, Newton, again mainly upon grounds of reason and established scientific knowledge of natural processes, tends to "trim" Christianity of its mysterious elements. A portion of his work, therefore, is in keeping with the general latitudinarian movement of the seventeenth and eighteenth centuries, which reduces Christianity to "natural religion" and grounds it in "natural reason." This third strand grows from both of our scientifically inspired motifs—the comparison of religious dogmas with scientifically established laws of nature, and from the more general metaphysical and logical properties of science. It is rationalistic in rejecting inconsistency and mystery; it rejects any claim that conflicts with scientifically established knowledge; and it is empirical in epistemology.

Newton's views formed, therefore, the basic point of departure of the age. His system of the world made explicit a number of conceptions which ultimately involved a metaphysic, an epistemology, and a methodology, all of which were related to religion and theology by his followers and contemporaries. His mechanistic view of physical nature became the accepted view. His dualism of matter (atomistically construed) and spirit also formed a dominant theme of the period. His Platonism, while not so clearly recognized to be present in his thought, was a subtle but nevertheless pervasively accepted point of view, as we have seen. Epistemologically, the empirical, a posteriori character of science came to be accepted as the dominant way of conceiving of the arguments which infer the existence and attributes of God, and of viewing God's relationship to the universe and to man. Finally, the "analogy of nature," the principle, in particular, of argument by analogy, characterized as intrinsic to scientific method, was taken to be the key technique of deducing God's existence and attributes.

These sometimes unified and sometimes disparate ideas —metaphysical, theological, methodological—provided a meal to sustain the theological appetites of several generations. Some thinkers of considerable gustatory potential had the whole meal; some nibbled away at the specific metaphysical, logical, and theological dishes. There were, as we have seen, some occasional digestive upsets. I shan't attempt to review in general the ideas of Newton's contemporaries and followers, but I shall note some of the variations in taste and some of the upsets. First, there was the tendency on the part of some of Newton's followers such as Clarke, and Cheyne to pursue the mathematical method of Newton's system of the world into a metaphysical a priorism. This departure from Newtonianism involved, ultimately, a rejection of empiricism and mechanism, with the universe taking on, for them, a resultant Pythagorean and rationalistic character. These thinkers still made use of the design argument, of course, which is somewhat disinterested in this particular point; and, in addition, they were still empiricists with respect to the methods of science itself. But theology and religion and metaphysics tend in their work to become rationalistic, and they tend to claim certitude for their theological conclusions. For Clarke, indeed, the a posteriori design argument is regarded as an inferior sort of inference. Cheyne considered argument by analogy, and the design argument, to be certain in its conclusions. On the whole, however, Newton's followers adhered to his methodological and theological convictions.

This tendency towards rationalism also characterized John Locke's theology, and along with those thinkers to whom we have just referred he regarded arguments for God's existence as certain. He did use the design argument, but he rather referred to it than developed it, and his main theological argument was Cartesian and cosmological. Furthermore, although Locke's metaphysical thought is somewhat Platonic and dualistic, as are Newton's theories, his conceptions of natural reason and natural law are not to be understood in the light of Newton's laws of nature or his experimental and empirical methods. Newton's laws of nature are mathematically formulated descriptions of mechanical world processes—the laws of motion, etc. They are discovered by empirical and experimental techniques, and are probable rather than certain. Locke's notion of laws of nature is Stoic in origin. The laws are prescriptive ethical or moral rules, intuitively self-evident and certain. Thus it is a mistake to push very far the view that Locke's philosophy is an interpretation of Newtonian science, for science, whether in its methodological and epistemological components or in its conclusions concerning the system of the world, has little to do with Locke's point of view. "Reason," "law of nature," "empirical," "natural," are in the Age of Reason quite amorphous terms. In general, Locke's theology and philosophy are pre-Newtonian.

A similar analysis may be made of the Cambridge Platonists. While they clearly embraced much of early modern science, and while they contributed a great deal to Newtonian theology and metaphysics, i.e., the Platonism, the basic notions of the design argument, the concept of space as the divine sensorium of God, nevertheless their ideas differ quite violently from those of the Newtonians in many respects. Like Locke, they tended to be a prioristic; they were wont to refer to "innate truths," and "general consent," as grounds for certitude in theological and philosophical matters. Further, in that they tended to identify scientific and theological ideas, they failed to keep science and theology separate. Newton was much more careful in this respect, although even he was not altogether successful.

Some of the ideas came in for separate and singular treatment. As we have seen, analogy was the subject of extensive discussion, with Bacon, Butler, Browne, King, and Berkeley taking a variety of positions with regard to its methodological and epistemological character, including the certitude or probability of its conclusions. Bacon and Butler regarded it as probable and scientific; King, Browne, and Berkeley regarded it as more in the nature of abstract a priori reasoning of the Thomistic type. King, at least, attributed certitude to the conclusions of analogical inferences. And so we have discovered a number of variations in the notion of analogy. Except in the case of Bacon and Butler, and perhaps Berkeley, this dispute, it is to be remembered, involved many other thinkers as well, and shows little if any relationship to the new physical science, although a number of the terms involved are common to science and theology. The Thomistic variety of analogy will be treated at some length below.

Boyle is another example of pre-Newtonian thought. His metaphysics is quite similar to Newton's, and, again like Newton, his philosophy is dualistic with Platonic overtones. However, he manifestly failed to perceive the clear use of a mechanically conceived "system of the world"—mechanical laws of nature—as the grounds for an argument from design. His theories are predominantly teleological in nature—arguments to design—based upon the countless means-ends relationships found throughout natural processes. He went so far as to derogate those orderly movements of planets, so dearly a part of Newton's theology, because he could find no "uses" for them—indeed, no uses to man!

Our discussion of Deism exhibited again, I think, the point that the effect of science was often relatively unimportant in relation to significant trends of thought in the eighteenth century. Newton, Locke, the Deists, all exhibit one very important use of science in theology and religion. They all tended to reject those traditional components of religion which do not square with scientifically established knowledge. Miracles, revelation, the historical truth of much of the scriptures, tend to go by the board. Of course, as has become clear, there appears to be little difference between Locke's intuitional "natural light of reason," also appealed to by the Deists and the Cambridge Platonists, and revelation. The attitude of these thinkers, however, is fundamentally different from that of those who accept revelation, and entails a rejection of the mystical element in traditional religion. Philosophical empiricism played an important part in the Deistic tradition—ideas were expected, by the Deists and by Locke and Newton, to be derived from sensations and perceptions. These views represent an important, if dominantly negative, use of scientific ideas; but Deistic positive thought in the main follows the intuitive and ethical vein that we have seen in Locke's thought. Only Newton, in fact, and some of his scientific followers, such as Keill, Pemberton, Whiston, Maclaurin, seem to have any sort of clear conception of inductive and deductive "reason", and thus of what reason can be said to establish in the way of knowledge. One paradoxical point concerning the Deists: as with all the major thinkers of our period, they used the design argument. And although the English Deists were, for the most part, disinterested in arguments for the existence and attributes of God, insofar as they did become interested in them, they are theists!

Some comment seems to be called for concerning the much-discussed "climate of opinion" of the late seventeenth and early eighteenth centuries. I suppose that it is perfectly proper to conceive of the opinions of an age, if the age can be in some sense isolated for inspection, in terms of weather and other climatic conditions. Certainly the seventeenth and eighteenth centuries had a considerable amount of cognitive rainfall, and most assuredly the period can be characterized in terms of verbal windiness. Indeed, we have considered a number of the periodic storms that pervaded the scientific, philosophical, and theological atmosphere. There is a remarkable repetition in the words used by the thinkers of the period. Reason, rational, natural, natural law, design, design argument, natural philosophy, natural religion, natural theology, physico-theology, empiricism, analogy, a posteriori, a priori, and so on, into the night. Our study, however, has, I think, shown that there is less agreement in meaning and understanding in the positive sense than the verbal chorus would seem to indicate. Newton and his scientific followers had, as we have seen, rather clearly expressed and conceived ideas concerning the mathematical-mechanical, and empirical-experimental nature of scientific methods and scientific conclusions. But even they often disagreed among themselves concerning the implications of these ideas.

Generally speaking, it might be agreed that there was an extremely vague "climate of opinion" which involved more or less the following ideas, each of which, however, almost immediately upon inspection breaks down into a number of differing, and often conflicting, conceptions. First, there is a generally accepted dualistic view of reality. This metaphysics conceives of reality as of two radically disparate stuffs—one material, corporeal, and dead; the other spiritual, dynamic, divine, alive. The latter is identified with God, and is conceived as the intelligent cause and creator of the former, including its order and processes. How the connection between the two stuffs (although the divine in some sense "perceives" everything in the natural world) is effected is either left hanging or is vaguely identified with some sort of mechanical force or energy such as gravity or the laws of motion. Neither of these, of course, does more than beg the question or cause it to be repeated one step further back. In addition, God is depicted both as a person and not as a person. He is both identified and not identified with gravity. He is a platonic architect, a geometer, a biologist, a mathematician. The whole business, even at first inspection, is quite vague.

There is a general acceptance of "reason" as the source of truth and knowledge, but upon study it is found that this term covers a multitude of not altogether similar and sometimes quite dissimilar notions. The only agreed-upon meaning of it is negative—it is opposed to revelation, faith, to mysticism of any sort, or at least of the sort traditionally identified with religion. But even here certain intuitionist themes, such as that of Locke concerning knowledge of natural law, appear little different from revelation in the epistemological sense at least. The difference in attitude, of course, is considerable, for the upshot is to reject traditional religious ideas concerning knowledge of the divine. "Reason" means self-evident innate ideas; it means self-evident truths such as the principle of causation; it means intuitions of laws of nature; it means deduction and demonstration; it means a variety of inductive procedures, including argument by analogy; it means logical consistency, or agreement with common sense; it means consistency with scientific knowledge of nature; it means general consent; it means observable; it means reducible to sense-data; and in the Cambridge Platonists it means human goodness. It therefore appears that when one finds an eighteenth-century thinker appealing to the verdict of "reason," including its numerous synonyms such as light of nature, natural reason, etc., it is not always clear just what he is referring to. The only clear use, it seems to me, lies in the inductive and deductive, experimental and mathematical techniques of the scientists. Whenever it is used with respect to other subjects, such as religion and theology and philosophy, it becomes very murky indeed.

A similar situation was discovered in the references to "laws of nature." In Newtonian science this phrase clearly connotes ideas such as the law of gravity: it refers to orderly sequences in the processes of nature expressed as causal laws, and is often formulated in terms of mathematical equations. Even here, however, Newton, his followers, and his contemporaries vary in their treatments of the implications of these laws. Some regard them as intrinsic to God's nature, some take them to be prescriptions, and some consider them to be descriptions. Locke, the Cambridge Platonists, the continental natural law theorists such as Grotius and Pufendorf, and quite often the Deists, usually use the phrases "natural law" and "law of nature" to connote something quite different from the scientific conception of Newton. To these people natural law covers intuited, self-evident ethico-moral or political laws. Such rules or principles are identified with the providence of God. Newtonian scientific laws cannot, of course, be transgressed except in the somewhat peculiar sense that nature gets "out of whack" and requires the attentions of the cosmic plumber. Perhaps this shows that even Newton from time to time confused descriptive scientific laws of nature with prescriptive moral laws. Lockean laws of nature, of course, can be broken. Often such normative laws of nature are seated in common or general consent—*vide* the Cambridge Platonists.

Our study has, in addition, shown that while there is a rather general acceptance of some formulation of the design argument, nevertheless an inspection of such formulations unearths a good deal of variation. Newton argued for a "designer" both from the systematic order exhibited in the scientifically established mechanical view of the world and from the purposive means-ends relations exhibited by organisms and objects in nature. His followers tended to repeat him with the possible exception that they emphasized the latter, less scientifically inspired, form of the argument. Of course, all tended to construe the latter sort of argument in terms of the former, mainly by interpreting the purposive relationships of the parts of organisms, as well as the purposive relations between objects in the world, as mechanical in nature. The upshot of all this is that although these arguments appear to be based upon final causes or purposive relationships, in fact, such relationships are simply interpreted as special types of mechanical or efficient causal relations. Men like Clarke, Boyle, Bentley, and others clearly placed more emphasis upon the teleological form of the design argument; and Locke and Clarke, among others, seemed to feel that the design argument was less *philosophically* compelling than other, a priori, arguments.

Indeed, with respect to the logical status of the design argument and its related theology, we have found radical dissimilarities. Most of our thinkers have held to the a posteriori and analogical character of the design argument, no doubt because it was felt that in this sense the resultant theology is scientific; but from there on it becomes increasingly muddled. Some thinkers held that its conclusions are certain, some that they are probable. Some give it a Thomistic twist. Some say it is not an argument at all. Even the commonly used terms "a priori" and "a posteriori" were discovered to be not altogether clear in designation, with the latter often taken to afford certitude in its conclusions. The sort of theology covered by the design argument went under a number of titles—"natural theology," "natural religion," "physico-theology," to name the most important. But care must be taken here, for the first two, "natural theology" and "natural religion" often do not refer to the same sort of thing. "Natural religion," as we have seen, often if not predominantly refers to ethical or moral theories, as in Locke, the Cambridge Platonists, and the Deists. Other terms used for similar subjects are "rational religion" and "rational theology"; and again there is no assurance that they have in any two thinkers the same referents. And so again the "climate" seems more verbal than real.

Last, the term "scientific" is perhaps the most vague of all, although it was no more vague, perhaps, than it is at present. Any number of things, leaving aside for the moment its clear meaning in Newton's *Principia* and *Optics*, could be intended by its usage. It might mean "a posteriori," but, as in Clarke's mathematicism, taken, he believed, from Newton, it might mean "a priori." It could refer to a mechanistic and materialistic metaphysics; it could and often did mean "mathematical"; it could denote "empirical," "analogical," "rational." Even "Newtonianism" had several meanings during this period. In particular, it might mean one drawn from the mathematical character of the *Principia*, where it designated the mathematical-mechanical view of the universe. On the other hand, it could derive from the *Optics* and designate the empirical and carefully experimental character of his scientific methodology.

Now my conclusion is this: that when one uses the notion of a "climate of opinion" of the Age of Reason and defines it in terms of "reason," "natural theology," "Newtonian science," etc., care must be taken to show that these terms had exceedingly diverse meanings, and that if such care is not taken, one gets from such characterizations a view of the age that exhibits it as having much more unity of belief than actually prevailed. There is, in addition, another danger in historical interpretations of a period in terms of a "climate of opinion." That is that they tend to be circular and thus only apparently informative. First, one describes an age, say the "Age of Reason," in terms of some of its major thinkers, for instance, Locke. Then, when it comes to discussing Locke's work, his work is in turn interpreted by the original description. Thus it is very easy to read into Locke's ideas meanings which are in fact quite foreign to them. An example would be to take Locke's phrase "law of nature" to mean the same as Newton's "law of nature"—that is, to make Newton's meaning characterize the age, and then apply it to Locke, or to make Locke's meaning characterize the "climate" and then apply it to Newton. Thus interpretations based upon the notion of a climate of opinion tend to obscure differences in ideas which are quite important in a proper description of the growth and development of the thought of an age or period.

Some mention should be made in this summary of the obvious blind spots in the philosophy of the Newtonians. First, there is the tendency to identify analogical reasoning of the type found in the design argument with scientific reasoning. Obviously experimental verification, generalization, prediction, control, fundamental to scientific reasoning and its conclusions, depend upon the principle of the uniformity of nature and the principle of analogy: like causes, like effects. But whereas Newton's scientific conclusions as exemplified in the *Principia* and the *Optics* are subjected to experimental verification, the conclusions of the design argument formulate a hypothesis which is not subject to verification. And this quandary leads to another—the ambiguous status of a posteriori reasoning. Newton, of course, makes both his theological conclusions and his scientific conclusions *probable*; nevertheless, it appears, although not clearly, that he would distinguish between a posteriori arguments which are verified, as in scientific reasoning, and a posteriori arguments which are not verified, as in the design argument. But what the difference would be is not attended by these thinkers—this problem had to await Hume's penetrating analysis. As we have seen, Bacon presaged this point, saying that analogy at best provides suggestions for hypotheses, which, in order to be scientific, must in turn be verified.

Then, too, the Platonism in Newton and others of the time is exceedingly unsophisticated. How this spiritual stuff, the divine, is related and relatable to the material stuff, the world of nature, is left hanging. Although Descartes' "pineal gland" connection between the two has been the subject of endless philosophical humor, it at least indicated that Descartes was aware of the problem. Mind and matter are viewed as related, of course, by some sort of power or efficient causality, but, as can be seen, this simply sets the problem back one step and forces the question to be asked as to what kind of mechanical power can relate a spiritual with a divine stuff. This sort of question leads to a cognitive miasma but was not even recognized, in effect, by Newton and most of his followers. Of a similar nature is the problem of conceiving of God as in some sense extended throughout space, where space is taken to be the "sensorium" of God. Originally, in Aristotle, the common sensorium is the place in the organism which brings together the data of the various sense organs of the human organism—but since God has no such organs of sense, this notion cannot

be applied to God without some peculiar consequences. Finally, the
Newtonians were content to ignore the difficulty that if design in the world
implies a designer, then the mental order, or intelligence, of God, itself
implies a designer, which forces one into an infinite regress. Actually, it was
the atomistic metaphysics, taking the world as "dead" in its ultimate
particles and thus necessitating a mover and orderer, which made early
modern science so very congenial to abstract theology. There were, in
addition to the points just listed, other loose ends. Providence becomes
shaky, since the machine apparently needs only an original orderer and
starter. Any acceptable metaphysics which makes the world alive would
seem to question the need for even original controls. If the world is a
machine, where is its fuel ? We have seen Newton attempt to keep God "in"
the world by making him a cosmic repairman who intervenes in the world
in order to repair its breakdowns; but even this conception had its Achilles'
heel in that it indicated a lack of power or foresight or both on the part
of God.

Indeed, it is clear that the design argument based upon science gives
very little to its users in the way of traditional Christian belief, even if we
were to accept its validity as a proof for the existence and a few of the
attributes, such as intelligence and goodness, of God. It will be Hume, of
course, who makes this point so terribly clear. It should be emphasized,
however, that the Unitarian and Arian type of religion accepted by Newton
and the other radicals of the time, and they were radicals, did not pay
much attention to, or put much importance upon, these traditional details
of received Christianity. They were, as we have seen, "trimmers."

Finally, the Newtonians generally accepted the primary-secondary
quality distinction, and in addition the empirical epistemology connected
with it, drawn from Locke, Gassendi, Bacon, and Galileo. They apparently
had little idea of the difficulties and complexities which these ideas involved,
deficiencies which would be glaringly exposed by the criticism of Berkeley
and Hume.

Now. Where did design theology come from—where did Newton and
his contemporaries find it ? This is our next question.

PART TWO

The Ancient and Medieval Context of the Design Argument

As I said at first, when all things were in disorder God created in each thing in relation to itself, and in all things in relation to each other, all the treasures and harmonies which they could possibly receive.

—PLATO, *Timaeus*

CHAPTER 6

In Classical Thought
Plato, Aristotle, the Stoics, Philo

We have seen that while the warp of early modern Christian theism was science, the woof was the design argument. There are, of course, designs and designs, orders and orders. Design can mean a mathematical arrangement, as in Pythagorean metaphysics; it can be mathematical-mechanical, as in Descartes and Newton; it can be artistic or esthetic, as in Plato; it can be means-ends or process-product, as in Aristotle—and all can be muddled together, particularly since any and all formulations of "order" depict some variety of uniformity which is easily connected, by analogy, with the human experience of manipulating materials in the production of something. It is easy to comprehend, therefore, the pervasive acceptance of some sort of design argument for the existence and attributes of a Deity in all sorts of radically differing metaphysical positions. Our theological and philosophical weavers drew their yarns and patterns from many suppliers.

A good part of the discussion in this chapter will range rather far afield, especially in the medieval section. But it is important to remain true to the aforementioned interest in seeing early modern natural theology in its intrinsic nature, in its origins, and in its outcome. Up to this point we have seen in some detail the complex context of early modern natural theology, and the profound place in it occupied by the design argument. We shall have to await the section on Hume to see what became of the design argument, what its fate was. The section we now begin will investigate where the design argument came from, i.e., the sources and development of the design argument and its logical correlate—argument by analogy.

As has been said, the design argument is pervasive and credible, is easily surrounded with an emotive aura which gives it a distinctive religious character, and, in its scientific form at least, it specifies one of the properties of God in a clear manner—mathematical and mechanical intelligence. Almost any organized set of beliefs which tend to show some sort of order

or harmony in the world or in any of its processes will provide a basis for it.
A peculiar blindness, of course, prohibits our design theologians from
attention to the equally obvious instances of disorder and waste in processes
of the world. The eyes of our subjects, just as with most of us, are trained
strictly upon what they are prepared to see.

Many differing formulations of the design argument have already been
discovered. Its general form, however, has come down through the ages
with scarcely a change. The differing formulations of the design argument
will be found to be due to changed conceptions of the nature of the world
order, and to changed ideas concerning the ways of knowing nature's
processes and structure—in other words, to new metaphysical and
epistemological views. The men with whom we have already dealt, then,
for the most part simply took a very old argument and refurbished it in
terms of the methods and metaphysics of Early Modern science.

The use of the design argument in order to combat the materialistic
views of Hobbes and Spinoza, as well as the Pyrrhonists, was noted in the
works of thinkers of the seventeenth century, and in the work of eighteenth-
century theologians from Richard Bentley onward. Interestingly enough,
at its very inception in the writings of Plato, particularly in the *Laws*, the
design argument served the same purpose. Plato and his mentor Socrates,
like Newton and his followers, were bent on rescuing traditional notions
from skeptical attack. Thus in Plato we will find the design argument used
in opposition to the same conceptions of mechanism and chance construction of the world order that provided the target for the Newtonians.
"Natural theology" in its eighteenth century sense meant "scientific"
theology, theology based on scientific notions and developed by methods
believed to be similar to those of science. In its more general sense, however,
natural theology, as distinct from revealed or mystical theology, has
through the ages meant theology based upon some theory of nature, upon
ways of conceiving of God or the gods in terms of certain kinds of ideas
about nature, and by certain cognitive means.

In this sense, Plato was the inventor of natural theology.[1] He felt that
certain characteristics of the gods could be demonstrated from premises
drawn from his conception of nature and its origin. In the *Timaeus* he
produced a conception of God as the original efficient cause of the world.
The formal cause, of course, is the forms.[2] This theological element in
Plato's thought is extremely important in that it provides him with a

[1] A. E. Taylor, *Plato: The Man and His Work* (6th ed.; London: Methuen and
Company, Ltd., 1949), p. 441.
[2] *Ibid.*, p. 442.

solution to the problem of relating the forms to their particular exemplifications in the world of the sensible flux—it provides the connection, the
participation, between these two aspects of reality. In this way Plato
counters the criticism of Parmenides and the Sophists.

Plato's main theological arguments, found in Book X of the *Laws*, could
easily be placed in the mouths of Butler, Locke, or Newton, as indeed they
probably were. In his opinion, insolence toward God arises from three
sources: (a) the belief that God does not exist, (b) the belief that although
the gods exist they have no interest in man, and (c) the belief that the gods
can be turned aside from justice and the good by sacrifices and prayers.[3]
All of these beliefs could be found among fourth-century Greek thinkers.
Of particular importance is (c), because it shows that Plato virtually
identified God with the uniform processes of nature, and excluded a
particular providence. Plato, as usual, shows more sophistication than those
who filched his ideas, including the Newtonians.

In response to the proposition that the gods exist, the one which
particularly interests us, Plato's character the Athenian asks: "How would
you prove it?" and Cleinias replies:

> How? In the first place, the earth and sun, and the stars and the universe,
> and the fair order of the seasons, and the division of them into years and
> months, furnishes proofs of their existence; and also there is the fact that
> all Hellenes and barbarians believe in them.[4]

Putting aside the interesting proposition that this argument might be
one of those useful lies that Plato in the *Republic* claims to be necessary for
the maintenance of order in the state, this passage clearly presents the
argument from design. The last sentence proposes none other than the
venerable argument from universal or general consent, an argument which
became the main basis of the Stoic conception of natural law, and which
we have noted above with respect to the Cambridge Platonists and the
continental rationalists. Locke's rejection of universal or general consent
will also be recalled.

Following Plato's formulation of the design argument in the *Laws*, we
discover that he argues that all corporeal movements are finally dependent
upon motions of soul. According to this principle, the order and arrangement of the world is due to the work of soul or mind. Not to allow any
modern theory to escape its humble or exalted origins, we should also

[3] Plato, *Laws*, in *The Dialogues of Plato*, tr. B. Jowett (New York: Random
House, 1937), Vol. II, x, 885. The following quotations and citations from Plato
refer to these volumes.
[4] *Ibid.*, x, 886.

mention that Plato defined atheism in terms of the belief that the world and its contents are the products of nonintelligent motions of corporeal elements. This charge is directed against the theories held by Atomistic and Skeptical philosophers, but here he is specifically arguing against those Ionian scientists [5] who attempted to account for the order of nature by means of mechanical principles. [6] We will recall Newton's contention that the attempt to derive the order of the world from mechanical principles is "inconsistent with my system." It is clear that eighteenth-century thinkers were presaged by the thinker who presaged everyone—Plato. Change the names and span two thousand years, and you have an essential part of seventeenth- and eighteenth-century theology. Mechanistic philosophers would say, according to Plato, that the sun, moon, stars, etc., are the products of chance and mechanism:

> They say that the greatest and fairest things are the work of nature and chance, the lesser of art, which, receiving from nature the greater and primeval creations, moulds and fashions all these lesser works which are generally termed artificial. [7]

External motion, as in heavenly bodies, comes after interior motions, as in soul and mind, and therefore the motion and order of the universe comes after, and is the work of, mind or soul. ". . . the whole path and movement of heaven, and all that is therein, is by nature akin to the movement and revolution and calculation of mind, and proceeds by kindred laws. . . ." [8] The Greeks tended to identify any sort of order with mind. For these reasons, among others, the guardians in Plato's *Republic* are to study astronomy well and thoroughly. Mankind went astray, and Athens lost its cause in Greece, according to Plato, by neglecting this principle and putting matter before mind.

And so we see Plato using the design argument to good effect, criticizing the mechanical and atomic theory which sought to explain the order and origin of the world in terms of ultimate mechanical natural laws and chance. As we should expect in the greatest early mathematician-philosopher, Plato argues *from* rather than *to* design. On the other hand, he appears to believe that the argument is what we should call a priori, and therein is in disagreement with many of our early modern design theologians.

He seems not to have connected the design argument with the principle of analogy. It is well known, of course, how very important the principle

[5] *Ibid.*, x, 889.   [6] Taylor, *Plato: The Man and His Work*, p. 490.
[7] Plato, *Laws*, x, 889.   [8] *Ibid.*, x, 897.

of analogy is in his work—many of his most important arguments were couched in analogical terms, as is evident from a bare reading of the *Republic*. But he does discuss the principle of analogy in the *Statesman* in connection with what he calls "example." Aristotle later gave precisely the same name to a similar kind of reasoning. Another reference to analogy in Plato should not be left unmentioned, for it is of the same form and name as the kind of reasoning which Aristotle later called "analogy," and still later was called "proportion." In *Republic VII*, where he discusses the division of mind into intellect and opinion, Plato runs this little analogy:

> . . . and so to make a proportion:
> As being is to becoming, so is pure intellect
>   to opinion.
> And as intellect is to opinion, so is science
>   to belief,
> and understanding to the perception of shadows. [9]

So the idea of proportionate analogy, a type of analogical thinking essential to Thomistic theology, and drawn largely from Aristotle, was, as we shall see, not original to Aristotle.

In summary, we can say definitely that Plato used the argument from design. The world was, to Plato as well as to Newton, inexplicable in terms of chance collisions of atomic particles. Further, the order of astronomical bodies is of such a kind that it could only be put into effect by mind, since matter cannot order itself or move itself originally and since the specific order and movements of these bodies implies initiation by mind. In these beliefs Plato agrees with all the design arguers that came after him. Newton and his followers held that the order, harmony, and beauty of the world, evidenced by mechanical law, could not be the result of natural mechanism and chance alone. So the different formulations of the argument from design as proposed by Plato and Newton follow from their different metaphysical and epistemological positions, although, as we have seen, there is an element of Platonism in Newton and most of his contemporaries. For Newton the material world is a machine. For Plato it is an organism and a work of art. Both views, however, are amenable to the design argument, for both machines and works of art or skill bespeak intelligent contrivers. Methodologically, Plato regarded the design argument as demonstrative and certain, "dialectical," a type of inference later called a priori, while the Newtonians, as we have seen, generally disagreed.

Aristotle, following his master, maintained similar views. He gave the

[9] Plato, *Republic*, in Jowett, *op. cit.*, Vol. I, vii, 534.

name "theology" to that highest of sciences, the science of Being, which combines substantial, self-dependent existence with freedom from change.[10] The conception of God Aristotle gives us in *Metaphysics* 5 is therefore that of an impersonal God, based upon metaphysical notions. Beginning with the conception of substance, the ground of all existing things, he held that it must be either perishable or not. If it is, then since all things are contingent upon substance, all things are perishable.

But is there anything which is indestructible? Yes, two things are not perishable: time, eternal with no before and no after, and change, continuous, if not identical with, time.[11] The only continuous change is change of place, and change that is so continuous is circular motion.[12] If the above reasoning is correct, according to Aristotle, then there must be an eternal circular motion,[13] together with an eternal substance which produces this eternal motion. Such a contention is further borne out, notes Aristotle, by the facts of observation and by the unceasing circular motions of the starry heavens. Now the movement of the starry heavens in an eternal circular motion necessitates an unmoved mover,[14] a mover who moves the heavens by the power of his efficacy as an object of desire. Everything in the world yearns for this pure actuality.

This is a short summation of Aristotle's dominant or major argument for the existence of God. This Deity is of a peculiarly nonreligious sort, however. While the argument deals with the orderly circular motion of the celestial bodies, still it is properly a cosmological rather than a design argument. The fact that Aristotle used the design argument, however, is quite plain, although W. D. Ross thinks it is a secondary argument and even contradictory to the cosmological one given above. Ross holds that in Aristotle's mature metaphysics, design and adaptation are ascribed to the unconscious teleology of nature, rather than to the working out of a divine plan. God as pure actuality merely contemplates himself, "thinks about thinking," and therefore has no influence upon the world in the sense of constructing it. God operates upon the world solely as forming the object of its desire. If this is true, then Aristotle's teleology is an immanent teleology,[15] and God is not a creator in the sense of an artist or mechanic.

[10] Aristotle, *Metaphysics*, in *The Works of Aristotle*, ed. W. D. Ross (Oxford: Oxford University Press, 1908–1952), Vol. VIII, vi, 1026a10–19; ii, 1064a33. The following references to Aristotle are to these volumes.

[11] Aristotle, *Physics*, 219b ff., 184a–199b, 200a–267b.

[12] *Ibid.*, 261a27–263b26, 264a7–265b12.

[13] Aristotle, *Metaphysics*, 1071b4–22.   [14] Aristotle, *Physics*, 257a, 231b13.

[15] W. D. Ross, *Aristotle* (New York: Meridian Books, Inc., 1959), pp. 123–127. Aristotle, *Study of Animals*, 641, 696b24–32.

But whatever his intentions or later views, in the dialogue *On Philosophy* he used the design argument.

> Aristotle used to say that men's thoughts of Gods sprang from two sources
> —the experiences of the soul, and the phenomena of the heavens. . . .
> But the heavenly bodies also contributed to this belief; seeing by day the
> sun running his circular course, and by night the well-ordered movement
> of the other stars, they came to think that there is a God who is the cause
> of such movement and order. Such was the belief of Aristotle.[16]

> . . . so those who first looked up to heaven and saw the sun running its
> race from its rising to its setting, and the orderly dances of the stars,
> looked for the craftsman of this lovely design, and surmised that it came
> about not by chance but by the agency of some mighty and imperishable
> nature, which was God.[17]

The sun's progress across the skies, the "dance of the stars," the craftsmanship implied in such a lovely design, the reference to the inability to believe that such a harmonious system could have been produced by chance; all the facets of the design argument are here just as they were in Plato. Anyone who thinks about the evidence will "surely reason that these things have not been framed without perfect skill, but that there both was and is a framer of this universe—God."[18]

This dialogue, it is true, is one of Aristotle's lost works, and probably was written after his connection with the Academy had ended. His break away from Platonic theory is shown by the heavy attack upon Plato's doctrine of transcendent ideas or forms.[19] Apparently written about the same time as the early sections of the *Metaphysics*, the dialogue nevertheless, as we have seen, does not represent a complete break away from the Academy on theological matters. Therefore, although it may well be that these conceptions represent Aristotle's more immature thinking on the subject, this does not prejudice the fact that historically his use of the design argument was a powerful support to its extensive acceptance by later theologians. The fragments to which we have referred are located in the work of Sextus Empiricus, Cicero, Seneca, Philo, Diogenes Laertius, and others, all of whom, aside from their own use of Aristotle's views, were important sources for later thought, and were thus responsible for transmitting the design argument to later generations of philosophers and theologians. References to these early thinkers can be found in the texts of

[16] Aristotle, *Select Fragments*, in *Works*, Vol. XII, 12a.
[17] *Ibid.*, 12b.
[18] *Ibid.*, 13.
[19] Ross, Introduction to *Select Fragments*, p. x. Ross, *Aristotle*, p. 6.

practically every thinker of any note in the early modern period. The Cambridge Platonists, Locke, Berkeley, Butler, are no exceptions to this generalization, and we shall see that this is also true of Hume. Indeed, we have seen it already in our opening quotation from Hume's *Dialogues Concerning Natural Religion.*

The basic point of departure in that form of the design argument which was used by Aristotle is in the conception of the world as an organism and as a product of art.[20] The premises are drawn from the observed sequences of change in the motions of the sun and other heavenly bodies. Such celestial phenomena are compared by analogy to the work of human skill and art. This represents the second source of human knowledge of God. (This is in addition to the first, or cosmological argument, referred to above.) In our first quotation he infers a God who is the creator of the world order, just as we infer a human creator from an object of artistic design. The second quotation reinforces this interpretation, with God taken to be a "craftsman." This conception does not necessarily depend upon an idea of "fine art," but upon the idea of skilled craftsmanship in general. To this is added another important notion: the belief that the doctrine of chance does not furnish an adequate explanation of the world order and its harmonious and systematic motions. There must, according to Aristotle, have been some "agency" involved. So we find in Aristotle's views, as in those of Plato, the anti-chance doctrine endemic in all the design theologians heretofore considered. Beauty and power, and the conception of an eternal and immutable uniformity of the motions of the celestial bodies, are also considered in the second quotation. The world system is comprehended as a settled, systematic, and harmonious order of interrelated motions. The third quotation considers the world system to be the result of the "perfect skill" of a "framer of the universe."

Aristotle apparently did not specifically analyze the logical form of the design argument. But it is of interest, as it was in the case of Plato, to note his ideas about argument by analogy and argument by example because these elements were brought together by later thinkers. It is in Aristotelian ideas that we have the source of later beliefs concerning induction and analogy, although they were transmitted to posterity in terms of Stoic and other interpretations. There was, however, an interesting development of terminology and conception with regard to the design argument before these later thinkers appeared.

[20] H. A. Wolfson, *Philo: Foundations of Religious Philosophy in Judaism, Christianity and Islam* (Cambridge: Harvard University Press, 1947), II, 76.

"Analogy" is a term found often in the writings of Aristotle and found in many different contexts. It runs the gamut of meaning from mere general comparison to the idea of mathematical proportion, and fulfils different functions in his metaphysics, biology, and rhetoric, as well as in his logic. For instance, he considered metaphysics a dialectical science, a science not treating of any one specific class of being, but of being in general. And the principles to be applied to all things, i.e., being in general, are not literal and univocal (unambiguous) but analogical.[21] In the *Metaphysics* Aristotle speaks of actual and potential being as the "same by analogy" in all things. For example, the statue is to its material as the waking man is to the sleeper. Analogy here takes the form of a mathematical proportion: A is to B as C is to D. Being itself must, therefore, be conceived analogically. With respect to the classification of things in the sphere of biology, Aristotle held that the parts of animals are not the same, yet in a real sense they are not different. They are similar, or analogous. Such analogies hold between hands and claws, fingernails and hoofs, feathers and fish scales. What the feather is to the bird, the scale is to the fish.[22] The highest genera in the classification of things are linked only by analogy—that is, the objects have only analogous characteristics in common. This represents the third grade of likeness. The first grade has to do with objects in infima species. These objects are immutable and not evolving. Their differentia are accidental—based on irregularities of matter, and not on essence and design. The second concerns species of the same highest genus, where there are identical bodily parts, and the differentia relate only to size and degree of possession of the same fundamental qualities. The highest genera, however, are linked only by analogy—that is, the things agree only in having analogous organs.

But for our purposes the most important conception of analogy is found in Aristotle's *Prior* and *Posterior Analytics*, although some important elements are located in the *Rhetoric*. The term "analogy" in fourth-century Greek means the same as our term "proportion," or the identity of ratios. So we see that his use of the term was rather different from the usages we found among Enlightenment thinkers, with the possible exceptions of King, Berkeley, and Browne. We have seen that Aristotle felt that the highest genera often have nothing in common; that is, they have no common essential characteristics. It is in the light of this view that he

[21] See Mckeon, Introduction to *The Basic Works of Aristotle*, ed. R. Mckeon (New York: Random House, 1947). Aristotle, *Metaphysics*, iv, vi, vii.
[22] Aristotle, *A History of Animals*, 486b16–23; *Parts of Animals*, 644a12–21.

states in the *Topics* (Book I, Chapter 17) that "likeness should be studied, first, in the case of things belonging to different genera, the formula being A is to B as C is to D (e.g., as knowledge stands to the object of knowledge, so is sensation related to the object of sensation), and, as A is in B, so is C in D (e.g., as sight is in the eye, so is reason in the soul, and as in a calm in the sea, so is windlessness in the air)." Here we have a formula that is called "analogia," that is concerned with an identity of relations between quantities, and is what we refer to as "proportion." Aristotle has here taken a quantitative formula and replaced the elements, or interpreted the variables, with qualitative data. It is basically a mathematical way of looking at things. In Book I, Chapter 18, he points up the use of likeness with respect to inductive arguments and to definitions; because it is from like cases that we move from particulars to universals, and because in hypotheticals, what we find among similars to be true of one is true of the rest. Likeness is useful in definition because if we can comprehend similars among things at a glance in each of a set of individual cases, then we will not be at a loss with regard to locating the object within its genus when we define it.

In the *Metaphysics*, Aristotle makes a statement similar to the one above. Some things are one (the same) in number, others in genus, others by analogy. In number the matter is one; in species those things are one whose definition is one; in genus those things to which the same figure of predication (category) applies are one; and by analogy those things which are related as a third thing is to a fourth are one. Here, of course, analogy is again represented as proportion, with mathematical form. Things that are one in genus are not all one in species, but are one by analogy (common properties), while things that are one by analogy are not all one in genus.[23] A little further on in the *Metaphysics* (1018a13–15) he notes that we can also apply the term "different" to those things that are similar by analogy. As we will see in the *Posterior Analytics*, this means that while the human nail and the bird's claw are analogous, yet they are different. In Book 9, Chapter 6 (1048a1–8), he repeats the formula of analogy as proportional relation with respect to definition and induction. If there is no likeness evident between things related by induction, we can move to analogy. His point here is to explain the identity and difference between actuality and potentiality; as "that it is as that which is building to that which is capable of building, and the waking to the sleeping, and that which is seeing to that which has its eyes shut but has sight, and that which has been

---

[23] Aristotle, *Metaphysics*, 1017a.

shaped out of matter to the matter. . . ." But all things are not said in the same sense to exist actually, but only by analogy—for some are as movements to potency, and others as substance to some sort of matter. Here is the same analogical form, used in metaphysical construction. Being, as noted above, is in its hierarchical structure only analogically the same in all things. This latter point is made again in Book XII, Chapter 4.[24]

In the *Ethica Nicomachea*, Aristotle deals with proportion or analogy with respect to the determination of the utility of the distribution of desirables. Equality must be considered with respect to proportion.[25] Political justice is found among men who are proportionately or arithmetically equal.[26] This is the principle of analogy as applied in ethical matters, with the mathematical form retained and the whole thing looked upon in mathematical terms.[27] Injustice, therefore, is a violation of proportion.

The subject of analogy is taken up in the *Posterior Analytics* in a number of places. Aristotle notes that of the basic truths used in the demonstrative sciences, some are peculiar to each science, and some are common to all; but those basic truths that are common to all are common only in the sense of being analogous, that is, usable only insofar as they fall within the genus constituting the province in question.[28] The basic truths are to Aristotle those propositions which cannot be proved, such as the meaning of terms, and those concerning existence. With respect to definition, and the various methods of selection of characteristics in forming definitions, he believed that beyond the compositive method of adducing common characteristics, and differentiation, lay the method of analogy.[29] With respect to the connections that are to be established by means of the demonstrative syllogism, i.e., essence and property, cause and effect, substance and attribute, Aristotle held that connections requiring proof which are identical by analogy have middles that are also analogous.[30]

It is evident that the concept of analogy, in the sense of proportion or identity of ratios, played a considerable part in Aristotle's philosophy—indeed, in nearly every aspect of it. We have seen that he brings the conception to bear in his metaphysics, his ethics, his logic, as well as his biology. Analogy is an ontological conception in his metaphysics and

[24] *Ibid.*, 1070a; *Posterior Analytics*, 98a20–24.
[25] Aristotle, *Ethica Nicomachea*, 1134a, 1134b.
[26] *Ibid.*, 1131a30–35, 1131b1–8.
[27] *Ibid.*, 1131a10–12, 1136a, 1106a36, 1132a.
[28] Aristotle, *Posterior Analytics*, 76a31–39.
[29] *Ibid.*, 98a20–24.   [30] *Ibid.*, 99a16–17.

rhetoric, it is a mode of selection and a type of inference in his logic, and it presents a way of constructing metaphors in his theory of rhetoric.

The main reason for this somewhat extended discussion of analogy in the mathematical sense of proportion of ratios is to make clear the change in meaning of terms which occurred during the period from Aristotle to the eighteenth century. Except for Browne and King, along with others who followed Aquinas, the term came to mean what we in modern times, exclusive of Thomistic theory, mean by it, and what Aristotle called not "analogy" but "argument by example." The conception of analogy as proportion was taken up by Aquinas and the Thomists who followed him as the principal method of conceiving God and his attributes. Even in Newton there is, as we have seen, a residuum of this proportionate analogy. However, it involved, as we shall see in Aquinas, a way of conceiving of God's attributes rather than an inference which proves God's existence.

Aristotle did consider a form of reasoning which is similar to what Enlightenment thinkers usually called "analogy," but he attached the name "example" to it. He quite correctly connected this kind of inference to inductive procedures, and exemplified it, interestingly enough, by means of a proportionate analogy. Example is to induction as the enthymeme is to syllogism.[31]

> We shall first treat of argument by example, for it has the nature of induction, which is the foundation of reasoning. . . . The speaker may argue thus: "we must prepare for war against the king of Persia and not let him subdue Egypt. For Darius of old did not cross the Aegean until he had seized Egypt; but once he had seized it, he did cross. . . . If therefore the present king seizes Egypt, he also will cross, and therefore we must not let him."[32]

Note Aristotle's recognition that the idea of similarity or analogy is the basis of the principle that like causes have like effects. Therefore, it is basic to generalization and prediction—indeed, to the whole notion of induction.

The above formulation of the doctrine is consistent with his other discussions of it. In the *Prior Analytics*, however, we get a more precise differentiation of example and induction. Example differs from perfect induction in two ways: (1) it does not proceed from all the similar instances; and (2) it ends by applying its general conclusion to a new particular.[33]

[31] Aristotle, *Rhetoric*, 1356b4–5; *Posterior Analytics*, 71a10. Ross, *Aristotle*, p. 271.
[32] Aristotle, *Rhetoric*, 1393a–b.
[33] Aristotle, *Prior Analytics*, 68b37–39, 69a1–19.

Taking the premise that war against neighbors is evil, Aristotle deduces that for Athenians to fight against Thebans is an evil. The evidence for the premise that fighting against neighbors is evil is drawn from the similar case, e.g., the war of the Thebans against the Phocians. It is not argument from part to whole (particulars to universals—or inductive generalization). Nor is it argument from whole to part (universals to particulars—syllogism). Rather, it is argument from particular to particular. Argument from example does not, as does induction, proceed from all the particular cases bearing resemblances. Since the war of Thebes against Phocia was evil, and it was a war against neighbors, then a war of Athens against Thebes, which would be a similar case in that both were wars against neighbors, would also be analogous in the other respect, i.e., it would be evil. It is an imperfect induction in that there is no complete enumeration of instances of wars against neighbors, all of which are found to be evil. Thus we see Aristotle's idea that example is related to induction as enthymeme is to syllogism, for an enthymeme is a truncated syllogism, a syllogism with one or another of its premises unstated, whereas example is an inductive inference with the generalization left unstated.

Now the formal basis of Newton's variety of the argument from design is similar to that of Aristotle's conception of example. All cases of order which we know (and yet we do not postulate that the enumeration is complete) have involved an intelligent creator. The world is a system which exhibits order (as in mathematical principles like the law of gravitation), and therefore also implies the analogon, an intelligent creator. In Aristotle's terms such an argument would be an imperfect induction because all the possible instances of order and related creators could not possibly be experienced. Further, it is an argument by example because it is an inference from one particular—the world order—to another particular —God. To put it another way, it is argument from one system, a machine, which in man's experience involves a constructor, to the world machine, with the inference that here also there is a constructor. This notion of example in Aristotle appears to be the ultimate source of the modern conception of analogy, unless one wishes to credit it to Plato on the grounds mentioned above concerning his discussion of example.

The proximate source of the modern conception of analogy is in the work of the Stoics, who seem to have begun to use the term "analogy" for what Aristotle called "example." It is my belief that Early Modern thinkers were influenced by both Aristotle and the Stoics, but that they followed in particular the Stoic terminology with respect to analogy, just as they followed the Stoic use of the design argument.[34] As did Ray and other eighteenth-century thinkers, they worked the purposive argument to design into the ground. Along this line, the Stoics showed in detail how plants and animals, and the parts and organs of plants and animals, are connected by means-ends relationships. They related things in particular to man, finding utility in practically everything. It was their idea that everything in nature is ultimately for the benefit of rational beings. As we have seen, this view was held by so many modern thinkers that even Boyle, who was himself quite infatuated with this kind of argument, nevertheless protested against such wild attributions of benefit to man of everything in the universe. The Stoics, however, most assuredly did consider man to be at the very apex of the hierarchy of beings, and felt that the rest of the universe was geared to his benefit.[35] This represents the teleological facet of the physico-theological argument, which we have seen to be a characteristic aspect of seventeenth- and eighteenth-century theology. According to this position, nature embodies means-ends relations similar to those in man's productions. The relation of the parts of the eye to the function of sight, the liver to digestion, etc., are analogous to the doors and windows of houses, the wheels of water clocks. No means-ends without purposes or intentions, as in man's artifacts; and no intentions without minds which have them. In effect, this means that there is no purpose without a purposer. Nature was, for the Stoics, an organism, with all parts purposively related.[36]

But they did not neglect order and symmetry, which to them as to the Newtonians implied intelligence.

> And just as the man who is familiar with ships, as soon as he sees in the distance a ship with a favouring wind behind it and with all its sails well set, concludes that there is somebody who directs its course and brings it into its appointed havens, so too those who first looked up to heaven and beheld the sun running its courses from East to West and the orderly processions of the stars sought for the artificer of this most beautiful array, conjecturing that it had not come about spontaneously but by some superior and imperishable nature, which is God.[37]

This resembles very much the statement from Aristotle, above. The order and harmonious movements, the symmetrical arrangements of the heavenly bodies, demonstrate for the Stoics the existence of the gods. The inference, at least in this fragment, is also held to be hypothetical or conjectural, that is, probable. A world exhibiting such divinely ordered

[34] Cicero, De Natura Deorum, ii, passim.
[35] Ibid., ii, 5, 53.   [36] Ibid., ii, 19.
[37] Sextus Empiricus, Vol. III, Against the Physicists, i, 27.

phenomena could not be a result merely of chance collisions of material elements, even were there no determinate benefits or purposes resultant from the order. This is the argument from design, from the order and harmony of astronomical bodies.[38] It is, in characteristic form, the analogy of God and the world to man and his products of skill, and it includes, in addition, the notion of direct providence. That is, in this analogy the pilot is in continuing and direct control of the process of sailing the ship—he did not just set it off in one direction and let it set its own course. In this sense of the activity of piloting a ship, art is inseparably linked to intelligence. Since the world exhibits in even greater degree the characteristics of works of human production, then by analogy we can infer that it had an intelligent producer. All sorts of analogies are mentioned: statues, houses, water clocks, even gravitational attraction. All are made by art and intelligence, and "with what possible consistency can you suppose that the universe which contains these same products of art, and their constructors, and all things, is destitute of thought and intelligence."[39]

In Stoicism the doctrine of analogy came into its own as one of the fundamental sources of knowledge. As with Plato and Aristotle, however, the Stoics do not seem to have related it to the design argument, although the design argument as used by them certainly fits into its form. At the basis of their epistemology lay the doctrine of the sensory origin of knowledge, the concept of the *tabula rasa*. All knowledge, believed the Stoic, rises from "sensuous presentations." Some of these presentations, or "ideas" in the terminology of Locke, rise from sensation, and some rise from reflection and introspection.[40] Yet in these *sensa* alone no knowledge is contained at all; that is, in bare perception there is nothing true or false. Truth has to do with the relations of ideas, and therefore is a characteristic of judgments. Sensation and perception are mere passive receptions by the mind of impressions.[41] Knowledge is something more, and comes only as a result of relating these sensa. Knowledge, then, has to do with relations of ideas, and it is only in the activity of judging that ideas are related.[42]

But the mark of truth in judgments is not the mere combination and

[38] *Ibid.*, i, 60, 111. Cicero, *De Natura Deorum*, ii, 21, 34–36.

[39] Cicero, *De Natura Deorum*, ii, 34.

[40] *Sextus Empiricus*, Vol. I, *Outlines of Pyrrhonism*, Introduction, p. xxv. Diogenes Laertius, *The Lives of Eminent Philosophers*, tr. C. D. Yonge (London, 1853), Sections vii, xxxvi. See St. George Stock, *Stoicism* (London: A. Constable and Company, Ltd., 1908), p. 22.

[41] *Sextus Empiricus, Outlines of Pyrrhonism*, ii, 70.

[42] *Sextus Empiricus, Against the Logicians*, ii, 397; i, 93; ii, 10. Diogenes Laertius, *The Lives of Eminent Philosophers*, Sec. xxxvi.

comparison of ideas preliminary to forming them into conceptions. True judgments are characterized by a sort of inner "assent" which amounts in our terminology to self-evident conviction.[43] The true is that which "subsists and is opposed"—judgments comparing ideas and concepts whose agreement or disagreement is immediately clear.[44] Those true judgments which apprehend reality are laws of nature. Such laws of nature are "natural" because they are based in man's reason, and man's reason *is* his nature, his essence.

Now reasoning itself is divided by the Stoics into three parts: natural philosophy, ethics, and logic.[45] Under logic, they included what we would call psychology and rhetoric, as well as formal logic or dialectic.[46] Analogy was considered under all these headings, as it was with Aristotle. That is, ideas are combined psychologically by means of likeness; argument proceeds by means of examples of like situations and characteristics; and concepts and definitions are formulated in terms of the analogies and similarities of things.[47] In relation to logic and similitude and representation, the Stoics also developed a theory of signs. Analogy belonged to rhetoric only insofar as it was a mode of arguing used by orators.

Ideas, then, are formed by several means. They arise in sense, are produced by means of composition, transposition, opposition, privation, similarity, and analogy. The idea we derive, for instance, from a picture of Socrates is an idea based on similarity. Ideas rooted in analogy can be of several kinds. In the first place there are ideas based on increase or decrease of characteristics, such as the ideas of giants and pygmies which are derived by analogy from the characteristics of men. More appropriate to the conception of analogy in which we are primarily interested, the Stoic maintained that analogy is the form of thinking behind conceptions such as our knowledge of the center of the earth, knowledge derived from consideration of the characteristics of smaller spheres of which we have had experience.[48]

In this last type of case in particular we find that the Stoics used analogy in one of the ways in which we have seen it used in early modern science

---

[43] *Sextus Empiricus, Against the Logicians*, i, 257–259; i, 364–365; ii, 397; ii, 87–90; *Outlines of Pyrrhonism*, ii, 97–98.

[44] *Sextus Empiricus, Outlines of Pyrrhonism*, Introduction, pp. xxv ff.

[45] Diogenes Laertius, *The Lives of Eminent Philosophers*, Sec. xxxiii.

[46] Seneca, *Ad Lucilium Epistulae Morales*, tr. R. H. Gummere (London: G. P. Putnam's Sons, 1925), Letters 9, 17. Diogenes Laertius, *The Lives of Eminent Philosophers*, Secs. vii, xli, xlii, lxii. *Sextus Empiricus, Outlines of Pyrrhonism*, p. xxv.

[47] R. D. Hicks, *Stoic and Epicurean* (New York: Charles Scribner's Sons, 1910), p. 58. *Sextus Empiricus, Outlines of Pyrrhonism*, ii, 58–60.

[48] Diogenes Laertius, *The Lives of Eminent Philosophers*, Sec. xxxvi.

and theology. It is what Aristotle called "example." The term does not here connote Aristotle's proportional or mathematical conception of analogy, although the latter was not neglected,[49] and is implicit in the notion of pygmies noted above. An interesting sidelight concerns the fact that the Stoics became entangled with the Alexandrine School in an argument about grammar. The Alexandrines held that all declensions and conjugations of names, verbs, etc., should be governed strictly by the principle of analogy, i.e., analogous or like endings for like terms.[50] This argument passed from the Greek to the Roman stage, and in Varro's *De Lingua Latina* we have the argument threshed out again. And to top it off, with the development of scholarship in England in the sixteenth, seventeenth, and eighteenth centuries, it was perhaps inescapable that the whole matter be threshed out again with regard to the English language, and this is exactly what happened.[51] Analogy emerges as more and more of a pervasive topic, shot throughout the fabric of many contexts, from logic to language.

When we come to the consideration of Roman thinkers, we find a similar attention paid to analogy. Cicero and Seneca both consider it. Seneca stated that it is by the observation and comparison of likenesses in recurrent actions that one is led to inferences. With respect to moral knowledge and judgments, both the "good and the morally sterling were inferred by analogy."[52] Cicero repeats the Stoic idea:

> Now notions of things are produced in the mind when something has become known either by experience or by combination of ideas or by likeness or by analogy. The fourth and last method in this list is the one that has given us the conception of the good. The mind ascends by analogy from the things in accordance with nature till finally it arrives at the notion of the good.[53]

Varro's statement concerning analogy as proportion has already been cited; he also refers to the conception of analogy in the sense of example. So we see that the term "analogy" had by the first century before Christ

[49] Varro, *On the Latin Language*, tr. R. G. Kent (Cambridge: Harvard University Press, 1948), Vol. II, Book x, Sec. 3.

[50] Max Pohlenz, *Die Stoa* (Gottingen: Vandenhoeck and Ruprecht, 1948), I, 42, 183, 265.

[51] See Joseph Addison, *Spectator*, No. 135 (1712). Samuel Johnson, *Rambler*, No. 208. Preface to Samuel Johnson's *Dictionary* (1775). Joseph Priestley, *The Rudiments of English Grammar* (1761). George Campbell, *Philosophy of Rhetoric* (1776), I, 378-379. S. A. Leonard, *The Doctrine of Correctness in English Usage: 1700 to 1800* (1929). Sandys, *A History of Classical Scholarship*, under "analogy."

[52] Seneca, *Letters to Lucilius*, Vol. III, Letter 120.

[53] Cicero, *De Finibus, Bonoram et Malorum*, tr. H. Rackham (London: Wm. Heinemann, 1914), x, 2, 33.

(Cicero and Varro were contemporaries) come to mean both proportion and example. And it appears that it was the Stoics who began to use the term "analogy," rather indiscriminately, to cover Aristotle's concept of example,[54] as well as other kinds of likeness, similarity, and proportion. Seneca and Cicero both noted that the term "analogy" is used for arguments which infer that an object has some property because it is similar to another object or objects which have the same property. According to this kind of procedure, one deduces the goodness, or good effects, of an action because it is similar to another act which was good, or had good effects. In like manner one deduces the probable nature of the inner parts of the earth by analogy from what we know about the inner parts of other spheres. Thus the concept of example in Aristotle, included under the concept of analogy by the Stoics, was later transmitted directly from them to such early modern thinkers as Galileo, Locke, Bacon, and Newton.

In sum, arguments to and from design were the most important theological tools of the Stoics. It is of interest that these Stoic views are found in the writings of Cicero and Seneca, Sextus Empiricus and Diogenes Laertius, all of which were readily available to early modern thinkers. It is in these writings that there is constant reference to inference by analogy, as well as to the design argument. As pointed out in the material on the philosophers and theologians of the early modern period, Cicero and Seneca, Sextus and others, were required reading in the British universities, and they were constantly footnoted or referred to by early modern thinkers. I have already argued that Locke and the Cambridge Platonists were influenced by Stoicism, and I think that this influence was general throughout the Age of Reason. The continental thinkers Grotius and Pufendorf, who influenced the Cambridge men and Locke, admitted their debt to the Stoics. Cudworth's *True Intellectual System* alone was a huge compendium of ancient learning, with references to and quotations from all the ancients noted above. Put these facts together with the remarkable correlation between Stoic and Lockean ideas on epistemology and logic, and I think the case is rather complete.

Philo, really the first theologian in the sense of an attempt to harmonize speculative philosophical thought with a religious doctrine of divine revelation, also used the design argument. He lived during the first century before Christ, and devoted his efforts to the fusion of Greek and Jewish ideas. According to Philo, man was made in the image of God, and therefore we can conceive of God by analogy with man. Here again

[54] See Pohlenz, *Die Stoa*, II, 24–34.

there is the appeal to the principle of analogy. We know God from "created things; as one may learn the substance from the shadow,"[55] a statement which shows a mystical turn that is not emphasized in the views of most of our subjects, and this factor does indeed distinguish his theory from that of Aristotle and the Stoics. Furthermore, he held that in the last analysis we find that we cannot really know God at all. We can prove that He exists, but cannot know His nature. And here, in clear focus, is the old dilemma, running its difficult course throughout the history of theology, of anthropomorphism and agnosticism. God is reduced to nature, or to human nature, or it is claimed that knowledge of Him is impossible.

Within the limits of this type of theology, the problem of the knowledge that man may have of God reduces to two major questions, which, as we have seen, were somewhat muddled in the Newtonian period: one, does God exist? and two, what is His nature?

But in such searching two principal questions arise which demand the consideration of the genuine philosopher. One is whether the Deity exists, a question necessitated by those who practice atheism, the worst form of wickedness, the other is what the Deity is in essence. Now to answer the first question does not need much labor, but the second is not only difficult but perhaps impossible. . . .[56]

A considerable amount of the cultivation of Philo's theological garden is, by anticipation, to be left to the spade of revelation. It might be of interest to repeat the reasons why, in the confines of logic, this problem arises. It results from the Aristotelian dictum that in order to know something we must be able to define it; and in order to define it, we must find its genus and differentia. But God belongs to no genus, and therefore is undefinable. Thus He would appear, by this logic, to be unknowable. We can only imperfectly *conceive* of His nature or characteristics through the mediation of analogy with created beings. It might be asked just why this sort of problem is so warily approached by theologians—and the answer is that a number of the traditionally conceived attributes of God, such as omnipotence, omniscience, etc., are found to be incompatible when the traditional logical categories are applied to their consideration. Analogy in Philo, since it is of this "imperfect" way of conceiving of God, is not to be understood as a form of inference to God's nature and existence, or as the same kind of inference that we find in the design argument in Plato,

[55] Wolfson, *Philo: Foundations of Religious Philosophy*, II, 83.
[56] Philo, *Philo: Philosophical Writings*, ed. H. Lewy (Oxford: Phaidon Press, 1946), p. 59.

Aristotle, and the Stoics. For Philo God is unnamable, and, strictly speaking, unpredicable and unknowable.

But even here Philo borrows from the Stoics in order to prove God's existence:

> We see, then, that any piece of work always involves the knowledge of a workman. Who can look upon statues or paintings without thinking at once of a sculptor or painter? [57]

Here again, then, is the recurrent artistic analogy of the world, as in all major Greek philosophers following Socrates, with the exception of the Atomists and Epicureans. And Philo, notwithstanding his earlier protestations, used this analogy, together with the argument from design, to prove God's existence. He produces the usual Stoic analogies—clothes, ships, houses—and compares them, as did Chrysippus, with the world. ". . . the highest art and knowledge is shown in this universe." [58] But he believed that this argument proves only the existence of God, whereas the Stoics held that it proves the intelligent cause of the world, which is God. So at least one characteristic of God would seem to be proved; Philo, however, eschews it, maintaining that the divine essence is not knowable. [59] The world is a sort of "wax impression" of God in which the particular objects and processes, as in Plato's theory, imperfectly copy the forms. [60] Here we see the beginning of theological troubles, the stretching of philosophical ideas upon the rack of theology and religion, or vice versa. The resultant problem of vacillation between pantheism, anthropomorphism, and agnosticism has continued to occupy theologians within the confines of traditional belief right down to the present.

Something new is here. In Plato, Aristotle, and the Stoics we were not particularly aware of the problem which assails and troubles Philo. It is one thing to prove God's existence—and relatively easy—if you have in mind the abstract kind of God of Aristotle, the impersonal unmoved mover, or the limited God of Plato, who had to work with a somewhat intractable material. It is another to know or conceive of God. The conflict between philosophy and revealed theology began early, with Philo, a Jew. God, in accord with knowledge based upon revealed truth, upon scriptural authority, and upon miracles, is omnipotent, omniscient, perfect, eternal, one. But any application of rational techniques to the comprehension of God, as with the design argument or the cosmological argument, must place God in a class (craftsmen, geometers, mechanics). They will view

[57] *Ibid.*, p. 59.   [58] *Ibid.*   [59] *Ibid.*   [60] *Ibid.*, p. 61.

Him, by inference, in terms of characteristics (intelligence, power, art, skill) which denote *man's* capacities (intelligence, etc.), and refer to *man's* productions (art objects, machines, etc.). Hence the possibility of pantheism and anthropomorphism, the shattering of God's unity. These problems worried Plato, Aristotle, the Stoics, very little; but as we shall see, they tortured theologians throughout the Middle Ages, and on into early modern and modern times. The strain has thrown modern theologians back upon skepticism and mysticism, and ultimately spelled out the demise of natural theology itself.

CHAPTER 7

In Medieval Thought
Augustine, Aquinas, and Others

> Yet from every effect the existence of the cause can be clearly demonstrated, and so we can demonstrate the existence of God from His effects; though from them we cannot know God perfectly as He is in His essence.
> —AQUINAS, *Summa Theologica*, Question 2, Article 2

The problem of the knowledge of God just discussed was bequeathed, along with a similar frame of reference, by Philo to the theologians of the Middle Ages. They responded to its irritation by turning even more fully to Aristotle's theories, a choice which was understandable since it was Aristotle's logic which was largely responsible for the problem in the first place. Augustine, whose work exhibits the same antipathy between knowledge of God and Aristotle's logical categories that bedeviled Philo, agreed with him in the belief that no complete knowledge of God is possible. Since the essence of God transcends all attributes by which human thought comprehends its objects, Augustine found it necessary to appeal to another cognitive mode, intuition, in which the idea of God is part of the immediate certainty of consciousness. In the *Confessions* (Book 6) he rejects the idea that God can be conceived anthropomorphically or materialistically, because these terms connote concepts which apply to man and to this world and therefore cannot apply to God. Later (Books 7 and 10) he formulates the theory that things in nature speak to him that "God made us," a conception similar to Berkeley's acceptance of the idea that there is a "visual language" of God. He does use the design argument.[1] With regard to proportion, Augustine mentions it in a discussion of music.[2]

The most important Medieval use of the doctrine of analogy comes with

[1] Augustine, *The City of God* (New York: Cima Publishing Company, 1958), Book XI, Chap. 4. Wilhelm Windelband, *A History of Philosophy*, tr. J. F. Tufts (2d ed.; New York: The Macmillan Company, 1901), p. 280.

[2] Augustine, *Writings of Augustine* (New York: Cima Publishing Company, 1947), II, 201.

later thinkers. Most of them thought of reality as a chain of being arranged in a hierarchy in which each link, each level, up to God at the apex, contains more of being, excellence and reality than the one below. Knowledge or conception of the attributes of God rises from the consideration of this chain of being, and a doctrine of analogy formulates the method for properly arriving at this conception. Among these thinkers the most important was Thomas Aquinas, and therefore the following discussion will deal in particular with his views, although other thinkers, such as Bonaventura, Anselm, and Suarez will be treated more briefly.

Aquinas faced Philo's situation, and he interpreted it in a similar way. How we can know that God exists is one problem, and it is a comparatively easy one to solve, according to his persuasion. Philo, as we know, ultimately took the mystical view, and to a degree so does Aquinas—with respect to such things as the Trinity; but he did not take this view with respect to much of theology, in particular the knowledge of God's attributes. Like Philo, he sets forth the predicament in Aristotelian terms.[3] The context is logical, the problem epistemological and metaphysical in implication. Considered in terms of the subject-predicate logic, which holds that the terms in propositions must be defined in terms of genus, species, and difference, the problem of God's attributes seemed almost insuperable. Because of this requirement Christian thinkers faced difficulties which were not faced by Aristotle. To expand our point in more detail, how, for instance, can a Christian be expected to conceive of God as a genus? A genus is a class marked off from other classes by differentia, thus making God, if he were a genus, limited and plural. To define Him in terms of genus-species would be to include Him in some larger class, just as the definition of man as "rational" animal differentiates the species "man" from the genus "animal" by means of the difference "rational." Man is only one class within a larger class of things. It would seem, therefore, that God cannot be differentiated or specified, and hence cannot be defined; and if He cannot be defined, then He cannot be conceived; and if He cannot be conceived, then He cannot be known; and if He cannot be known, then He cannot properly be named by attributes which inhere in a subject.[4] We can know only *that* God exists; we cannot know *what* God is. The "what" of God is therefore not a genus, nor in a genus.

[3] Aristotle, *Topics*, 101b39; *Posterior Analytics*, 93b.

[4] Thomas Aquinas, "Summa Contra Gentiles," in *Selected Writings* (Everyman's Library; London: J. M. Dent, 1939), Pt. I, Chap. 24. Thomas Aquinas, *Summa Theologica*, ed. A. C. Pegis (New York: Random House, 1945), Vol. I, Pt. I, Question 88, Articles 2 and 3.

Since it is only by the above method that we are able to obtain "natural" knowledge, or "scientific knowledge" (in Aristotle's terms), Thomas quite consistently concluded that it is impossible to have any *natural* knowledge of God. Knowledge begins with sense, and out of the data derived from sensation our intellect forms definitions and demonstrations. But since we have no such basis in sensation for knowledge of God's attributes or properties, "It is impossible for any created intellect to see the essence of God by its own natural power." [5] Therefore, ultimate knowledge of God is attainable only through the usual channels of mysticism and revelation.

This being the case, it is the burden of Aquinas to show how it is possible to speak sensibly of God at all. What basis is there for our words and sentences concerning God, what sort of significances do they have? If we use in our demonstrations and descriptions similar terms which do not have the same meaning, such as "dog" (fish) and "dog" (animal), then the demonstrations and descriptions can easily fall into the fallacy of equivoca-tion. Now Thomas attempts to avoid this difficulty by means of a theory of remotion and a theory of analogy. By remotion he means the negative approach, knowledge of what God is not. [6] This is not our interest; our interest lies in analogy.

Analogy is a kind of knowledge of God, though not, as said before, a way of actually knowing Him. It is based upon God's relations to His creatures, or to created things. When we conceive God, we conceive Him in a limited way *in terms of* the things which He has created, i.e., the world of nature, including man. Terms which have the same form but which are used with more than one meaning are called "equivocal." If the terms which we use to describe God are of the latter kind, then it is absolutely impossible to have knowledge of God's nature, and reasonings using them will be guilty of the fallacy of four terms. [7] On the other hand, terms cannot be predicated univocally of God and his creatures, for this would imply pantheism and anthropomorphism. [8] So we must speak of God in another way— analogically—making use of terms which are neither univocal nor equivocal.

But what is the relation of God to creatures which allows the possibility of such analogical knowledge? How is God related to His creatures? First, He is related to them causally. God is the first and continuing cause of everything. In the *Summa Theologica* Thomas points out that we cannot

[5] Aquinas, *Summa Theologica*, Pt. I, Question 12, Articles 4, 7, 8; Pt. I, Question 88, Articles 2 and 3.

[6] *Ibid.*, Pt. I, Question 13, Article 1; *Summa Contra Gentiles*, Pt. I, Chaps. 14–15, 25.

[7] Aquinas, *Summa Theologica*, Pt. I, Question 13, Articles 5 and 10.

[8] *Ibid.*, Pt. I, Question 13, Article 5.

know God through likeness common to God and His creatures.[9] No created object, such as man, and no characteristic of man, such as intelligence or goodness, *represents* God to the viewer. But there must be some link, something in some way common between them, or there is no basis for knowledge of the divine. The word "agnosticism" applies to this situation. The relation of causation is not enough, for we do not call God good only because He is the cause of goodness. However, since God is the source of all perfections, every created thing is like God insofar as it is perfect.[10] In this way terms applied to creatures can be substantially applied to God. Every effect has some similarity to its cause, and the perfection or excellence of each creature, relative to its position in the hierarchy of being, is caused by God as source. Such terms, however, although predicated substantially of God, fall short of representing Him. Nevertheless, our intellects, insofar as they are able to know God, know Him as He is represented by His creatures. Now every creature represents God in whatever way it possesses some perfection, because God is absolutely and universally perfect, and the source or cause of all the perfections in His creatures. All names or terms applied to God, then, signify the divine substance in an imperfect manner, since they more correctly pertain to created beings, who have only limited perfections.

The basic possessor of perfection is being, and it is being that possesses degrees of perfection. The being of substance and accident, for example, is not a third term, but is proportioned to them insofar as they participate in being.[11] Therefore, we can say that the perfection of each creature is proportioned to its amount of being. Thus develops the notion of the hierarchy of existents, with each higher level having more being, and consequently more excellence and more perfection, than those below.

> But since our intellect knows God from creatures, in order to understand God it forms conceptions proportioned to the perfections flowing from God to creatures.[12]

The perfections which exist united and simple in God, however, are received divided and multiplied in creatures.

Having seen, although quite obscurely, since "perfection" in this sort of context is a very obscure word, the metaphysical basis of analogy and analogical predication, we may now proceed to a consideration of the kinds of analogy. There are presented in the writings of Aquinas at least two

[9] *Ibid.*, Pt. I; Question 12, Article 2.
[10] *Ibid.*, Pt. I, Question 13, Article 2.
[11] Aquinas, *Summa Contra Gentiles*, Pt. I, Chap. 34.
[12] Aquinas, *Summa Theologica*, Pt. I, Question 13, Article 4.

kinds of analogy, and since he seems to switch in his different writings, favoring first one or the other, it is difficult to know which one represents his final opinion. Modern day Thomists disagree on the question, and different groups among them are identified by which of the following types of analogical reasoning they accept.

First, there is what is usually called "extrinsic attributive analogy." "Health" is attributed to urine (as a sign), or what we would call a symptom, and to medicine (as a cause), with respect to the proper predication of health to animals. The name, of course, is predicated in different significations, since "health" applies properly only to animals; but it can by analogy be applied to urine (healthy urine) since urine functions as a sign of health (symptom, in more modern terminology). This kind of analogy, thus, represents an extension of the proper designation of a term—health. In the same manner one can apply the term "health" to medicine, on the principle that medicine is the cause of health. Extrinsic attributive analogy, the kind of analogy represented by our first example, is not properly applied to God,[13] since in effect there is no quality or property designated in common by the term "health" in the context of urine and animals. It is in the second sense that analogy is to be used with respect to God, where one thing is proportioned to another, as "healthy" is proportioned to medicine and to the body, since medicine is the cause of health in the body. This latter kind of analogy is usually called "intrinsic attributive analogy," or "substantive analogy." In Thomistic opinion it is based on something more than just a causal relation, for there is something essential involved. Something is actually held in common between God and creature, an intrinsic property related to the excellence or perfection of each. This property, of course, is held in lesser amount by the creature than by God. In this way the terms "good," "wise," etc., are applied to God not only because He is the cause of all wisdom and goodness, but because these attributes exist in Him in a more excellent way, in proportion to His greater amount of perfection. Yet, these attributes exist analogously, not univocally, in creatures, relative to the degree of their perfection or being.[14] Substance and accident are here proportioned to each other by being, as corporeal vision and intellectual vision are proportioned to one another by seeing. In this kind of analogy it is presupposed that "being," "good," "wisdom" are intrinsic or inherent to the terms proportioned, or, as Thomas states it, "essential" in their relation. The term "wisdom," for instance, does not refer to or

[13] Aquinas, *Summa Contra Gentiles*, Pt. I. Chap. 34. *Summa Theologica*, Pt. I, Question 13, Article 5.

[14] Aquinas, *Summa Theologica*, Pt. I, Question 13, Articles 2, 6–8.

designate something *totally* diverse when used for both man and God; this would imply equivocation and the ineffability of God—agnosticism; neither is it univocal, that is, "wisdom" does not, when applied to God and man, designate *the same* attributes or properties, for this would lead to the equally if not more onerous ideas of pantheism or anthropomorphism. There is evident in this tortuous dialectic the cognitive tight-rope-walk between pantheism and agnosticism occasioned by the application of logical techniques to religious belief. Both terms, wisdom with reference to man and wisdom with reference to God, participate in that to which they are proportioned. They are not applied, either to God or to man, merely extrinsically (as signs or causes), but by community of excellence which is held proportionately in the sense that God has more excellence and being than the creatures in terms of which we know Him. There is a degree, therefore, of participation operant, and this is what is meant by the Thomistic idea that terms are not applied *merely* to God as cause, but also essentially because there is some degree of good, wisdom, etc., held in common by man and God.

> Hence it must be said that the word 'knowledge' is predicated of God's knowledge and ours, not altogether univocally, nor purely equivocally, but analogically; this is the same as to say that it can be predicated proportionately. Conformity according to proportion can be two-fold, and thus we have two kinds of analogy; there may be conformity between two terms which are proportionate to each other according to a fixed ratio, as between 2 and 1; 2 is the double of 1. Or again, there may be a conformity between two terms not proportionate to each other, but which are proportional, as between 6 and 4, for 6 is to 4 as 4 is to 2. The first kind of conformity is a proportion, the second kind is a proportionality or similarity of proportions. According to the first mode of conformity we may say that being applies analogically both to substance and accident which is proportionate to it. But being could not apply the same way to creatures and to God; between the two there is but a similarity of proportionality, such as exists between our intelligence and the sense of sight; the intelligence is to the intelligible being what sight is to color; and this similarity of proportions can be expressed by the word 'knows.'[15]

This quotation seems inconsistent with the view of proportion which Aquinas put forth in the *Summas*. Both conceptions come ultimately from

[15] Aquinas, *Disputed Questions on Truth*, Part II, Question 11, Article 6, in Garrigou Lagrange, *God: His Existence and His Nature*, tr. Dom Bede Rose (St. Louis: B. Herder Book Company, 1949), p. 271. See also Thomas de Vio Cardinal Cajetan, *The Analogy of Names*, tr. E. A. Bushinski (2d ed.; New York: Duquesne University, The Ad Press, Ltd., 1959).

Aristotle: the first from his *Metaphysics* and the second from the ideas of analogy we noted in the *Rhetoric* and the *Ethica Nicomachea*. Both are quasi-mathematical conceptions. So in this example we find Aquinas rejecting the idea he later accepts, and adding a third kind of analogy, that of proper proportionality. This last quotation is from the *Disputed Questions on Truth*, written between 1256 and 1259. The *Summa Contra Gentiles* was written between 1258 and 1260. The *Summa Theologica* was written between 1267 and 1273. In the *Summas* Thomas seems to hold that the real basis for the principle of analogy is the causal relation, as between substance and attribute, God and creature, which makes for a community of excellence in that the effect must resemble the cause, however imperfectly. Thus we can know God, though imperfectly, from creatures having different levels of perfection from God, but having some perfection in common with Him. In the last quotation, however, God is related only to Himself.

If the chronological development is of any weight, the analogy presented in the *Summas* is Aquinas' final opinion. The one presented in the *Disputed Questions* is useless. It does not seem to me that a proportion of the form A is to B as ? is to ?—man's knowledge is to man's being as God's knowledge is to God's being—is inferentially significant. Further, as later theologians have pointed out, even if it were not vacuous it would not avoid the fallacy of four terms, or equivocation, on the term "knowledge." Modern Thomists, however, tend to accept this kind of analogy as the basic one.

The substantive or intrinsic attributive analogy of Aquinas seems to be similar to the hierarchical idea of Augustine, that is, it grounds analogy in the similarity between God and His creatures in relation to the degree of being and perfection within the great chain of being. Anselm and Bonaventura agree with this view, which represents a doctrine of resemblance by emanation. Unlike Thomas, however, they hypostatize or reify the universal, such as good, wisdom, etc. This "copy" theory is different from the doctrine of Aquinas.[16] Actually, Anselm never faced the problem of how humans can know God in rational terms. Like Thomas, he held that all creatures derive their existence from God as emanating cause, but their similarities to God are extremely limited.[17] He would be surprised, Anselm says, if human names or words could be applied to Godly sub-

[16] Saint Anselm, *Monologium* (Chicago: Open Court Publishing Company, 1903), Chap. XXXI.
[17] *Ibid.*, XXVIII.

stance.[18] No relative terms, no terms of quantity or quality are applicable
to God. The first would subordinate Him to something contingent, and
the second and third would disrupt His unity and simplicity.[19] Anselm
followed Aquinas and Philo in refusing to subsume God under a genus, or
make Him a genus. In the last analysis he held that it is impossible for
created beings to know the unfathomable mystery of God,[20] a conclusion
that Aquinas refused to accept. Our terms, according to Anselm, are based
on some "likeness" which he does not further explore.

Scotus, on the other hand, held that the link between God and His
creatures is *being*, and that "being" has a common meaning in man and
God. As that which is absolutely universal in all things, being is the proper
object of human intelligence. According to Scotus, therefore, being is
univocal, and God is naturally knowable to man.[21] Whatever is subject to
the law of contradiction is univocal, and being, although it is not a genus
since it has no specific differences, does admit of degrees. Scotus rejected,
then, the kind of analogy that Aquinas accepted, and held that Aquinas'
view commits the fallacy of equivocation. Suarez followed him in this
interpretation.

Our excursion into Medieval thought has made it evident that the
problem of knowledge of God in terms of Aristotelian logic assumed large
proportions. In effect this means the problem of translating religious belief
into rational, logical, or scientific terminology, and in some sense sub-
mitting religion to rational justification. These theologians were in a
position somewhat like that of an animal in a maze. Many rationally
promising avenues presented themselves, causality, similarity, analogy,
but each choice bumped its chooser into a wall of pantheism, anthropomorphism or agnosticism with respect to knowledge of God's character,
and into conflict with other of the assumed (revealed or scriptural) traits of
God, such as His unity, simplicity, omnipotence, and omniscience. All these
Medieval theories more or less approach the problem in terms of a doctrine
of emanation of perfections from God to creatures according to degrees,
and according to the principle *that* God exists and is the cause of everything else in the universe. How much right this gives to talk of knowledge
of God is another subject, and Augustine, Philo, Anselm, Aquinas, all

[18] *Ibid.*, XV.
[19] *Ibid.*, XVI, XVII.
[20] *Ibid.*, XXVI, XLIII.
[21] John Duns Scotus, *Op. Oxon.*, I, d3, q3, n26, noted in J. Anderson, *The Bond
of Being: An Essay on Analogy and Existence* (St. Louis: B. Herder Book Company,
1949), p. 271.

seem to have believed that there is no possible "natural" or "scientific" knowledge of "what" God is. It is also clear that these Medieval conceptions of analogical knowledge of God's attributes do not represent the kind of analogy which we have found behind the design arguments, nor are they in the direct line of development of the scientific conception of analogy as linked to induction, which we have been following from Aristotle onward. They are ways of conceiving of, rather than arguments for the existence of, God. This point is supported by the fact that they argued for God's existence, the "that" of God, by cosmological and ontological arguments, with the exception of one of Aquinas' arguments, which was teleological and an example of the argument to design. "Hence it is plain that they [things, the governance of the world] achieve their end, not fortuitously, but designedly [*Summa Theologica*, I, 2, 3]." Whatever lacks knowledge cannot be moved toward an end except by some director endowed with intelligence. Aquinas seems not to have noted that this is also an analogical argument, not, however, in the "proportion" sense. Still, this only goes to show the diversity between Thomistic "analogy" and that of the Stoics and Early Modern thinkers. The elements involved, of course, are similar, and have to do with God's existence and attributes as based upon inference by analogy; but the modern design argument changed its basic analogy to that of the machine and the machinist. It drew its support not from the analogy of the artist which was favored by the Stoics, Plato, and Aristotle, but from physical science; still, the modern machine is also a product of art or skill. The major difference between the arguments of the Early Moderns and the Greeks lies in the organistic metaphor involved in Greek thought—their way of thinking of the world as a living organism. For the Early Modern theists, the ultimate elements of the material world are dead and inert. For all this, the arguments have the same form, and the appeal to the movements of the heavenly bodies is uniform from Plato through Aristotle down to Newton and his contemporaries. The other difference relates to the manner in which the order of the heavenly bodies is described and understood, to whether knowledge of the order is conceived as demonstrative and a priori or as conjectural and a posteriori. Some aspects of the argument thus change radically.

The argument *to* design, the teleological argument, changed but little down through the ages. As we have noted several times in the preceding chapters, eighteenth-century minds tended to consider purpose in mechanical terms, since even machines have functional or means-ends relations among their parts. One thing seems very clear, and that is that the concept of analogy is historically ambiguous.

Seventeenth- and eighteenth-century acceptance of the scientific character of the design argument because of its analogical pattern of inference, however, was not due wholly to Stoic or Medieval sources, or to Bacon's influence. There was in the work of Galileo a consistent use of analogy as a source of suggestion and hypothesis; indeed, his signal arguments for the heliocentric theory of the solar system and for the motion of the earth, sun and planets rest at bottom on analogical reasoning. In 1609 he heard of the invention of the telescope, constructed one for himself, and using it very quickly made a series of important discoveries. First, he found that Jupiter has satellites or moons which rotate around it. Second, he observed spots on the sun which revolve with it. He then used these materials in order to argue that the solar system is a larger version of a system such as Jupiter and its moons, wherein the planets are *analogous to* the moons and the sun is analogous to Jupiter.[22] The rotation of the earth, of the moon, and of the other planets is held to follow *by analogy* from the motion of the sun and Jupiter's moons. Strictly speaking Galileo did not prove, experimentally or otherwise, that the earth moves or that the sun is the center of a rotating system of planets. What he did was to argue by analogy that such properties belong to these bodies. Further, throughout his mechanical treatises and in his *Dialogue Concerning the Two Chief World Systems* he repeatedly used the term "analogy" to stand for theories and hypotheses about the objects and processes of nature. Analogy, therefore, was used consciously by a very great and famous scientist as a basic method of discovery; as a fundamental means of suggesting hypotheses; and as the method for demonstrating the epoch-making heliocentric theory of the solar system. These points were not missed by our design theologians.

Galileo's relations to Early Modern thought are by no means restricted to scientific matters. It was inevitable that his scientific ideas be attacked on theological and religious grounds, since Medieval science and theology were irretrievably intermixed, and he found it necessary to defend himself by arguing that his scientific ideas were consistent with Christianity. Since his great contribution to science lay in terrestrial and celestial mechanics, it would naturally follow that his theological ideas were formulated in terms of a mechanical view of the world. It is scarcely necessary to say

[22] Galileo Galilei, *Dialogue Concerning the Two Chief World Systems* (Berkeley and Los Angeles: University of California Press, 1953), pp. 46–47, 51, 62, 65, 68, 107–108, 114–115, 118–120, 325–326, 397. See also Galileo's *On Motion and On Mechanics* (Madison: University of Wisconsin Press, 1960), pp. 20 ff.

that his theology was thus based upon the design argument. In his *Letter to the Grand Duchess* he discusses theology, saying "Nor is God any less excellently revealed in Nature's actions than in the sacred statements of the Bible."[23] His science had convinced Galileo that God made the world, that He had created an immutable mathematical system, that God is the most creative of creative geometricians.[24]

Thus the ancient design argument, in company with its logical partner, analogical inference, in effect leaped a thousand years, becoming, in the process, attached to Early Modern science. Virtually ignored by Medieval thought, argument by analogy and the design argument were revitalized, given new uniforms and accoutrements, and in general fitted out for battle in the theological lists of the Enlightenment.

[23] Galileo Galilei, "Letter to the Grand Duchess," in *Discoveries and Opinions of Galileo*, tr. Stillman Drake (New York: Doubleday and Company, Inc., 1957), p. 183.
[24] Galileo Galilei, *Dialogue Concerning the Two Chief World Systems*, pp. 102–104.

CHAPTER 8

Conclusions to Part Two

As we have traced our theological fabric down through the ages it has become clear that its weavers gathered their yarns and patterns from many sources of supply. In this section attention has been directed toward answers to the questions when, where, and how concerning the origins and development of the design argument, both in its structure and in its materials, its data, and its form. The conclusion, I am convinced, is quite clear—the design argument as well as its analogical form is undeniably ancient. The variations which have been discovered in its use are mainly connected to shifts in metaphysical theories and in emphasis.

One item found almost universally in our design theologians is their rejection of, indeed, their horror of, materialistic and mechanistic attempts to explain the ultimate origin and processes of the universe. All these thinkers are in opposition to (a) materialistic monism of the mechanistic variety, and (b) its corollary, the view that the ultimate origin and structure of the world could have come about by chance. Such ideas would not, our philosophers feel, do justice to the "dance of the stars," to the "exquisite contrivance" of the world apprehended in human experience. Few of them were willing to pay homage to Tyche.

Where Newton's enemies were the "horrid Hobbes and Spinoza," Plato's foes were Democritus and Leucippus and the Sophists. Plato believed that the world is an organism created out of a pre-existing, somewhat intractable, stuff by a divine artificer. The order and uniformity of the stars and the seasons, the cognitive and rational character of a world which seeks to exemplify more perfectly the forms, could not possibly be the product of nonintelligent motions of corporeal elements. Plato was dialectically certain that the world is a rational order similar to mind or spirit. With respect to theological methods, however, Plato, although his argument is undoubtedly analogical in form, did not to my knowledge discuss analogical argument specifically with respect to his theology. He did use the early modern form of analogy, which he refered to as "example," a term used also by Aristotle for the same argument. Similarly, he refers to "proportion," which later became the basis of the Thomistic conception of God. And so it was found that Plato shares with Newton both the antagonism to materialistic explanations of the ultimate character of the universe and the design argument. But they do not share the view that the material world is mechanical in nature. For Plato the world is through and through teleological, pervaded with purpose and with processes and objects striving to copy their respective forms. This is not to ignore Newton's Platonism. It is almost as if his mechanical analogy melts into the organistic, since the mechanical arrangements and contrivances in the world, mechanically categorized and related, exemplify God's purposes. Both Newton and Plato viewed things in the world as exemplifications of forms. Let us put it in the following way: In Newton, as we have seen, things in the world function so as to exemplify the forms, the "protoplast" as Newton called it. But the processes of the material world are *mechanical*, that is, an onion seed does not seek or desire to become an onion. It becomes an onion because of built-in efficient physical and chemical causes which mechanically work to produce the onion. God, of course, intended that the onion seed become an onion, take the final form of an onion, but for the rest the process is purely mechanical, even to the point that there might be a breakdown in the process which God would have to step in and repair. On this point Plato avoided many of Newton's peculiarly Christian difficulties. Newton, in assuming the Christian doctrines, which hold among other things that God made the world out of nothing, was hard put to explain why an all-powerful God should construct an imperfect machine. For Plato the imperfection and evil of the world can be put off on the intractability of the original material out of which God was forced to construct it. Things in this world, the onion for instance, possess according to Plato a formal and final cause. As can be seen in Plato's *Symposium*, each thing in a sense desires to more perfectly embody its form. Its basic cause is therefore formal and immanent, whereas in Newton the causes of all things are external and efficient.

Many of the comments made about Plato's use of the design argument can also be applied to Aristotle, although Aristotle's mature theological position seems to entail an impersonal Deity. In this mature position he uses the cosmological argument to prove the existence of the unmoved-mover. The design argument typically concludes that the first cause is a person, a self-conscious mind, an artist or artisan. Again, for Aristotle the design in the world order is immanent rather than external and mechanical

—there is no "divine plan" in the sense of self-conscious intentions carried out by an artist or mechanic.

Nevertheless, in an early work Aristotle does use the design argument, however inconsistent this is with his later theological views. Like our other theists, he views with distaste the theory that the ultimate order and origin of the world are products of the chance concourse of atoms. Rather he refers to the "lovely design" of the universe, and the "dance of the stars." Again, like Plato, Aristotle does not specifically link the logic of analogy with the design argument, although analogy is implicit in the argument. However, as we have seen in some detail, he did formulate in his logical theory various principles of analogical reasoning which were used in a number of ways throughout his philosophy. He distinguished between "example" and "proportion," two formulations of analogical reasoning the latter of which becomes the basis of Thomistic theology and finds its way into the work of Early Modern theologians such as Browne and Berkeley. This proportional analogy has also been found to characterize Newtonian theology, but it is to be distinguished from the actual inference to God's existence and attributes. Newton's argument, which he calls a "similitude" appears to be an instance of Aristotle's "example."

Both Plato and Aristotle maintain theological positions in the tradition of natural theology. Both use rationalistic formulas for proving the existence of the cause of the world order, and both appear disinterested in "revealed" theology. This point should be qualified with respect to Plato. Plato's knowledge of the good is a kind of intuition which resembles revelation; and the soul apparently gets knowledge of the forms in a prior and purely spiritual state, if we take the *Phaedrus* seriously. This prior knowledge, lost at birth and recovered through recollection, might be interpreted as a kind of revelation, particularly since Plato's discussions of its acquisition are often expressed in mythological form with considerable religious flavor. In addition the process of dialectic seems to be a sort of "releasing" of innate knowledge, and this, I suppose, would encompass the design argument as Plato develops it. These mystical overtones so characteristic of Plato, however, are not at all evident in Aristotle.

The design argument found its greatest early protagonists in the Stoics. Convinced for a number of ethical and epistemological reasons that the world is rational, orderly, infused with "logos-sperkatikos," they developed the design argument in terms of any and every analogy, including machines, ships, houses, water clocks, etc. Like Plato and Aristotle, the Stoics rejected the view that the world is a mechanism in favor of the belief that it is a living organism. On the other hand they were, in contrast with Plato and Aristotle, metaphysical materialists. They appear to have believed that the design argument is conjectural and probable, but they placed the same emphasis upon the rational character of theology, in contrast to revealed theology, that is evident in Plato and Aristotle. They seem to have begun to use the term "analogy" to cover both of Aristotle's formulas, "analogy" and "example." It is likely that our Early Modern thinkers, including the Newtonians, took a good deal of their theology from the Stoics, including their formulations of the design argument, as well as their use of the term "analogy." The Stoic theology tended to be pantheistic, however, and not transcendental.

The contrast between the mystic or "revealed" theology and natural theology was clearly noted by Philo of Judea. Although he used the design argument, he was exceedingly wary of its tendency towards pantheism and the identification of God's intelligence with that of man. He was also very much concerned about the logical and epistemological problems consequent to the application of Aristotle's logical categories to the understanding of God. As a result, Philo left as a legacy to the Medieval period some of its theological problems. Thus generation after generation of theologians wrestled with the problem of defining God. Definition of God in terms of His being a genus or the member of a genus would seem to limit His perfection, or fracture Him into pieces. The result was that Philo's formulation of the design argument is exceedingly mystical and shadowy in presentation. There is no knowledge, in the Aristotelian sense of knowledge, of God's essence. God is thus above reason. But this is not the only kind of problem envisaged by Philo. He was also aware of the difficulty of making consistent the various beliefs concerning God's character as omnipotence, omniscience, benevolence, unity, etc., difficulties which dogged later theologians. Because of the epistemological and logical problems spelled out in the work of Philo, Augustine simply maintained that knowledge of God's existence is intuitive. He used the design argument in its Stoic formulation, and proposed a sort of intuitionism which takes the experience of the world and its order to be a "divine sign language," telling us directly and immediately that God exists. We have seen this sort of thing in Berkeley's theology.

The wary attitude towards the application of "scientific" principles to the understanding and comprehension of the existence and attributes of God became traditional in the theologians of the Middle Ages; in consequence they tended to separate the knowledge of divine *existence* from knowledge of divine *attributes*. Human minds could know *that* God exists; but not *what* His characteristics are. In their approach to these problems Medieval theologians had to beware on the one hand the chasm of agnosticism—no possibility of knowledge of God, and on the other hand the cliff of anthropomorphism and pantheism—the identification of goodness, power, and intelligence in God with those same traits in man and the world. God's characteristics or attributes must be knowable in some way; but they must not be the *same* properties that are denoted by the terms used with respect to man's intelligence, power, etc. In attempting to avoid these alternate pitfalls, Medieval theologians had recourse to the principle of proportionate analogy, a principle with whose complications and problems we have become familiar. Suffice to say that the Thomistic view of analogical knowledge of God's characteristics is a way of conceiving of, rather than an inference to, the nature of God. Therefore it is quite a different tradition from that of the Early Modern Newtonians, although, as we have seen, the Newtonians were aware of the fact that terms such as "good" and "intelligent" must mean something infinitely greater when applied to God than they do when applied to man. Nevertheless, they would not, I think, object to applying such terms to God—"geometer," for instance, is geometer as applied to human intelligence; it is just that God is supremely intelligent, the Geometer of geometers. Aquinas would, I think, have objected to this description, since it would lay its proponents open to the charge of anthropomorphism and perhaps to pantheism. If geometrical intelligence in God and man means the same thing and has the same denotation (although quantitatively greater in God of course), then God's nature is identified with one aspect of ordinary nature—human mind; and God is therefore identified with ordinary nature. The same type of analysis may be applied to terms such as "good," "power," "knowledge," etc.

Therefore Aquinas' "natural theology," leaving aside the ultimate mystical and revealed character of knowledge of God's essential attributes, lay in his cosmological proofs for the existence of the first cause, and in addition in his argument to design, which is the fifth of his famous proofs "that" God exists. Aquinas' "analogy," of course, is drawn from Aristotle's notion of "proportion"; and this notion shows up again in the work of Browne, King, and Berkeley. Mysticism, revealed knowledge of religious truths, has a place in Medieval theology which was largely lost in Early Modern times. It is obvious in Stoicism, and almost absent in the Epicureans and the early Atomists, but is fundamental to the position of

Aquinas and most other Medieval theologians. In Aquinas there is not the shift from reason back to mysticism and irrationalism which characterizes Philo, the Neo-Platonists and Augustine. Reason is, however, kept in what he believed to be its proper sphere. It is, in short, a philosophical treatment of religion that makes up the theology of Aquinas, but it is nothing like the rather wholesale decamp to rationalism current in the Early Modern period. For Thomas and most of the Medieval theologians, a scientific knowledge of God and His attributes is proclaimed impossible.

In many ways Galileo exhibits the resurgence of ancient Greek ideas which are different from those of Plato and Aristotle—Lucretius, Democritus, the Stoics, and ancient and seminal scientists such as Archimedes. Galileo, I suspect, provided the main source of the identification of analogy with those scientific methods sketched out above, the methods that became so significant in the eighteenth century. His ideas, along with those of Bacon, in particular their common antipathy to Aristotelian science and logic and their common espousal of empiricism, became the common inheritance of Early Modern science, philosophy, and theology.

And now to Hume's critique of the total tradition of the design argument, both ancient and modern.

PART THREE

The Denouement
Hume and the Design Argument

Is it not hard and tyrannical in you, more tyrannical than any Act of the Stuarts, not to allow me to publish my Dialogues?

—HUME, Letter to Eliot, 1763

CHAPTER 9

Hume's Critique of Natural Theology

It is quite evident that Early Modern versions of the design argument were adaptations of a very ancient theological tradition. Hume recognized that his target was ancient and eclectic, as well as modern, both in metaphysics and in epistemology; that the newness of Newtonian theism lay rather in its having taken over the forms and prestige of the new science than in its originality. For the rest the distinctions are mainly in mood and in attitude. Our two strands of design theology, then, come together in the work of David Hume, whose critique is directed against natural theology, particularly of the design variety, in both its ancient and modern forms. Specifically, his argument is destructive of the attempts of design theologians to appropriate the a posteriori methods of science. But he does not limit his aim to this point. Design theology is gently but thoroughly excised of its dualistic metaphysics, its use of the principle of causation, its application of the method of analogy, its confusion of ceremonial and emotive prejudices with rational evidence, and of some of its claims concerning good and evil. When the philosophical dust has settled, not only the design argument but natural theology in general is found to be completely disarmed.

I should like to pursue this subject in two distinct steps. The first deals with some historical aspects of Hume's *Dialogues*. The second analyzes his criticism of natural theology. As a beginning, then, I should like to establish the fact that in his *Dialogues Concerning Natural Religion* Hume is directly attacking Newton and Newton's followers.

I. HUME'S OPPONENTS

Few philosophers have exhibited the critical acumen of David Hume; indeed, it seems quite permissible to say that he was, if not one of the greatest philosophical critics of all time, at least the greatest of the eighteenth century. It is natural to depict incisive critics as sharp-visaged men of small and lean stature, of piercing and gimlet-eyed glance. As is usually the case in important instances which confound the general, such was not true of David Hume. Hume's was a rapier intellect hidden behind folds of fat, masked by a round, bovine face dominated by large eyes whose dead stare shook some men such as Rousseau to the very core.

Hume's general critical philosophy is universally cited in our own times, an indication of his truly profound influence upon contemporary philosophy. His theological and religious criticism, exemplified in the *Natural History of Religion* and in the *Dialogues Concerning Natural Religion*, is also well known. His critical work in other fields, however, is not so famous. He was, for instance, a Tory historian in an age of Whigs and Whig historians, as would befit a Scotchman. He was also a supporter of Scottish literature, a capacity in which he stood against the formalism of the Johnsonians. So it is clear that whichever dominant trend we attend to in the intellectual currents of the eighteenth century, we find Hume as at least a minority of one, standing in its path, puncturing its sacred cows. Our earlier discussion of eighteenth-century theology made clear that one of these sacred cows was natural religion or natural theology. And, in addition, it was recognized that the existence of such a strongly knit binding dominating the thought of the age shows clearly how very important is Hume's position in the history of thought. Kant's philosophical slumbers, from which he was awakened, represent only a part, albeit a most significant part, of the dogmas of the age with which Hume dealt so rudely.

Therefore, to read Hume's *Dialogues Concerning Natural Religion* without the knowledge developed heretofore, and without the recognition of the significance of the scientific interpretation of it, is similar to the experience of coming into a theater and seeing only the last act of Hamlet. These *Dialogues*, subtle and yet obvious, profound and yet whimsical, but destructive in all guises, appear as a great production on the stage of philosophy; for they present, in the history of theological and philosophical religion, the last act in the drama of the design argument, although there was a nineteenth-century curtain call in the work of Paley and the writers of the *Bridgewater Treatises*.

Historians of thought have directed much attention to Hume's masterpiece, with the purpose of interpreting the doctrines expounded by its various speakers and associating them with the ideas of Hume and other thinkers. I take the definitive treatment of the subject to be that of N. K. Smith, who in his *Hume's Dialogues Concerning Natural Religion* maintains that the theories propounded by Philo are those of Hume. It is generally agreed that the views of Demea represent the a priori school of theology as exemplified in the doctrines of Samuel Clarke. There is no such agreement, however, concerning the ideas advanced by Cleanthes, and these ideas form the most significant subject of all in that Cleanthes' theories are the main target of Philo's criticisms. Kemp-Smith identified these ideas with those of "the contemporary users of the design argument," and with Balbus the Stoic, a character in Cicero's *De Natura Deorum*. David Mossner holds the view that the ideas asserted by Cleanthes are those of the Lockean school, particularly Joseph Butler.[1] Charles Hendel considers Hume's theological position to be ambivalent. It is his opinion that both Philo and Cleanthes represent Hume's beliefs, and that their historical source is Berkeley. Of these interpretations I think that of Kemp-Smith is most nearly correct, but his phrase "contemporary users of the design argument" needs elucidation.

Specifically, the views proposed by Cleanthes in the *Dialogues*, to sum them up, represent: (a) the kind of theology developed by Sir Isaac Newton and his followers, and (b) the ancient design arguments of the Stoics, particularly as represented in Cicero's *De Natura Deorum*, traceable at least to the work of Plato, and accepted by most of Hume's contemporaries.

At the very beginning of Hume's examination of natural theology in the *Dialogues* certain important questions are raised. What is demonstrable by reason in matters of theology? Do methods of reasoning in theology differ from those of common life and of science? Is it possible to use scientific knowledge about nature, and the methods of observation, as bases for inferring the existence and attributes of God? In response, Cleanthes argues that theological reasoning does not differ in method and assurance from scientific and practical reasoning; and in support of these contentions, he presents the following argument:

> Look round the world: contemplate the whole and every part of it: you will find it to be nothing but one great machine, subdivided into an infinite number of lesser machines, which admit of subdivisions, to a degree beyond what senses and faculties can trace and explain. All these various machines, and even their most minute parts, are adjusted to each other with an accuracy, which ravishes into admiration all men, who have ever contemplated them. The curious adapting of means to ends, throughout all nature, resembles exactly, though it much exceeds, the productions of human contrivance; of human design, thought, wisdom, and intelligence. Since therefore the effects resemble each other, we are led to infer, by all

[1] David Mossner, "The Enigma of Hume," *Mind*, n.s. 45 (1946).

the rules of analogy, that the causes also resemble; and that the Author of Nature is somewhat similar to the mind of man; though possessed of much larger faculties, proportioned to the grandeur of the work, which he has executed. By this argument *a posteriori*, and by this argument alone, do we prove at once the existence of a Deity, and his similarity to human mind and intelligence.[2]

A second passage continues the same line of thought. Together the two constitute the main positive doctrine of natural theology stated by Cleanthes in the *Dialogues*.

To exclude all argument or reasoning of every kind is either affectation or madness. The declared profession of every reasonable skeptic is only to reject abstruse, remote and refined arguments; to adhere to common sense and the plain instincts of nature; and to assent, wherever any reasons strike him with so full a force, that he cannot, without the greatest violence, prevent it. Now the arguments for natural religion are plainly of this kind; and nothing but the most perverse, obstinate metaphysics can reject them. Consider, anatomize the eye; survey its structure and contrivance; and tell me, from your own feeling, if the idea of a contriver does not immediately flow in upon you with a force like that of sensation. The most obvious conclusion is surely in favor of design; and it requires, reflection and study, to summon up those frivolous, though abstruse objections, which can support infidelity. Who can behold the male and female of the species, the correspondence of their parts and instincts, their passions and the whole course of life before and after generation, but must be sensible, that the propagation of the species is intended by nature?[3]

And, Cleanthes continues:

But is the whole adjustment of means to ends in a house and in the universe so slight a resemblance? The oeconomy of final causes? The order, proportion, and arrangement of every part? Steps of a stair are plainly contrived, that human legs may use them in mounting; and this inference is certain and infallible. Human legs are also contrived for walking and mounting; and this inference, I allow is not altogether as certain, because of the dissimilarity which you remark; but does it, therefore, deserve the name only of presumption or conjecture?[4]

We notice our old friends again. This presentation of the design argument is formulated in the two ways with which we have become so

---

[2] David Hume, "Dialogues Concerning Natural Religion," in *Hume: Selections*, ed. G. W. Hendel, Jr. (New York: Scribner's Selections, 1927), p. 302. Quotations from Hume's *Dialogues* are all taken from this volume, unless otherwise indicated.
[3] *Ibid.*, p. 316.   [4] *Ibid.*, p. 304.

familiar in preceding pages—the arguments *from* and *to* design. Also made perfectly clear is the connection with science claimed by the supporters of the argument. The method of discovery and proof, the "analogy" of nature which proved the motion of the earth, and the similarity of motions among bodies upon the earth and in the heavens, is analogical, a posteriori, observable, scientific. Quite naturally, therefore, Hume links analogy to Galileo and to the new sciences of astronomy and mechanics.

> But Galileo, beginning with the moon, proved its similarity in every particular to the earth; its convex figure, its natural darkness when not illuminated, its density, its distinction into solid and liquid, the variations of its phases, the mutual illuminations of the earth and the moon, their mutual eclipses, the inequalities of the lunar surface, etc.[5]

> Is not the moon another earth, which we see to turn round its center? Is not Venus another earth, where we observe the same phenomena? Are not the revolutions of the sun also a confirmation, from analogy, of the same theory?... These analogies and resemblances, with others, which I have not mentioned, are the sole proofs of the Copernican system: and to you it belongs to consider, whether you have any analogies of the same kind to support your theory.[6]

Here the linkage between science and theology is made the fundamental point of departure. Here is Newtonian theology, with its allied claim that the analogical methods employed in such reasoning are those which science uses in discovering the motion of the earth and the principles of motion in bodies upon the earth. These two alleged similarities between scientific theism and physical science are presented in support of the contention that the world has a designer. The two-fold influence of science upon theology which we explored above among Newton's contemporaries and followers is therefore clearly the object of critical attack in Hume's *Dialogues*.

The first quotation, with its obvious emphasis upon the machine analogy, is weighted toward the argument from design. It proceeds from the mechanical order and symmetry of the world, to infer that there must, as with men's machines, be an intelligent cause responsible for the order and symmetry. Nature "resembles exactly" the productions of human contrivance. By means of such inference, not only the existence, but one of the attributes—intelligence—of God is proved. Now Cleanthes holds that this argument is based upon the evidence of sensory observation. Further, like certain astronomical proofs of the earth's motion, it is based upon analogy. On these and other grounds it is contended that the argument is a posteriori

[5] *Ibid.*, p. 313.   [6] *Ibid.*, p. 312.

in character and similar to the reasoning of science and practical life. Finally, Cleanthes holds that it is *only* upon this scientific basis that belief in the existence and attributes of God is justifiable. Theology is like science. It proceeds from premises based on scientifically established propositions—the laws of motion, etc. This is the machine analogy based directly upon Newtonian science. It envisions the world as a system of material bodies, bodies composed of particles which are moved, ordered, and adjusted in accordance with forces described by the law of gravity and other scientific laws of nature. "Order" here means, therefore, the processes of nature functioning according to laws of nature. Such order might be called "pure" mechanical order. Much is also made of the "curious adapting of means to ends," of purposes as basic to nature—both in the whole and in the individual things which exist as its parts. We see this particularly in the second and third passages, where the eye is anatomized in order to exhibit its mechanical structure. A similar treatment is given to the sexual structure, both physical and psychological, of animals. The two arguments, from and to design, are run together; the means-ends relationships are predicated of objects which, technically, are not sentient and thus have no intentions. Both sorts of argument, it is maintained, proceed according to the principle of analogy. Purposive relationships are interpreted as mechanical relationships, and such arguments, actually to design, are thus converted into arguments from design. In this context purposive order, the means-ends relation, concerns functional or process-product relations rather than intentions. Machines like clock-works, for instance, have functional relations among the parts that make them up, but no intentions. Generally speaking, then, when the mechanical order of the planets and other astronomical bodies is interpreted in the functional sense, and organic bodies are interpreted, as explained above, in the mechanical sense, both kinds of argument tend to be brought under the concept of the argument from design.

In each of the first three passages there is presented the view that the design argument is scientific in that it proceeds a posteriori, is from effects, is based upon observation. The logical form is that of analogy—the method of discovery of Galileo and Newton. As is apparent from the last two quotations, Hume, in the person of Philo, immediately attacks this analogical form, claiming that while its validity is clear in Galileo's inferences concerning the motion of the earth, it is not evident in the design argument. In addition, in the earlier passages there is the somewhat equivocal claim that the belief in the intelligent creator is forced upon the mind in a way similar to that of sensation. In one sense this appears merely to be a way of emphasizing the empirical and a posteriori character of the design argument; but in another sense there is one added notion. In the statement "Look round the world!" and in the appeal to the "plain instincts of nature," there is the suggestion of an intuitive rather than an inferential process, a point which will demand analysis later on. This is, again, the emotive aspect of the design argument to which we have referred from time to time.

Now these arguments are clearly of the Newtonian variety. The conclusive point lies in a comparison of these passages with some of those quoted from other theological writers of the time, writers we have seen to closely follow Newton in their beliefs. Take, for instance, the passage of Cheyne, on page 33. In the quotation there is explicit reference to the mechanical view of the world, to the analogical nature of the inference to God's existence. Nature is the "vast, if not infinite machin of the universe ... consisting of an infinite number of lesser machins"; and the laws of nature are "those laws of motion, by which natural bodies are commonly govern'd in all their actions upon one another...." The inference is secured by "they who are masters in the noble art of just analogy," who "may from a tolerable knowledge in any one of the integral parts of nature, extend their contemplations more securely to the whole of any other integral parts less known." Here again is the "analogy of nature" to which so many of our authors so pointedly refer. The similarity between this passage and that which sets forth Cleanthes' notions as presented on page 137, where he asks Philo and Demea to "contemplate the whole and every part" of the world, is obvious. Further, Cleanthes submits that "you will find it to be nothing but one great machine, subdivided into an infinite number of lesser machines"; and, finally, he contends that "we are led to infer, by all the rules of analogy," that since the effects of man's labours, machines, are so similar to the world, then the world machine must have a similar cause. Note also Cheyne's view that the argument can proceed from the part to the whole, which becomes one of the targets of Philo's criticism in the *Dialogues*. The similarity of the views of Cleanthes and Cheyne appears quite obvious: Cleanthes not only says he is going to make use of scientific notions, or those in common with science, he actually does so. As has been shown, there is no question concerning the Newtonian source of Cheyne's theory; neither, it seems to me, should there be any further questions concerning the source of Cleanthes' theory.

The most conclusive passage, however, is from Colin Maclaurin. First,

he emphasizes the a posteriori basis of the design argument as does Hume's
Cleanthes. ". . . but it is only *a posteriori* that we thus infer the necessity
✓ of his existence, and not in the same manner that we deduce truth in
geometry";[7] as compared with Cleanthes' "By this argument *a posteriori*,
and by this argument alone, do we prove at once the existence of a Deity,
and his similarity to human mind and intelligence." Maclaurin also
emphasizes the scientific character of these theological methods, a subject
of fundamental significance in Hume's *Dialogues*. Often returning to this
point, Maclaurin holds that it is only from observation and experiment
that we get knowledge, even in matters theological. Fortunately, natural
theology is based upon observation and experiment and is, therefore, a
rational endeavor like any other part of science and practical life. These
elements, of course, are characteristic of the views set forth by Cleanthes
in the *Dialogues*.

Compare Maclaurin's statement, quoted on page 42, with that of
Cleanthes on page 138. Here are mentioned exactly the same examples:
"plain argument," and "plainly of this kind"; "perverse obstinate metaphysics," and "nice and subtle reasonings"; "strikes us like a sensation,"
and "flow in upon you with a force like that of sensation"; the anatomy and
structure of the eye as connected with design; sexual arrangements. All in
all the passages are so similar that we may say the argument of Cleanthes
in Hume's *Dialogues* is probably a paraphrase of Maclaurin's Newtonian
argument. The likelihood of coincidence is lessened when we remember
the close agreement (see page 40), noted just above, concerning the
observational and experimental basis of theology. Whether or not Hume
took the material from Maclaurin, the similarity here and with Cheyne
and the other Newtonians is enough to show that Cleanthes certainly is
asserting a species of Newtonian theology. This is the main contention.
Happily there is even more evidence in support of it, in the form of proof
that Maclaurin specifically provided the source of some of Hume's
materials. The following quotations should be carefully compared. First,
from Maclaurin:

> The abstruse nature of the subject gave occasion to the later Platonists,
> particularly to Plotinus, to introduce the most mystical and unintelligible
> notions concerning the Deity, and that our most perfect worship of him
> consists, not in acts of veneration, reverence, gratitude or love; but in a
> certain mysterious self-annihilation, or total extinction of our faculties.
> These doctrines, however absurd, have had followers who, in this as in

[7] Maclaurin, *An Account of Sir Isaac Newton's Philosophical Discoveries*, p. 405.

other cases, by aiming too high, far beyond their reach, overstrain their faculties, and fall into folly or madness. . . . [8]

Now for the parallel statement from Hume:

The ancient Platonists, you know, were the most religious and devout of all Pagan Philosophers; yet many of them, particularly Plotinus, expressly declare, that intellect or understanding is not to be ascribed to the Deity, and that our most perfect worship of him consists, not in acts of veneration, reverence, gratitude or love; but in a mysterious self-annihilation or total extinction of all our faculties. These ideas are, perhaps, too far-stretched; but still it must be acknowledged. . . . [9]

It seems to me that parallels such as this cannot be charged to coincidence. Beyond the manifest similarity of the conceptions employed, there is a word-for-word identity in the last passage, which makes it highly probable, even if we consider the possibility of a common source, that Hume took his material from Maclaurin. Since Maclaurin, as we have seen, was in all these passages simply restating Newton's theory, it is difficult not to accept the hypothesis that at least some part of Cleanthes' arguments in the *Dialogues* represents scientific theism. When this evidence is brought together with that which was presented above concerning Cheyne and the many other examples of Newtonian theism, I think we can with considerable confidence assert that Hume was attacking Newtonian theism.

There are many other parallels between the *Dialogues* and Maclaurin's work. Some, such as the a posteriori and experimental character of theology, have already been mentioned. Maclaurin, like Cleanthes, constantly reiterated his belief in the worth of the new discoveries in science with respect to their use in theology. This view, common among the Newtonians as well as other theologians and philosophers of the age, is indicated by characteristic discussions of Copernicus, Galileo, and others, found in both Maclaurin and Cheyne. The Brahmin idea of the spider spinning the world from his bowels, the idea that chance gives no explanation of the world, the circulation of the blood, the "great mysterious being," Bacon on atheism and religion, the inability to completely account for nature mechanically, Galileo's method of discovery as analogy, the revolution in learning, Galileo and Copernicus on Jupiter and Saturn, the doctrine of the "microcosm and macrocosm," all are common to Maclaurin and the *Dialogues*. For this reason, in addition to the convincing evidence brought together above, I believe it to be perfectly obvious that in Hume's *Dialogues*

[8] *Ibid*, pp. 397–398.
[9] Hume, "Dialogues Concerning Natural Religion," p. 318.

the character of Cleanthes is used mainly to set forth Newtonian theology, and that Maclaurin's book received the attention of Hume during the composition of the *Dialogues*. The important point is that Hume's sources for the design arguments found in the *Dialogues*, the scientific theism involved, lie in the work of Isaac Newton and thinkers who agreed with him and followed him.

Now is such a position on the part of Hume in any way remarkable? No. As we have seen, this was the age of Newton and the laws of motion, and Newton was the most celebrated figure in the intellectual world. Hume was not immune from impression by a great scientist. In other of his writings there is ample evidence of the influence of Newtonian science, i.e., his experimental and natural philosophy. For instance, in *An Enquiry Concerning the Human Understanding*, Hume tried to formulate principles and laws of human understanding analogous to the Newtonian mechanical principles of nature,[10] and the famous laws of association represent his conclusions on this subject. A similar intention is evident in the earlier *A Treatise of Human Nature*, where he attempted to apply Newton's experimental methods, so successful in mechanical philosophy, to the analysis of human experience. More optimistic than in the later *Enquiry*, Hume wished to develop a system of human nature analogous to the system of physical nature found in Newton's *Principia*. Finally, the principle of the inexplicability of ultimate causes, one of Newton's methodological postulates in science, is fundamental in Hume and he specifically credits it to Newton.[11] This principle is also integral to the *Enquiry*, where again Hume specifically credits Newton for the principle of analogy, and to the *Dialogues*. There is, therefore, nothing unusual in the fact that Hume made use of Newtonian ideas concerning theology, for Newtonian ideas permeate the whole of Hume's thinking. The only peculiarity lies in the fact that if we identify Hume's accepted ideas with those presented in the *Dialogues* by the character Philo, then Hume appears to have been in disagreement with Newton on theological matters, whereas the points mentioned above strongly suggest that he was in hearty agreement with Newton's science and methodology. The key lies in the fact that Hume was not religious in the traditional sense. Therefore he applied Newtonian principles consistently, where Newton did not. Newton did not demand experimental verification on matters theological, nor did he submit his speculations to his own logical tests. Hume did, hence the *Dialogues*.

[10] Hume, *Enquiry*, Sec. I, pp. 11–12. See also Hume's *History of England*, Chap. LXXI.   [11] Hume, *Enquiry*, Sec. VII, p. 79.

Something more should be said about analogy. A great deal of attention has been given to its role in Early Modern design theology, and to its origins and development. As we have seen, the concept of analogy had, in Hume's part of the eighteenth century, come to play a relatively greater part in disputations concerning theology than it had with Newton and other theorists at the turn of the century. Newton stated that his theology was founded upon the principle of "similitude," [12] and also that the principle of analogy was very significant in science. [13] Maclaurin followed Newton. Cheyne made analogy the fundamental principle of metaphysics and theology, in a sense which appears to have been partly stimulated by Aquinas. Butler's use of the principle, so famous during his time, is well known. Berkeley treated it at length, and other lesser figures, such as King and Browne, spent their time in protracted disputes concerning it. Hume was conversant with the work of these men, and he supported his ideas about analogy by appeal to Newton. We have seen the importance that Hume places on scientific discoveries and the kinds of reasoning behind them, including analogy, which was specifically mentioned by Galileo as his method of inference. There was, it must be remembered, no direct proof of the motion of the earth until Foucault's pendulum. From evidence garnered by telescopic observations, which showed that the sun, Venus, and Saturn move, Galileo argued by analogy that the earth must move. Saturn has moons, and moves; therefore the earth, since it has a moon, must move. The importance of this sort of thing, so simple in retrospect to an age which is so engrossed in scientific sophistication, may easily escape the modern reader. But for seventeenth- and eighteenth-century thinkers the heliocentric theory was most momentous, and it completely shattered pre-existing views of the universe. Naturally the method associated with such momentous discoveries would gain wide attention. This, then, is one of the main reasons we have found so many theologians maintaining that the design argument, because it is based upon the principle of analogy, is scientific.

And in this we also have the explanation for Hume's emphasis upon the principle of analogy, both in the theology of the *Dialogues*, and in his general philosophy. Perhaps more than any thinker of the age, Hume was interested in methodology and logic. If one inspects the beginning paragraph of Section IX of the *Enquiry*, "Of the Reason of Animals," he will find a passage concerning analogy which is quite similar to the one in the

---

[12] *Mathematical Principles*, p. 546.
[13] *Ibid.*, pp. 398–399.

Dialogues.[14] A close inspection of Hume's philosophy shows that the principle of analogy, in the scientific and non-Thomistic sense, probably is of more importance to his epistemology than to that of any other philosopher of the time, for he makes it the basis of matter-of-fact reasoning. "All our reasonings concerning matters of fact are founded on a species of analogy, which leads us to expect from any cause the same events, which we have observed to result from similar causes. Where the causes are similar, the analogy is perfect, and the inference, drawn from it, is regarded as certain and conclusive."[15] All in all it is manifest that Hume placed considerable importance upon the principle of analogy. It is likely, in view of the general interest in the principle, that he drew inspiration with regard to it from several sources, including Galileo, Bacon, Newton, Butler, and Berkeley; and it is in addition obvious that the conception of analogical reasoning, tied as it was to the new science, had become traditional.

I think, in the light of the evidence, that we can regard our first hypothesis as well and convincingly established. The theories put forth by Cleanthes in the *Dialogues* represent mainly the kind of natural theology expressed by Sir Isaac Newton and his followers, and have to do with the attempt to use science, both as a method and as a body of factual and theoretical knowledge, in support of the Christian religion. Hume was criticizing such doctrines by means of the views of the character Philo, and was thus criticizing the dominant theological trend of the age—Newtonian theism.

There is, of course, the ancient source of the design argument, a source that is also clearly discernible in Hume's *Dialogues*. The Stoic and Aristotelian antecedents of the doctrine of analogy and of design theology, traced above, show up in Hume's work. As noted earlier, the Stoics considered analogy to be one of the principles of the derivation of ideas. Hume, in a discussion of resemblance, used one of their common examples, the similitude of a man to his picture.[16] "That these principles will serve to connect ideas will not, I believe, be much doubted. A picture naturally leads our thoughts to the original. . . ."[17] There are other indications that Hume was interested in Stoic doctrines. The Stoic argument served Early Modern theologians as a form upon which they could engraft, for theological purposes, the ideas of science. Many of them simply restated Stoic views with little or no change, and in connection with this point it is interesting to note the names of Hume's *Dialogue* characters. Philo and

[14] Hume, "Dialogues Concerning Natural Religion," pp. 303–304.
[15] Hume, *Enquiry*, Sec. 7, p. 114.
[16] *Ibid.*, Sec. V, p. 54.   [17] *Ibid.*, Sec. III, p. 23.

Demea, for example, each represent a type of philosophy and theology. Cleanthes is, in the work, a champion of design theology, both in its modern sense and in the ancient Stoic sense. It seems perfectly fitting to discover that Cleanthes was the name of an ancient and important Stoic philosopher, the second head of the school in fact. Balbus the Stoic in Cicero's *De Natura Deorum* is presented as following his teachings.[18] Philo, the skeptic in the *Dialogues*, reflects Cicero's work in that the historical Philo, an early skeptical theorist, was a mentor of Cotta, the representative of skepticism in Cicero's *De Natura Deorum*. These correlations lead to the conclusion that Hume probably drew the ancient theological doctrines presented in the *Dialogues* from Stoicism and skepticism. His particular sources were probably *De Natura Deorum* and the works of Sextus Empiricus, although Hume was familiar with most of the available sources of ancient thought. A considerable number of Hume's skeptical views can be found in the works of the ancient skeptics, as a cursory examination of Sextus Empiricus will show, including the critique of causality, the problem of inductive generalization, and the difficulties surrounding prediction of future events.[19]

A structural analysis of the *Dialogues* finds that in their arrangement, the introductory "agenda" so to speak, and in the concluding points, the form is similar to that of Cicero's *De Natura Deorum*.[20] Both begin by hazarding the significance of the subject, and subtly fencing in the author so as to protect him against the charge of ungodliness. Both present the skeptic as desiring refutation, and as believing that the received propositions which he disputes are nonetheless true. Both end by saying that the design theologian is probably nearer the truth; and both verbally, but not actually, restrict the questions at hand to the attributes of God other than his existence. As we have seen above, the argument immediately is concerned with the existence of God, although the disputants verbally agree in the beginning to assume it and argue only concerning his attributes. All in all, it appears very likely that the formal structure of the *Dialogues* was inspired by Cicero's work; and some evidence has already been presented to the effect that the Stoic, Epicurean, and Skeptical content may also owe something to Cicero.

[18] See *Hume's Dialogues Concerning Natural Religion*, ed. Norman Kemp-Smith (2d ed.; London: Thomas Nelson and Sons, 1947), p. 60.

[19] For the development of skepticism in the Early Modern period see Richard Popkin, *The History of Scepticism: Erasmus to Descartes* (New York: Humanities Press, 1960).

[20] *Hume's Dialogues Concerning Natural Religion*, ed. Norman Kemp-Smith, pp. 60-61.

The Stoics, as brought out above, made detailed use of the design argument in both its forms. The analogies most popular with them were those comparing the world to ships, horologes, and buildings; and in addition they presented detailed enumerations of things on earth and in the heavens with regard to means-ends relations—final causes. The motions of the planets, etc., were held to show the world to be a work of art similar to those things produced by men; therefore, from the world, since it is analogous to the things produced by men, we can confidently infer a builder, designer, constructor, artificer. Now there are found in Hume's *Dialogues* recurrent references to such examples and analogies, and Cicero's work contains them, as do most Stoic fragments. (It is not maintained that Cicero was a Stoic, although he drew much from them. He is probably most correctly characterized as an eclectic.) Cleanthes, as well as Philo, compares the world to houses, paintings, sculptures, ships, clocks, all Stoic examples. Philo notes in Part I, page 299, how all the modern divines "talk the language of Stoics, Platonists, and Peripatetics, and not that of Pyrrhonians and Academics." (The latter two refer to groups of skeptics.) In Part II, page 304, Philo asks Cleanthes to show how the world is analogous to a house, and a little later, page 306, brings up the same question in regard to the watch; then it is a Stoic favorite, the ship. The ancient and modern come together in the following: "But can you think, Cleanthes, that your usual phlegm and philosophy have been preserved in so wide a step as you have taken, when you compared to the universe, houses, ships, furniture, machines; and from this similarity in some circumstances inferred a similarity in their causes?"[21] In other places Hume seems to draw directly from Cicero. The references to Tully's use of the design argument, and to Simonides and Hiero, are examples. The vast conglomerations of the uses of things to which the Stoics constantly refer are neglected in the *Dialogues*; still, much space is devoted to the teleological structuring of organisms. The adaptations of parts of organisms, such as the eyes for sight and the sexes for reproduction, are found in Cicero as well as in Newton and his followers. It should be remembered that in Hume's time such functional relations were thought of predominately in mechanical terms.

Now I think the conclusions are clear. Hume's *Dialogues Concerning Natural Religion* most obviously deal with natural theology in general, and proceed by an attack against the design argument. The attack is mounted primarily against the Newtonian formulation of the argument, which is set

[21] Hume, "Dialogues Concerning Natural Religion," p. 308.

forth by Cleanthes; and it is extended to the design argument in all its forms, including those traditionally proposed by eminent philosophers and schools of philosophy, beginning at least with Plato. It is also clear that the dominant form of the design theology under attack was inspired by the methods and discoveries of the new mechanical and physical scientists of the age, great and small, who used the design argument in its Newtonian formulation, or at least in what they understood to be his formulation. It is important to grasp the point that Hume was able to attack the entire tradition of natural theology—all of it, old and new. Argument by analogy is the keystone; when it falls, as Hume knew well, the whole theological edifice crumbles, although as usual the ruins will continue to be occupied by a few who are immune to the discomforts of logical inconsistency. It is also important to see that the design argument was begging for such treatment. It was no purely "philosophical" topic, whose consideration was restricted to the private discussions of a few intellectuals by secluded firesides. Hume's *Dialogues*, perhaps the most conclusive and definitive piece of philosophical criticism ever produced, hit home in the vulnerable area of general acceptance, in the area of religious belief accepted by most educated people of the time, and by practical preachers as well. They came at a time when religion seemed to have been conclusively established by the new science. They concern themselves with a generic and well-entrenched position with a venerable history of acceptance accounting in its defense most of the most formidable names in the history of thought such as Plato, Aristotle, Bacon, Locke, Berkeley, Butler, Aquinas, and such great modern scientists as Galileo, Newton, and Boyle. For these reasons Hume's *Dialogues* represent a milestone in the history of philosophy and philosophical theology. The outcome was of considerable importance.

Our problem now is this: how successful was Hume's criticism of the design argument? If successful, it means the destruction of hallowed beliefs, their removal from the lists of philosophically defensible views of God. This is now our topic for consideration.

II. HUME'S CRITIQUE

Since it has been established that the design argument in both its ancient and modern forms, as well as the question of its relation to early modern science, is the subject of Hume's *Dialogues*, we can proceed to a consideration of his attack. While Hume, by the dialogue form, and by numerous artifices of form and character, masks the negative tone of the destructive arguments, nevertheless, I think we shall find that close analysis of the argument of the *Dialogues* exhibits its deadly anti-religious efficiency with respect to any rational or natural foundation for religious belief. I shall follow the subject in terms of the distinctions developed in the course of the preceding pages. First, the design argument under Hume's inspection is composed of both ancient and traditional, as well as Early Modern elements. Common to both of these strands of argument is the analogical form of inference; in its ancient form the analogy is between the world and the work of art as well as to simple machines. In the Newtonian form the analogy is between the world and the machine. In both forms the world is taken to be similar to the contrivances of man. And whenever the purposive structure of organs and organisms, eyes, bodies, etc., are considered they are also interpreted as machines. In this way the world is taken to be a large machine made up of many smaller machines.

Now it is clear that the key factor in the design argument is its form—the analogical form of inference that it employs—and therefore it is natural that it is the main point of Hume's attack. Prefatory to our analysis, however, several points should be borne in mind. First, the design argument in each of its forms is actually a species of the cosmological argument, and thus depends upon the principle of causality, that is, it involves the principle that whatever exists (even world machines) must have a cause. Further, it depends upon the principle of uniformity, that is, like causes produce like effects. Finally, as we have seen, the scientifically oriented argument from analogy claims a posteriori status, in the two senses discussed above, i.e., in that the laws of motion are based upon observation and experiment, and in that the analogical form of reasoning is the basic method of discovery in the physical sciences.

The schema of analogical reasoning is as follows: Object A has properties 1, 2, 3, 4; Object B *resembles* A in having properties 1, 2, 3; therefore, object B, since analogous or similar to A in three properties, also has property 4. According to the design argument, Object A, a man-made machine, say a watch, has orderly and purposive relationships between the parts and is made by a watchmaker; Object B, the world, has orderly and purposive relationships between its parts; hence object B, the world, must have a watchmaker-type creator who is God. Now modern logicians would, I think, agree that analogical reasoning is a valuable tool in the development of hypotheses. Galileo's argument that the earth moves because analogous bodies—the moon, sun, Saturn, Jupiter—move, would be, according to this view, well taken. But, and this is important, analogy is not considered to be a method of proof or verification. We shall see that this is precisely the point of departure taken by Hume in criticizing the design argument. It is in addition granted that analogical arguments, while not deductively valid, are nevertheless very strong psychologically, particularly when the similarities between the analogons are extensive.

Specifically, Hume's main contentions, which will be developed in order, are as follows:

(1) The design argument is *not* scientific in that it offers no evidence for the *causes* of the world order. The world is one particular, not a member of a species a great number of whose members have been observed. In order to demonstrate a cause for any effect it is necessary to have observed the cause and effect in conjunction, indeed, in constant conjunction. And no one has seen the origin of one world, let alone "worlds." A priori (since no a posteriori evidence is available concerning the cause of the world), it may have caused itself. The doctrine of evolution provided precisely the filling for this pie, arguing that natural selection provides a law which explains how the world and the organisms in it took on their form. It was devastating in its effect, as we shall see below.

(2) Hume points out that the analogy is weak—that is, it isn't even a good example of the method of analogy as suggesting a hypothesis. At most, therefore, the argument would offer extremely low probability in the suggestion of a hypothesis, and none as proof.

(3) Directly in connection with the second point above, Hume devotes a considerable amount of space to *reductio ad absurdum* arguments. These arguments are calculated to show that, even if we grant that such analogy does allow demonstration, and that it is a posteriori, one can, by precisely the same methods of analogy, and from the same kind of evidence, deduce a number of conclusions about the proposed cause of the world that are remarkably obnoxious to those who accept traditional religious doctrines. The world is like a vegetable, hence is caused by a seed or plant; the world is disorderly as well as orderly, hence implies a disorderly cause; the world is full of evil as well as beneficent purposive-relationships, and hence implies an evil cause; machines and houses are often made by many artisans, hence the world has multiple causes—many gods. In other words, in these *absurdum* arguments Hume shows that arguments of precisely the same form and of equal validity demonstrate conclusions radically at variance with those accepted by the users of the design argument. Of course, these *absurdums* are made possible by the rather unique neglect of negative evidence which constantly characterizes the thought of the users

of the design argument, as in the case of Newton's argument that the anomalies of certain planetary motions imply the necessity of a cosmic repairman.

Finally, when Cleanthes in discouragement retreats to the emotive-intuitive force of the design argument, to the claim that despite Hume's critique in the words of Philo, people nevertheless find the argument a conclusive source of conviction, Hume, admitting the *ad hominem* character of his argument, tells him that this is to confuse emotion with evidence. Early training and antecedent convictions lead the users of the design argument to emphasize the ways in which the world is analogous to man's machines. For the rest, it is mostly verbal confusion. The arguments will be considered in order.

At the beginning Philo allies himself with Demea in protesting the essentially unknowable and mysterious character of God's nature against Cleanthes' efforts towards developing a rational and empirical approach to theology. As the discussion wears on, however, Demea, little by little, becomes aware that Philo is playing him like a fish—that Philo is in fact a skeptic of the first order, and that his skeptical views are wont to destroy not only Cleanthes' natural theology, but also Demea's a priori and mystical theology:

> Hold! Hold! cried Demea: Whither does your imagination hurry you? I joined in alliance with you, in order to prove the incomprehensible nature of the Divine Being, and refute the principles of Cleanthes, who would measure everything by a human rule and standard. But now I find you running into all the topics of the greatest libertines and infidels; and betraying that holy cause, which you seemingly espoused. . . .[22]
>
> And are you so late in perceiving it? replied Cleanthes.[23]

It is one thing, as Demea sees, to destroy natural theology in order to espouse mysticism and rationalism, but another indeed to reach conclusions which destroy all possible rational conviction about theological matters, and yet this is precisely what Philo has done. He begins by a sustained attack upon the design argument. Cleanthes maintains that the design argument has the logical status of science and common sense, and underscores this claim (pages 294–296) by reference to Galileo, Newton, and Copernicus. In addition it is claimed (page 299) that the argument proceeds in the language also of Stoics, Platonists, and Peripatetics. After some preliminary skirmishing in which Philo and Cleanthes agree with Demea that it is only the "attributes" of God, and not his "existence," which are

[22] *Ibid.*, p. 382.   [23] *Ibid.*

to be discussed, they get down to the main battle, with Cleanthes proposing the scientific variety of the design argument we saw above. Despite the agreement to assume God's existence and argue only for his attributes, Cleanthes' first argument, as we have seen, immediately infers his existence plus some attributes (intelligence, benevolence).

It is claimed (page 302), thus, that the argument is scientific in that it follows "all the rules of analogy"; that it employs the same analogical and a posteriori methods (pages 302–303) in precisely the same way that Galileo's arguments concerning the motion of the earth are analogical and a posteriori. Philo loses no time in his attack, nor does he immediately reject the a posteriori character of the argument. But he does claim that the arguments are not the same, that Cleanthes has not at his disposal, as did Galileo, a full analogy. All cases, he says, in which we scientifically argue from effects to causes must refer to (a) effects of exactly a similar nature, effects which can be shown to belong to members of the same species; and (b) the causes as well as the effects of the analogons must be experienced.

> That a stone will fall, that fire will burn, that the earth has solidity, we have observed a thousand and a thousand times; and when any new instance of this nature is presented, we draw without hesitation the accustomed inference.[24]

But, in the design argument of Cleanthes, which says that the world is a machine, we do not have the requisite experience of similarity. The world is a particular; it does not belong to a species; it is unique; it is on the surface not a member of the class of machines.

Further, in machines, houses, etc., *the cause is observed*, time after time, to be responsible for, to be the condition of, the effect. But in the design argument this condition does not hold. ". . . order, arrangement, or the adjustment of final causes is not, of itself, any proof of design; but only so far as it has been experienced to proceed from that principle."[25] Since we have no such experience of the origin of worlds, ". . . will any man tell me with a serious countenance, that an orderly universe must arise from some thought and art, like the human; because we have experience of it?"[26] Since this key aspect of scientific induction is missing—the experience necessary to correct causal inference—we can only proceed a priori; and "For ought we can know *a priori*, matter may contain the source of spring of order originally, within itself. . . ."[27] This eventuality came to pass, almost on the heels of Hume's suggestion, in Darwin's theory of evolution.

---

[24] *Ibid.*, p. 303.   [25] *Ibid.*, p. 306.   [26] *Ibid.*, p. 311.
[27] *Ibid.*, p. 306.

Note that Philo's contentions are not at all unfair. The claim of Cleanthes is that the analogical argument from design is the same as those of common sense and science. And Hume, in the words of Philo, has clearly exposed the fact that in important ways the design argument is not like a posteriori scientific and common sense inferences. Cleanthes, in the midst of the argument just referred to, complains that if Philo's strictures are accepted, then Galileo's argument concerning the earth's motion is invalid. ". . . a caviller might raise all the same objections to the Copernican system, which you have urged against my reasonings. Have you other earths, might he say, which you have seen to move ? Have. . . ." But Philo's response is swift. "Yes!" cried Philo, interrupting him, "we have other earths. Is not the moon another earth, which we see to turn around its center ? Are not the revolutions of the sun also a confirmation, from analogy, of the same theory ? . . ."[28] The reference to Galileo is specific: "But Galileo, beginning with the moon, proved its similarity in every particular to the earth; its convex figure, its natural darkness when not illuminated, its density, its distinction into solid and liquid, the variation of its phases. . . ."[29] "Cite your experience, and deliver your theory," says Philo. It is clearly improper to claim that the analogy used in the design argument is scientific—it is not for the simple reason that scientific analogies are based upon detailed and supported similarities. In addition the causal relationships between scientifically supported causal relations are observed sequences—both the cause and effects are observed in conjunction. Note that according to Philo's point on observing causes and effects, Galileo's argument would offer a hypothesis, rather than a proof—it is the "sole" proof, according to Philo.[30] But the similarities between the earth and the moon, etc., are full and complete. Both are members of the species of planets, and there is evidence enough to justify great probability in the hypothesis that the earth moves. Cleanthes, Philo rightly observes, does not have such similarities at his disposal. The world is not experienced to be the effect of either a machine or a work of art. Both sorts of inference argue to a first cause, and therefore both are subject to Philo's critique that neither involves the observation of causes. Nobody has observed or seen the origin of worlds. Indeed, a supernatural cause could not be observed even if it did cause the world.

Empirical arguments and proofs, says Philo, follow the logical rule that negative evidence is as relevant as positive evidence. Cleanthes, however, continues to accept the hypothesis of a designer despite negative evidence

<hr />

[28] *Ibid.*, pp. 311–312.   [29] *Ibid.*, p. 313.   [30] *Ibid.*, p. 312.

which is logically more powerful and compelling than the positive evidence. This means, of course, that those who accept the design argument neglect negative evidence and overgeneralize. To put the point another way, they maintain their hypothesis in the face of any possible negative evidence. The upshot is that logically the hypothesis is compatible with any empirical events whatsoever; and this is not a condition that is allowable if the hypothesis is to be considered empirical. No facts could possibly disprove it, and yet it is not, clearly, an a priori hypothesis, since its negation does not involve one in a self-contradiction.

Now Philo, in the quotations above, clearly proposed one sort of test—the standard of observation with respect to the relationship of causes and effects. The hypothesis that the world is created, is *caused*, by a designer-mechanic-purposer is verified by observing that worlds are created by designers. But, we find, no worlds-in-creation have been observed; and there is in addition some question, since God is defined as nonmaterial and spiritual, whether it would be possible to observe him even if he were producing a world. Strictly speaking we can observe only physical events, or those objects and events subject to sensation and perception. Even more difficult and metaphysical is the problem of whether or not material and spiritual realities can be causally related. Leaving out this latter problem, and rejecting, perhaps without justice, Descartes' view that the physical and spiritual come together in the pineal gland; and granting on common-sense grounds that mind and matter can be so related; it remains true that in principle it would seem to be impossible to observe the creation of a world by a God of the variety accepted by the design theologians. Hume, in the expressions of Philo, is clearly claiming that the design argument is not an empirical hypothesis in the scientific sense.

Ultimately, the supporter of the design argument as an empirical hypothesis in some sense would probably attack the verification principle here employed. This principle is yet unsettled in modern philosophy as respects its general relation to cognitive statements. But it seems clear that it is acceptable with respect to *scientific* statements, and, it would seem to me, to common-sense statements. It should be remembered that in the very beginning of the *Dialogues*, Cleanthes makes the claim that the reasoning is the same in the design argument as it is in science and common sense, and it is obvious that the theologians shared this view.

But Cleanthes is not allowed to rest his case even here, for his brief is matched by a series of *reductio ad absurdum* arguments. Developed by means of the same logical form and the same sort of evidence that was used by Cleanthes, Philo infers, with precisely the same logical propriety, a number of conclusions which are heinous to the counselor for the design argument. Under the principle that what is logical sauce for the theological goose is also logical sauce for the skeptical gander, Philo appeals to the following points:

First, a priori, any consistent explanation of the world and its origin is acceptable so long as its denial does not involve a contradiction. Remember, there is, as it has been shown, no a posteriori way of verifying the source of universes. Therefore, in the absence of observed or observable evidence of the causes of the world, for all we know it might very well cause itself. "[pages 306–311] For all we know *a priori*, matter may contain the source or spring of order originally, within itself. . . ." As has been noted, on the very heels of Hume's argument came Darwin's doctrine of evolution, with its law of natural selection, which makes the claim that the world causes and orders itself seem quite reasonable. *Ad hoc* appeals to God's use of natural selection as His method of creating the world order serves only to set the problem back one or more steps—either to an infinite regress (since the orderly plan in God's mind itself necessitates an orderer); or to the quite conclusive logical point of Occam's razor—that God is an hypothesis which is no longer necessary. "[page 323] . . . a mental world, or a universe of ideas, requires a cause as much, as does a material world, or universe of objects. . . ." Cleanthes' weak rejoinder is "[page 326] I know not, I care not; that concerns not me. I have found a Deity; and here I stop my inquiry. Let those go farther, who are wiser or more enterprising." I shall introduce some more material on this question in Chapter Ten, in the nineteenth-century curtain call of Paley, Whewell, and the *Bridgewater Treatises*.

Philo turns next to certain other aspects of the world order. He develops a set of analogies which produces quite disturbing conclusions, but which are nevertheless fully as valid as those offered by Cleanthes. The world order appears as similar to an animal or a vegetable as it does to a machine or a house. The causes of the universe, therefore, are vastly different from minds or intelligence. "[page 334] Now if we survey the universe, so far as it falls under our knowledge, it bears a great resemblance to an animal or an organized body, and seems actuated with a like principle of life and motion." The circulation of water, the repair of waste, the close sympathy of the system, the parts preserving the whole, all are similar to aspects of animal organisms. By analogy, then, the world should be created by procreative generation. "[page 341] . . . we should suppose this world to be an animal; a comet is the egg of the animal; and in like manner as an ostrich lays its egg in the sand, which, without any further care, hatches the egg, and produces a new animal...." Notice that in addition to providing analogical arguments for a cause of the world order which is obnoxious to theologians, these inferences also weaken the design argument in that they exhibit aspects of the world order which are *dissimilar* to mind or to machines. Since an analogical argument depends for its strength upon the number and force of the characteristics which the analogues have in common, the design argument is vitiated to the extent that dissimilarities are pointed up. Philo's discussion, thus, is double-barreled in its shot at the design argument.

Cleanthes becomes quite exercised at this line of argument, and opposes it on the ground that we find many important similarities between animals and the world missing. The world has "[page 336] no organs of sense; no seat of thought or reason; no one precise origin of motion and action." And then, with catastrophic results, he blunders on into Philo's rather unsophisticated trap: "In short, it seems to bear a stronger resemblance to a vegetable than to an animal, and your inference would be so far inconclusive in favor of the soul of the world." This is a catastrophe for the simple reason that it affords more grist for Philo's critical mill. He has only to leap to the acceptance of Cleanthes' proposition, for to hold to the view that the world is a vegetable, rather than an animal, puts the design argument in even worse straits than before. Cleanthes clacks on, in a somewhat extended discussion of trees and plants in Europe and Asia, adding fuel to Philo's torch. As we have it in Philo's statement:

> If the universe bears a greater likeness to animal bodies and to vegetables, than to works of human art, it is more probable that its cause resembles the cause of the former than that of the latter, and its origin ought rather to be ascribed to generation and vegetation than to reason or design.[31]

And how would such a world-vegetable be created? "In like manner," says Philo:

> As a tree sheds its seed into the neighboring field, and produces other trees; so the great vegetable, the world, or this planetary system, produces within itself certain seeds, which, being scattered into the surrounding chaos, vegetate into new worlds. A comet, for instance, is the seed of a world....[32]

Since for any of these alternative hypotheses no empirical data can be shown which provides a verification or demonstration, no cosmogony can

[31] *Ibid.*, pp. 339–340.   [32] *Ibid.*, p. 341.

be established, and any number of contrary hypotheses is as good as the other. It is of no avail to argue that seeds, etc., were the designer's ways of creating worlds, a point brought up in agony by Demea (page 343), for plants create their own seeds—"A tree bestows order and organization on that tree . . . An animal, in the same manner, on its offspring. . . ." Even reason itself, insofar as we experience its origin, is derived from generation, from its animal source (page 345). "Hesiod, and all the ancient mythologists, were so struck with this analogy, that they universally explained the origin of nature from an animal birth, and copulation. . . . The Brahmins assert, that the world arose from an infinite spider, who spins this whole complicated mass from his bowels. . . ." Even if plants did not procreate themselves, Philo could trap Demea into an infinite regress of ordering causes.

The principle of analogical argument is an indifferent friend to theology and to the Christian point of view. Therefore many analogies are logically on the same footing, and, indeed, allow the theologian to be hoisted by his own methodological petard. Certainly none of the above conclusions are friendly to the Christian notion of an omnipotent geometer-mechanic. And yet, this is not by any means the worst treachery on the part of the fickle friendship of analogical reasoning. Philo turns from animal-vegetable analogies to those which involve God's other characteristics—His unity, power, goodness. Following out the analogies of mechanic-watch-makers, ship-builders and house-carpenters, Philo argues that in none of these cases is the cause that single or unified artisan which the religious position of Cleanthes demands. "[page 330] A great number of men join in building a house or ship, in rearing a city, in framing a common-wealth: why may not several deities combine in contriving and framing a world?"

And what about intelligence? Again granting the validity of analogical reasoning of the type Cleanthes espouses, Philo says that the analogy of machines, houses, and ships proves no specific intelligent cause.

> But were this world ever so perfect a production, it must still remain uncertain, whether all the excellences of the work can justly be ascribed to the workman. If we survey a ship, what an exalted idea must we form of the engenuity of the carpenter, who framed so complicated, useful, and beautiful a machine. And what surprise must we feel, when we find him a stupid mechanic, who imitated others, and copied an art, which through a long succession of ages . . . had been gradually improving. Many worlds might have been botched and bungled. . . .[33]

And this is, unfortunately, not the end of embarrassment: the world is not

[33] *Ibid.*, p. 330.

by any means a perfect production. There are (page 329) "many inexplicable difficulties in the works of nature. . . ." The world is so far imperfect that it appears beyond understanding. "[page 360] Observe too," says Philo, "the curious artifices of nature, in order to embitter the life of every living being. The stronger prey upon the weaker. . . . The weaker, too, in their turn, often prey upon the stronger. . . ." Philo rubs it in (page 372)— "Did I show you a house or palace, where there was not one apartment convenient or agreeable; where the windows, doors, fires, passages, stairs, and the whole economy of the building were the source of noise, confusion, fatigue, darkness, and the extremes of heat and cold; you would certainly blame the contrivance, without any further examination. The architect would in vain display his subtlety, and prove to you, that if this door or window. . . ." Where, then, is the argument for God's power?

> None of these parts or principles, however useful, are so accurately adjusted, as to keep precisely within those bounds, in which their utility consists; but they are, all of them, apt on every occasion, to run into the one extreme or the other. . . . Rains are necessary to nourish all the plants and animals of the earth: but how often are they defective? How often excessive? Heat is requisite to all life . . . but is not always found in the due proportion. The irregularity is never, perhaps, so great as to destroy any species; but is often sufficient to involve the individuals in ruin and misery.[34]

We know, of course, that species have been destroyed by many factors— Hume's argument grows still stronger with advances in knowledge. But it is strong enough as he presents it:

> The whole presents nothing but the idea of a blind nature, impregnated by a great vivifying principle, and pouring forth from her lap, without discernment or parental care, her maimed and abortive children.[35]

In this last section of the *Dialogues*, almost all pretense at literary balance gives way before Philo's onslaught. I have remarked that Philo was rubbing it in. Here he proceeds to grind out the whole miserable implication—still clinging to the precise logical form claimed by Cleanthes, whose good philosophical temper must show some strain. The last argument shades into another. As we have repeatedly seen, the mechanical and purposive arrangements in the world have been offered by practitioners of the design argument as evidence for the *benevolence* of the cause of the world. The unity and power of the cause have already been brought into question;

---

[34] *Ibid.*, p. 379.   [35] *Ibid.*, p. 381.

and now the same sort of evidence, and the same sort of argument, that Cleanthes uses in order to prove God's benevolence are used in order to prove his *malevolence*. If, says Philo, those factors, processes, purposive relationships, objects in the world which benefit man can be used to argue the goodness of the cause; then, by the same token, those factors which hurt him imply a malevolent cause. Philo joins Demea, who again stupidly rises to the bait, in a description of the horrors of the world.

> Our sense of music, harmony, and indeed beauty of all kinds, give satisfaction, without being absolutely necessary to the preservation and propagation of the species. But what racking pains, on the other hand, arise from gouts, gravels, megrims, toothaches, rheumatisms; where the injury to the animal-machinery is either small or incurable? Mirth, laughter, play, frolic, seem gratuitous satisfactions, which have no further tendency: spleen, melancholy, discontent, superstition, are pains of the same nature.[36]

Notice that these arguments are not exactly the same as the traditional incompatibilities poetically described by Epicurus, although Philo, to be sure, points these up.[37] It is, more precisely, that arguments for God's plurality, stupidity, and malevolence are as well grounded in observation and in analogy as are His unity, intelligence, and benevolence; perhaps they are even more well founded, since the disorder and misery of the world seems even more evident than its order and benevolence. One cannot have it both ways, asserts Philo. If observed goodness in the world constitutes evidence for a good cause, then observed badness constitutes evidence for a bad cause; if observed order in the world constitutes evidence for an orderly and intelligent cause; then observed disorder constitutes evidence for a disorderly and stupid creator; if observed machines and ships have a number of creators who have produced them through trial and error, and possibly bungling techniques; and if their creators are unintelligent copiers, then the causes of the world machine or ship are also blundering copiers. Even Newton, we will recall, became involved in a similar logical discontinuity: the order in the world, the laws of motion and optics, etc., imply an intelligent mechanic-geometer; but the disorder, the variations in planetary motions, etc., imply not, by a similar logic, a disorderly cause, but the need for cosmic repairs! He did not note that an all-powerful and intelligent God would supposedly make a machine that needed no repairs. Unless he were malicious, a thought which naturally would never enter the pious Newton's head.

[36] *Ibid.*, pp. 365–366.   [37] *Ibid.*, p. 365.

These arguments bring about a change in Cleanthes' position. He finds himself forced to admit that the creator is not all-powerful, not omnipotent. We must, he says, rest content with more moderate theological claims, considering the evidence. "[page 371] . . . in a word, benevolence, regulated by wisdom, and limited by necessity, may produce just such a world as the present." In this light God is viewed as neither omnipotent nor infinite, and Cleanthes retreats to the contention that religion, whatever its cognitive status, is "useful" in matters of behavior and morality.[38] Philo does not let this pragmatic argument go by, but more on that later.

There is a final appeal to which Cleanthes returns. It is not in any one place in the *Dialogues*, indeed, it is a constant thread of argument which runs throughout the discourse. It is the final court of appeal of the theologian—the psychological compulsiveness of the design argument. If its cognitive character is so weak, then why, asks Cleanthes, is there such universal acceptance of the design argument?

> The comparison of the universe to a machine of human contrivance is so obvious and natural, and is justified by so many instances of order and design in Nature, that it must immediately strike all unprejudiced apprehensions, and procure universal approbation.[39]

Notice that the machine analogy is incidental to this statement—its logic has already been exploded. Early in the *Dialogues* we found Cleanthes claiming that a survey of the anatomy of the eye leads one "irresistibly" to the idea of a contriver. "[page 316] . . . tell me, from your own feeling, if the idea of a contriver does not flow in upon you with a force like that of sensation." Note the terms "flow in," "feeling," "force like that of sensation." "[page 317] . . . no language can carry a more intelligible, irresistible meaning. . . ." "And if the argument for theism be, as you pretend, contradictory to the principles of logic; its universal, its irresistible influence proves clearly, that there may be arguments of a like irregular nature." Note that the emphasis here is placed upon the immediacy of the conclusion in favor of a designer, and not upon the inferential character of it. The question of logical validity, of the propriety of the argument's inferential character, is all but read out of court in favor of the general acceptance of the belief. I am sure that the intention herein is not to appeal to *consensus gentium* in favor of the conclusion, but rather to appeal to it as evidence for the intuitive conclusiveness of the design argument. It is like a language speaking to us, an Augustinian variety of

[38] *Ibid.*, p. 391.   [39] *Ibid.*, pp. 386–387.

intuitive certitude, of self-evidence, beyond the reach of argument or inference.

And thus we rediscover that interesting claim, met many times before in alliance with the design argument, that it "points to," "speaks to us," that in some sense the design argument is the occasion of a direct and self-evident knowledge of God's existence that is somewhat noninferential. It "carries a force like that of sensation." Along with this claim, which reflects intense psychological conviction, go a multitude of *ad hominems*, those all but inevitable associates of claims to intuitive knowledge, against all who are so blind, prejudiced, stupid, as to not be aware of such intuitions. Cleanthes' arguments against Philo are constantly clogged with such question-begging epithets: only "obtuse metaphysicians" can reject the design argument; those who are skeptical of the efficacy of the design argument are "cavillers" and "raillers." Now although Cleanthes is a kindly and personable, non-Warburtonian dogmatist, nevertheless he is a dogmatist in the constant claim that there is in effect something wrong with the skeptic, psychologically if not morally, because he does not accept the very argument at issue.

And this is where the design argument ends up in the *Dialogues*. Two arguments of precisely the same analogical character, one moving from the benevolent properties in the world order to a benevolent designer, and one moving from the malevolent properties in the world order to a malevolent designer, are not treated with the same respect. Nor is it possible to combine them and argue to a designer who is both benevolent and malevolent, or who is, in addition, weak. To the dogmatist, skeptical derogation of the design argument is another instance of "cavilling" and of "raillery"—of the wrong-headed and perverse character of the skeptic. The dogmatist, of course, sees nothing wrong with ignoring the skeptic's argument, nor with excusing himself from attending to it by calling his opponent names. The same procedure is followed in regard to other aspects of Philo's skeptical contentions; the disorder of the world, the multiplicity of designers, etc., are examples. One must, says Cleanthes, "[page 316] . . . adhere to common sense and the plain instincts of nature; and to assent, whenever any reasons strike him with so full a force, that he cannot, without the greatest violence, prevent it." And the arguments of natural religion are, in his opinion, of this type.

They are of this type, rejoins Philo, only if you have been taught to look at nature in this way. It is clear that there is no logical refutation possible for an argument which makes its appeal to psychological compulsiveness.

For the kind of logical illness which allows a thinker to select one rather than another of two arguments, both of which have equal logical validity, there is of course no logical remedy; and if the argument selected has even less logical validity, there is even less logical recourse. Since the appeal is *ad hominem*, the response is of the same character. Cleanthes himself, like so many of his intellectual cohorts, has changed the rules of the game. He has decamped from his logical position; he has said, in effect, to Philo: (a) If the logic is so bad, then why do so many people find it so convincing? and (b) Why does it strike people with such forceful conviction? Philo's answer is that people have been conditioned to be religious. They elect to accept the design argument because it fits what they already believe and what they wish to continue to believe; and they wish to believe it because human life in general is so mean, unhappy and painful, so full of fears, longings, unsatisfied desires, and ignorance concerning death, that they incapsulate these desires into the belief in a perfect, eternal, just and merciful creator, who will be infinitely kind to them in an infinite future life. Demea and Cleanthes unwittingly help Philo along this road, the first by dwelling upon the emotive-intuitive element. "[page 358] . . . each man feels, in a manner, the truth of religion within his own breast; and from a consciousness of his imbecility and misery, rather than from any reasoning, is led to seek protection from that Being, on whom he and all nature is dependent." Following this up, Philo says that proof is unnecessary for "what every one feels within himself." Hence "strong imagery" and "eloquence," and not reason, are the source of religious conviction. So much for "natural propensity." Cleanthes himself alludes to the fact that the force of the conviction is supported "by early education," by training, in other words.[40] And so it comes to be a matter of emphasis—a verbal matter. Logically, there are remote analogies, and one whose prior training and experience so form him will elect to place emphasis upon the design hypothesis because it fits what he wants to believe.

Late in the *Dialogues*, after Demea leaves somewhat in disgust, the question of the sources of religious belief arises again, in a similar temper to that we have just been considering. Religious conviction is based upon emotion, persuasion, and fear. In a nutshell, there is no rational source for religious convictions about the existence and attributes of a divine being. Demea recognizes that he has been diddled; Cleanthes is, of course, not surprised at all.[41] The work ends on this sort of note, not, however, without further criticism by Philo. Here is the grudging agreement:

[40] *Ibid.*, p. 387.   [41] *Ibid.*, pp. 366, 382.

... if [a person of] *very limited* [my italics] intelligence, whom we shall suppose utterly unacquainted with the universe, were assured, that it were the production of a very good, wise, and powerful being, however infinite, he would, from his own conjectures, form *beforehand* a different notion of it from what we find it to be by experience ... he might, perhaps, be surprised at the disappointment; but he would never retract his former belief. ...[42]

If we rephrase Hume's quite deferential statements, a stupid and ignorant person, prejudiced in advance, would not give up his prior convictions even if he recognized their difficulties; he would excuse his prejudice by explaining his "blindness and ignorance."[43]

The argument is then resumed in the following terms: suppose that the man is *not antecedently* convinced of God's power, intelligence, and benevolence; i.e., suppose that there does not exist a favorable prejudice in advance of the facts. Then the case would be quite different. The utter meanness, disorderliness, viciousness of the world would lead him to no such convictions as that its cause was intelligent, good, and powerful. Indeed, just as a poorly built house would lead us to infer a stupid and incapable architect, a "poorly built" world would lead to the conviction of a stupid and incapable designer, even if we grant the contention that there is a designer.

The intention of the argument is quite clear. The only reasons for being convinced by the design argument, the only reasons for its psychological compulsiveness, lie in previously acquired and emotionally grounded prejudices in its favor. These prejudices derive from fear of the unknown, from terror of death, from inclinations based upon previous education and training, and they lead the theologian to neglect overpowering negative evidence. "Is the world considered in general, and as it appears to us in this life, different from what a man or such a limited Being would, *beforehand*, expect from a very powerful, wise, and benevolent Deity? It must be a strange prejudice to assert the contrary."[44] The phenomena do not allow us to conclude a good, intelligent, powerful being: hence the source of conviction to the contrary must be founded upon matters which are based upon emotions and other psychological causes. If religion reduces completely to "temper and education," in other words to attitudes conditioned by society, and is not based upon reasoned conclusions and empirical evidence, the melancholy aspects of life, its "gouts and megrims," can be ignored. But if evidence is the rule, then these sad situations are

[42] *Ibid.*, p. 371.   [43] *Ibid.*   [44] *Ibid.*

part of the evidence and must be given their due. A "firm conviction," yes; a rational conviction, no.[45] The orderly aspects of the world, its scientific laws of motion, its muscles and sinews of living organisms, do strike us with force—but, antecedent conviction is the key to this force, for the arguments based upon such order neglect similar arguments, of just as much *logical force*, based upon disorder and pain. The arguments in favor of the design hypothesis are psychologically compelling, but they are not "[page 386] in themselves, very numerous or forcible." In the last analysis it is a verbal disagreement, which depends upon one's emotional standpoint. But even here Philo excludes moral and natural benevolence.[46] Philo says his inclination is skeptical, and Cleanthes admits that his is contrary to skepticism. This initiates the final controversy, in which Philo disputes Cleanthes' attempt to milk a little more in his favor out of the small amount of cognitive agreement he has drawn from Philo. Before taking this up, perhaps we should recall just what Philo has admitted to. He has admitted only that there are remote analogies between the world of nature and the works of men. But this admission is qualified to death by the remark that everything in the world bears some remote analogy to everything else. A heap of sand and a man resemble each other in that they both occupy space. This admission in no way vitiates Philo's *absurdum* arguments showing that the same sort of evidence would also prove nothing about the cause of the world in terms of number, character, benevolence; that, in fact, similar arguments show an equal likelihood that the world is a vegetable or animal which has been constructed by a group of somewhat inept workmen. All of the received notions of God as omnipotent, omniscient, omnibenevolent, are out of the window. In addition, not even a smidgen of acceptance is given to the argument that the design inference is scientific—scientific inferences, it is still claimed, involve the experience of the causes as well as the effects, a condition that does not hold in the design argument.

At this place in the argument, to return to the point, Cleanthes appeals to the ancient pragmatic justification of religious persuasions. This view claims that, whatever its logical status, its status as true or false, and however corrupted, the acceptance of religion is better than its non-acceptance. The doctrine of an all-powerful, all-good, all-knowing God, and a future state dependent upon God's judgment, is so strong and necessary a security to morality (page 391) that "we never ought to abandon or neglect it."

[45] *Ibid.*, p. 384.   [46] *Ibid.*, p. 390.

This argument asserts that, true or false, religious belief does so much good in the world, so works upon the minds of men to make them behave morally, that its maintenance is worthwhile, whatever its cognitive character. But Philo will not allow Cleanthes even this small amount of satisfaction.

> How happens it then, said Philo, if vulgar superstition be so salutary to society, that all history abounds so much with accounts of its pernicious consequences on public affairs? Factions, civil wars, persecutions, sub-versions of government, oppression, slavery; these are the dismal consequences which always attend its prevelancy over the minds of men.[47]

Cleanthes immediately appeals to the distinction between "proper" religion, whose function is to ameliorate men's conditions, and religion as practised. Philo, of course, will not allow this perhaps pardonable sophistry. One cannot argue both that the effects of religion are good as expressed in peoples' actions, and that peoples' actions do not express religion. Religion is what is practised in its name.

> When divines are declaiming against the common behavior and conduct of the world, they always represent this principle as the strongest imaginable (which indeed it is) and describe almost all human kind as lying under the influence of it; and sunk into the deepest lethargy and unconcern about their religious interests. Yet these same divines, when they refute their speculative antagonists, suppose the motives of religion to be so powerful, that, without them, it were impossible for civil society to subsist.[48]

Even if religion were eminently successful in forming the morals of men so that they would behave in a more moral fashion than they would if they had not been so trained, nevertheless, it would have to be added to the list of nonrational arguments for, causes of, the belief in God's existence and attributes. What is shown, after all, is but another source of antecedent prejudice in favor of electing to believe the religious hypothesis. In addition, Philo argues that man's natural inclination to honesty and benevolence would, without its constant deflection due to superstition, stand him in much better stead with respect to orderly and responsible behavior. Indeed, Philo argues that in history we see progress almost wholly correlated with the control of institutionalized religion and its priests and officials.[49]

Cleanthes returns to the contention that the "chief, the only great comfort in life; and our principal support amidst all the attacks of adverse fortune" lies in belief in a kindly God and an immortal and good life.

[47] *Ibid.*   [48] *Ibid.*, p. 392.   [49] *Ibid.*, pp. 395–396.

Philo, of course, continues to assert that this is simply another instance of persuasion based upon emotion, that it is an added appeal to fear and terror and hope, and not to evidence. And this very irrational character of religious belief, he contends, makes religion continually subject to fits of terror. "Terror is the primary principle of religion," and, therefore, "passion predominates" in it.[50]

Now it is not of primary interest to me whether Hume is represented by Philo, Cleanthes, or Demea. It seems clear that he is represented by at least both Cleanthes and Philo, if we consider the materials of the *Dialogues* as repeating views we find in other of Hume's works. However, it can be remarked that, using this criterion, Philo's assertions and arguments are repeated in Hume's other works. A strict comparison of arguments, however, makes it abundantly clear that after this theological battle is over almost nothing is left of the forces of Cleanthes' arguments other than a few tattered shreds of the uniforms of the forces of design theology. If we ask the question "what is left of the design argument in its logical sense," surely, the answer must be very little indeed. Its office is not supported by any rational credentials. True, Philo does accept some part of the design argument, but in the following quotation we see how very limited an acceptance it is:

> That the cause or causes of order in the universe probably bear some remote analogy to human intelligence: If this proposition be not capable of extension, variation, or more particular explication: If it afford no inference that affects human life, or can be the source of any action or forbearance: And if the analogy, imperfect as it is, can be carried no further than to the human intelligence; and cannot be transferred, with any appearance of probability, to the other qualities of the mind: If this really be the case, what can the most inquisitive, contemplative, and religious man do other than give a plain, philosophical assent to the proposition. . . .[51]

Is this conclusion, to which Philo is ready to give a "plain, philosophical assent," of any succor to the views of received, traditional religion? The answer to this question is certainly no. Not one of the traditional properties of God is admitted. Nothing acceptable to traditional Christianity remains —no unity, no benevolence, no omniscience—only a "cause or causes" bearing some "remote analogy" to human intelligence. How remote this analogy might be is indicated in the examples of vegetables, animals, rotting turnips, all of which have remote analogies to man. And even this

[50] *Ibid.*, p. 398.   [51] *Ibid.*, p. 400.

meager concession is logically available only to the "religious man," one who, out of antecedent prejudice in favor of the evidence in support of his religious beliefs, elects upon nonrational grounds to accept the favored conclusion: one who rejects the equally logical conclusions that the world is an animal or vegetable, or that we know nothing about the cause of the world, or that the world causes itself, or that its cause or causes are stupid and malevolent. Surely this conclusion, even with all the emphasis that can be put upon its weak probabilities, and even disregarding the equally strong arguments *ad hominem* which can be arrayed against it, offers little comfort to the theologian. Indeed, at the hands of David Hume, natural theology meets a somewhat violent, although well mannered and reticently executed, death.

If the funeral has been delayed, or if the body has, like that of Lenin, been preserved; or if the body has, like some heroes and Pharaohs, been repeatedly exhumed; it is not because there is any logical life left in it. It is because, as Hume very well recognized, its acceptance has never been based upon its rational support. The design argument will be popular so long as religion is popular, and so long as unsophisticated theologians feel the need of rational pretense. As we shall see, it is in fact seldom affirmed by modern theologians.

Nevertheless, some kind remarks, in the way of eulogy, should be made about the design argument, and about natural theology in general. The attitude expressed in these remarks would, I think, be acceptable to Hume. The kind of broad-minded "latitudinarian" religion, which so often found its support in the design argument, was an amiable, kindly religion, lacking most of the hallmarks of mumbojumbo, mysticism, and authority which so often characterize traditional Christianity. Few ghosts and demons, few superstitions, were involved in it, and its conception of God as a sympathetic artist-mechanic-mathematician, working as best he can for the benefit of man, is certainly one of the more congenial supernaturalisms. Shorn of the jealousies and hatreds of the Calvinistic tradition, the God of design theology epitomizes the good qualities held in common by Him and His creatures. In comparison with modern reassertions of demonism, sulphur and brimstone, authority, bibliolatry and mysticism, Newton's view of God and man represents a breath of clean theological air, whatever its logical status.

We now turn to the place of design theology in the nineteenth century.

CHAPTER 10

The Curtain Call

Ocean, n. A body of water occupying about two-thirds of
a world made for man—who has no gills.
—AMBROSE BIERCE, *The Devil's Dictionary*

In the discussion which follows I shall assume what I feel to be quite
evident: the proposition that Hume's analysis destroyed the rational
foundations of the design argument as it was commonly presented in the
seventeenth and eighteenth centuries. The Newtonian as well as the ancient
variants of this argument were shown clearly in Hume's work to be an
instance neither of scientific nor common-sense reasoning. I do not assume
that Hume destroyed the other facet of the design argument—urged
explicitly and implicitly by Cleanthes throughout the *Dialogues* and
constantly affirmed by other writers of the age—the view that the existence
of God is in some sense an *intuition* which is triggered by the examples of
design in the world, and whose validity is not destroyed by counter-
arguments of equal logical status and validity. It seems clear to me that
this sort of claim, that is, the claim to some sort of mystic and intuitive
insight, is not rationally refutable. As Cleanthes said, "I have found my
God, and here I stop." It will be recalled, however, that Hume *explains
how* this belief arises. It comes from the emotional structure of man's
longings and needs, from his terror, his fear of death and the unknown,
and reflects attitudes formed by his education and training. In other words,
Hume offers an alternative explanation for the admittedly common
acceptance of the conclusions of the design argument and the neglect of its
manifest weaknesses. His explanation is couched in psychological and
sociological terms which assert that these very compelling religious beliefs
are founded not upon reason but upon prejudice and other emotional
(nonrational) grounds.

For the reasons listed in relation to these psychological and sociological
causes, Hume recognized that it is quite unlikely that the design argument,
which adds to these emotional causes the stimulus of analogical reasoning,

always a powerful aid to belief, would be removed from the human scene by his criticism. And he was correct. The design argument is still very commonly seen in popular discussion and in popular publications, so commonly that my assertion need not, I think, be supported by citations. I do not wish to discuss this particular phenomenon, since I feel that Hume's explanation of it, together with additional and similar materials from modern social science, which show the power and pervasiveness of social conditioning and training, accounts for it very well. What I wish to do in this section is, first, to deal with two nineteenth-century resurrections of the design argument in the work of Paley and Whewell, and second, to relate Hume's work in theology to nineteenth-century skepticism. I have named this chapter "The Curtain Call" because, with Hume's *Dialogues*, the cognitive or rational part of the drama of the design argument is over and done with. However, the writings of Paley and Whewell, and others not to be mentioned, are of interest for at least two reasons. For one thing, they illustrate the fact that the persuasiveness of the design argument continued unabated for another hundred years, even in academic circles. For another, they exhibit the fact that writers within a generation of the death of Hume (and bear in mind that Hume's *Dialogues* were published several years after his death in 1776), could resurrect the design argument in its logically weakest but psychologically most compelling form, as if David Hume's *Dialogues* had never been written.

The second main topic is the comparison of Hume's works with the rather radical movements towards skepticism which in the nineteenth century went on alongside the work of Paley and Whewell and many other authors. I shall argue that Hume's *Dialogues* presage in a theoretical sense nearly every line of attack which has been leveled against religion and theology in modern times. More generally, the view is that Hume's work in philosophy, generally admitted to be the seminal work of almost all of modern empirical and analytical philosophy, including positivism and the linguistic variety of ordinary language philosophy, is also in fact one of the most seminal works in the development of modern religious skepticisms.

I

William Paley, 1743–1845, was an English churchman. He is seldom mentioned today except in the antiquarian sense. Often listed as the purveyor of a theologically tinted variety of utilitarianism, with which we will not be concerned, he nevertheless was extremely well known in his own day for his works in theology, and his influence upon many important people was great. Cardinal Manning, for instance, writes that in his youth, after a study of Paley's *Evidences*, "I took in the whole argument, and I thank God that nothing has ever shaken it." [1] John Stuart Mill, in his *Three Essays on Religion*, felt it necessary to attack Paley's argument from analogy, and to comment, in almost exactly Hume's spirit, upon the weaknesses of its logical form.

In his *Natural Theology*, published in 1803, Paley set forth the design argument in immense detail. For the most part the book contains a complex discussion of the manifold uses and adaptations of the parts of plants and animals. Thus for Paley the argument from design is little more than an analysis of these vegetable and animal means-ends relationships. As in the case of Boyle, we have in Paley's work an example of the utilitarian doctrine of final causes with a vengeance. Two things should be said about his argument at this point. First, he combines the argument from design together with the argument to design—he regards all animal organisms as machines. Second, in so doing he uses the most singularly inappropriate form of the design argument. As Hume pointed out, animals are, empirically, the things in the world which most obviously organize themselves. Hence Paley's argument is a repetitive begging of the question.

His chosen analogy is a very familiar one—the watch—which we have seen in connection with Boyle, Clarke, Leibniz, Voltaire, and many others. As has often been the case, he derogates astronomical phenomena, Newton's favorite, since it is difficult to see how the motions of the stars and planets help man. Although Paley seems to have been a particularly thick-headed man, he was aware of the analogical character of his arguments, even when he was belittling the theological value of astronomy.

> My opinion of astronomy has always been, that it is not the best medium through which to prove the agency of an intelligent creator. . . . And what we say of their forms, is true of their motions. Their motions are carried on without any sensible intermediate apparatus; whereby we are cut off from one principle ground of argumentation—analogy. [2]

Peculiarly enough, Paley regarded purposive relationships as the defining characteristics of machines; even more peculiarly, he regarded the relationships of muscles and tendons, etc., as more obviously related by "intermediate apparatus" than the motions of the planets and other solar

---

[1] Lytton Strachey, *Eminent Victorians* (New York: G. P. Putnam's Sons, 1918), p. 6.

[2] William Paley, *Natural Theology* (Boston, 1866), pp. 212–213.

bodies. This shows that he totally missed the import of Newton's laws of motion, which show the mechanical interrelation of all bodies. Every plant, animal, and body on the globe was for Paley a machine.

> In crossing a heath, suppose I pitched my foot against a stone, and asked how the stone came to be there; I might answer, that, for anything I know to be the contrary, it had lain there forever: . . . but suppose I had found a watch upon the ground, and it should be inquired how the watch happened to be in that place; I should hardly think of the answer which I had given before, that, for anything I know, the watch might have always been there. Yet why should not this answer serve for the watch as well as for the stone ? For this reason, and for none other, viz., that when we come to inspect the watch, we perceive what we could not discover in the stone, that its several parts were framed and put together for a purpose. . . .[3]

Nor would it change the situation if we had never seen a watch made, or if the watch were inaccurate. Further, it would be impossible for any man in his senses to think that the watch had come out of a number of possible material forms.[4]

I think it is fair to say that Paley has added nothing to the design argument; indeed, his formulation of it is much weaker than that of Cleanthes in the *Dialogues*. But Paley magnifies his difficulties with the claim that the ability of watches to reproduce themselves would be even more evidence of contrivance! As a matter of fact, we can see even the charming and magnanimous Hume gasping at this cropper, for if watches reproduced themselves, there would be prima-facie evidence that they ordered themselves and all analogy to machines would be lost. We know when we look at a watch that there is contrivance, because we know that watches are manufactured by men; but, and this is the important reservation, we do not in the same way know that animals are manufactured— indeed, that is the very point at issue.

In the application of his principle Paley uses, among others, the example of the human eye, which we have seen before in Newton. To him it exhibits wonderful contrivance, as do the eyes of fish. Next comes a discussion of the generation of plants and animals.[5] These purposive connections, say the eye to the rest of the organism and to its behavior, are again compared with machines. Now it is one thing to claim that the *whole* human organism is a machine—even this view escapes none of Hume's retorts. It does not escape his argument that, a priori, we don't know what causes animals to be organized; nor does it avoid his contention that organisms are sufferers

[3] *Ibid.*, p. 5.   [4] *Ibid.*, p. 7.   [5] *Ibid.*, p. 30.

of many "non-organized" properties, such as gouts, megrims, etc. It is quite another thing to declare that the whole universe is a machine. As we have seen, Paley derogates this argument. It is a third sort of thing to do what Paley does—to deal in detail with a *part* of the organism, such as the eye. This sort of analogy is the worst possible form of the design argument, since the eye obviously grows and is organized as a part of a whole organism, and is not in itself a machine in any clear sense. If animals as a whole are not clearly examples of machines, then the parts of animals are even less so.

In 1828 the Earl of Bridgewater died, leaving by will the sum of 8,000 pounds for the purpose of publishing a work on the evidences in various natural phenomena of the power, wisdom, and goodness of God. The funds were entrusted to the Royal Society of London, which was to have the responsibility for appointing the scholars who were to do the writing. The eight volumes published, each by a different author, represent the ultimate exploitation of the argument from design.[6] The third volume of the series, concerning the evidences for natural theology in astronomy and general physics, was written by William Whewell, Master of Trinity College and Professor of Moral Philosophy at Cambridge University. The title of this work, published in 1833, is *Astronomy and General Physics Considered with Reference to Natural Theology*. It is not an example of the work for which Whewell should be most remembered. He was an important thinker on scientific method,[7] and wrote several works on the history of science and induction.[8] Be that as it may, the discussion of his theology can be initiated by the following quotation:

> . . . it may be interesting, after such an advance [in science], to show how the views of the creation, preservation, and government of the universe, which natural science opens to us, harmonize with our belief in a creator, governor, and preserver of the world. To do this with respect to certain departments of natural philosophy is the object of the following pages.[9]

Whewell's whole approach confused from the beginning the distinction between prescriptive and descriptive laws. This well-known ambiguity fails to discriminate between moral and legal laws, which are a result of legislation, either by a group or a single person, and laws of nature established

---

[6] Mossner, *Bishop Butler and the Age of Reason*, p. 203.

[7] Sir William Cecil Dampier, *A History of Science* (3d ed.; New York: Macmillan Company, 1943), pp. 456–457.

[8] William Whewell, *History of the Inductive Sciences* (3d ed.; New York, 1858).

[9] William Whewell, *Astronomy and General Physics* (London, 1862), p. 2.

by science, whose sources we are unaware of. He held, quite properly, that nature acts by general laws. In the world in which we live the occurrences and events which we experience result from causes which operate according to fixed and constant rules.[10] But then Whewell makes the unwarranted jump from the scientific to the moral and legal use of the term "law." He maintains that by observing these laws of nature we may find some method of detecting the nature of the *government* of the world. As is obvious, the question as to whether the world has a government is begged from the very beginning. Thus, according to Whewell, if we find balance and fitness in the modes of activity of the world and their *regulations*, then we will have the solution to our problem. In this manner we may be able to discover something of the nature of God.

> By observing the laws of the material universe and their operation, we may hope, in a somewhat similar manner to be able to direct our judgment concerning the government of the universe: concerning the mode in which the elements are regulated and controlled, their effects combined and balanced. And the general tendency of the results thus produced may discover to us something of the character of the power which has legislated for the material world.[11]

He recognizes some of the limitations of this sort of argument. We are, he says, "not to push too far the analogy thus suggested. There is undoubtedly a wide difference between the circumstances of man legislating for man, and God legislating for matter." Note, however, that it is not the logic of the argument that is troubling Whewell, it is the fear that he will become involved in too much anthropomorphism, that is, in the claim that God is too much like man. Hume had, of course, pointed out that we can ascribe no more properties to God, according to the principle of analogy, than we find in the world; but this again is not Whewell's worry. He wishes to hold to the traditional views of God's powers and properties, such as omnipotence, omniscience, omnibenevolence, unity; and the analogy simply will not support them.

Whewell's first interest, then, is in general laws as exhibiting final causes or adaptation, rather than in the argument from mechanical order alone. This interest in teleology to the relative exclusion of mechanical order has been common. He states:

> It will be our business to show that the laws which usually prevail in nature are, by their form—that is, by the nature of the connection which they establish among the quantities and properties which they regulate—

[10] *Ibid.*, p. 3.   [11] *Ibid.*, p. 5.

remarkably adapted to the office which is assigned to them and thus offer evidence of selection, design, and goodness, in the power by which they were established.[12]

These laws, according to Whewell, are all arbitrary in the sense that there is no reason why they should not be otherwise. Some ultimate being wished them to be the way they are in order to bring about the manifest benefits they give to living creatures. Whewell's intention is to show these adaptations:

> we shall, therefore, endeavor to point out cases and circumstances in which the different parts of the universe exhibit this mutual adaptation, and thus to bring before the mind of the reader the evidence of wisdom and providence which the external world affords.[13]

The main part of the book Whewell divides into two sections relative to the type of adaptations involved in the frame of the world. The first is devoted to *Cosmical Arrangements*. The second concerns *Terrestrial Adaptations*. Note the different terms: "arrangement" as distinct from "adaptation." There is no difficulty, he says, in recognizing the teleological nature of terrestrial organization and the creatures of the earth.[14] Following this lead he notes the vegetative cycle on the earth and its adaptation to solar movements. This is a clear proof, in his view, of design in the formation of the world. Note that "design" here means "intentions." "Why should the solar year last so long and no longer?"[15] Also placed in evidence is the obvious accommodation of organized bodies to the length of the day. In his view there is much evidence of adaptation in the laws of many terrestrial objects and activities: the mass of the earth, climates, plant geography, heat, water, air, electricity, magnetism, light and plants, sound, etc. One can see Hume's anguished expression at this sort of argument—no mention is made of animals eating animals, of disease, of drought, of earthquake. If animals did not fit themselves to the day-night sequence, Hume would say, they would not exist.

On the side of cosmical arrangements he makes clear that he regards them as different from terrestrial adaptations. Furthermore, the evidence drawn from cosmical sources does not offer such convincing proof of the existence and attributes of God as that from terrestrial adaptations.

> It has been observed by writers on natural theology, that the arguments for the being and perfections of the creator, drawn from the cosmical considerations, labour under some disadvantages when compared with

[12] *Ibid.*, p. 259.   [13] *Ibid.*, p. 11.   [14] *Ibid.*, p. 14.   [15] *Ibid.*, p. 24.

the arguments founded on those provisions and adaptations which more immediately affect the well being of organized creatures. The structure of the solar system has far less analogy with such machinery as we can construct and comprehend, then we find in the structure of the bodies of animals, or even in the causes of the weather. Moreover, we do not see the immediate bearing of cosmical arrangements which we most readily acknowledge to be useful and desirable, the support and comfort of sentient creatures.[16]

It is readily evident that Whewell is copying Paley. Even machines are defined in terms of purpose. The world as a cosmos does not seem to be a machine because we cannot find out the purposes (intentions) which are responsible for its construction. Order is not enough, even though the cosmical symmetry exhibits some of the most startling examples of universal law. The concept of utilitarianism comes strongly to the front in the statement referring to the "support and comfort of sentient creatures." The probable reasons for this emphasis upon final causes lie not only in the writings of Paley and others, but in the whole development of utilitarianism.

Not that Whewell completely ignores the notion of nonpurposive order as exhibited in laws of nature.

The laws of material nature, such as we have described them, operate at all times, and in all places; effect every province of the universe, and involve every relation of its parts. Whenever these laws appear, we have a mani- festation of the intelligence by which they were established. But a law supposes an agent, and a power; for it is the mode according to which the power acts.[17]

So we find Whewell echoing the arguments of the Newtonians, albeit he places more emphasis upon the sub-parts of organisms, and upon final causes. But this is not in itself unusual, for the world, organisms, parts of organisms, are all held to be analogous to men's machines and thus to imply a mechanic. Whewell follows Butler in adding to all this the legalistic notion of a lawgiver, but this does not make his argument essentially different from the other arguments—all of them involve arguments con- cerning things made by man such as laws, machines, and works of art. There is nothing in Whewell that is not in the argument of Cleanthes in Hume's *Dialogues*, and there is nothing in his work that would militate against any of Hume's destructive criticisms.

The work of Paley and Whewell, and those who followed them, offer exceedingly good examples of the fact that the design argument, while not logically cogent, nevertheless continued and continues to command a

[16] *Ibid.*, p. 127.   [17] *Ibid.*, p. 311.

good deal of respect. We have noted before the point underscored by all modern logicians, that arguments by analogy, at their strongest, offer no value as proof, although they may very well be of signal importance in suggesting hypotheses—"consistencies" in Hume's terminology. They are, nevertheless and paradoxically, extremely compelling sources of belief. And they are compelling even when, as in the case of the design argument in all its varieties, their inferences are retortable, weak, refutable. Analogies are "handles" for understanding things. Metaphors, similes, comparisons, all are excellent tools for exhibiting meanings in difficult contexts, and it is no surprise at all to find theologians fastening upon such tools. Our investigations continue to show that for those theologians who are armed with antecedent convictions as to the existence and nature of God, the design argument continues to be a very appealing way to express, to entertain, to argue, to present evidence in favor of, such convictions; while at the same time to ignore equally valid evidence against them.

Such arguments as those of Paley and Whewell, of course, did not exhaust the theological efforts of the nineteenth century. I should like to deal with some points of view which were, in fact, quite antithetical to those we have just been describing—the development of skepticism in the period. The purpose is to compare these points of view with the views of David Hume, and to continue the discussion of the downfall of natural theology.

As we have seen, the design argument fared well at the hands of most nineteenth-century believers, despite Hume's criticism. Nevertheless, theology and religion no longer could expect the kind respectful treatment from almost the entire community, academic and otherwise, which had characterized Hume's time. Hume was a member of an extreme minority, albeit this minority has received remarkable attention at the hands of historians. This group included, in addition to Hume, only a few Deists (a "tatterdemalion crew"), Spinoza, Hobbes, Shaftsbury, and some others. In the nineteenth century, to the contrary, the attack against religion and theology came from so many respectable quarters, and was of such intensity, that it generated considerable depression among the faithful. Witness Arnold, who bemoans the retreat of "the sea of faith," and Tennyson, who sadly comments that the stars "blindly run." This depression was shared by others than the literati—by famous government officials such as Gladstone, and by plain people. What was, thus, speculative and theoretical in the age of Hume was practical in the Victorian age, when the Pandora's box of skepticism was thrown open in earnest by Darwin's Bulldog.

The "noxious crop" scornfully indicated by Gladstone is of course old hat to the modern scholar; but it was relatively new then, new at least in its popular influence. Criticism was directed not only against the design arguments of Paley and Whewell and the other authors of the Bridgewater treatises, but against religious belief in general. Faith, in addition to reasoned natural theology; revealed religion, in addition to natural religion, make up the targets. In *Religion and the Rise of Scepticism*, F. L. Baumer portrays with considerable drama the ways in which six interlocking arguments were thrown into the critical scales, and shows how they, in effect, provided such a degree of counterbalance to the weight of faith that as a result our modern age harbors a residual skepticism which forms the backdrop against which many of the pressing anxieties of modern times can most clearly be exhibited. Baumer entitles the arguments as follows: the utilitarian (or pragmatic), the scientific, the anthropological, the psychological, the economic, and the historical. My contention is that it was Hume who ushered into the modern world most of these arguments— that in fact almost the whole of modern skepticism is theoretically prefaced in his work.[18] We are as yet, so to speak, as they were in the nineteenth century, feeding upon the leaven of his skeptical bread. In this sense, Hume began the sapping of the intrenched inner fortress of scientifically formulated religion.

Let us first consider the utilitarian or pragmatic argument. It was put forth by the Benthamites in great detail, by the secularists, and by the socialists. It does not relate to the *truth* of religious beliefs, but to their *usefulness*. Emphasized earlier by the *philosophes* in their claim that the church and priests had combined to hold down progress, this argument had strong social and political overtones; and it is at least in principle an empirical hypothesis which might be formulated in the following question: Does the general acceptance of religious beliefs have good or evil consequences? Our nineteenth-century skeptics emphatically contended that its consequences are, and have been, evil in balance. Bentham, writing under the lamp of Lucretius and Epicurus, claimed that religion in general obviously injures man, both individually and in general, causes him anxiety (an interesting claim, since modern existentialists argue with

---

[18] It is not argued that the specific arguments of skepticism are original in Hume. Many, if not most, of them have Academic and Pyrrhonistic sources. Hume's greatness lies in marshaling them so well, and also in recognizing their applicability to Early Modern religion and theology. Historically, Hume's work is the seminal source of modern philosophical and religious skepticism. See Richard Popkin, *The History of Scepticism: Erasmus to Descartes*.

considerable convincingness that the loss of religious faith has undermined man's sense of purpose in life, and thus causes him anxiety!), produces torment, and leads him into intolerance which impedes scientific progress.[19] He was joined by a mixed group of supporters in this argument, including Marx.

This argument, as we have seen, was no stranger to Hume. Cleanthes, we will remember (see page 165) argues that whatever the logical status of religious belief, it is so strong and necessary a security that "we ought never to abandon or neglect it." Philo, in Hume's place, does not allow this contention to pass uncriticized. History abounds, he says, with accounts of the pernicious consequences of religion upon public affairs—factions, civil wars, persecutions, subversions of government, oppressions, slavery, are invariably in its train. Man's natural aptitude for benevolence would serve him better, but it is constantly subverted by religion. Finally, Hume maintains that progress has been attained only when men and institutions have freed themselves from the control of institutionalized religion, its priests and its officials. It is worth remarking that Hume's ethical theory was a major source of utilitarianism, and thus it is only proper to find his views lurking in the background of the nineteenth-century utilitarian argument against religion.

The second general avenue of attack against religion in the nineteenth century came from the direction of science. This source of skepticism has been mentioned many times before. Unlike the pragmatic or utilitarian critique, although often allied with it, the scientific critique is directed at the truth of religious claims. It has two, or at least two, sides. One is epistemological, and one is metaphysical, although they are often difficult to separate.[20] Huxley, Leslie Stephen, Auguste Comte, the Mills, Spencer, all support the agnostic position, which declares that there is no rational way of settling the question whether God exists. Reason is dependent upon materials drawn from experience, and there are no experiences of Gods or of world creations. I should think that little need to be said in respect to Hume's use of this argument in one of its most basic and profound formulations. In the *Dialogues* and elsewhere in his writings, Hume consistently asserts that there is no way of knowing or proving ultimate causes, including the causes or cause of the world. Who, we will recall his asking, has seen the origin of worlds ? It was Hume who showed in detail that the

[19] Jeremy Bentham, *Analysis of the Influences of Natural Religion on the Temporal Happiness of Mankind* (London, 1822), p. 41.

[20] F. L. Baumer, *Religion and the Rise of Scepticism* (New York: Harcourt, Brace and Company, 1960), pp. 144 ff.

hypothesis which asserts the existence of a God who is a designer-mechanic-cause is outside the pale of scientifically establishable propositions. Where is the observable species, he asked, of which the world is a member, whose causes have been observed or experimented with; how would one verify the hypothesis that an omnipotent, omniscient, omnibenevolent, but unexperiencable, God is the cause of the world?

The other attack from science came from the direction of biology, and, of course, far and away the most influential biological theory was the doctrine of evolution. The principle of natural selection, which explained why and how organisms, through adjustment to their conditions, come to be what they are, probably did more to undermine the design argument than any other single force. According to this principle the world and its creatures adapt and order themselves. This, of course, rendered unnecessary the hypothesis that the order discernible in the world was due to, and necessitated, an orderer: the machine no longer needed a mechanic, and the work of art no longer needed an artist. The most typical attempt to avoid this unwelcome conclusion came in the interpretation of evolution and natural selection as God's way of ordering the world. This attempt comes to grief, unfortunately, on the principle of Occam's razor. God, as an explanatory hypothesis, is no longer necessary.

Now Hume, insofar as I know, used neither the notion of natural selection nor of evolution in general. Nevertheless, he made some interesting remarks which bear upon this sort of critique against religion. We will recall, for one thing, his suggestion that a priori, the world and the organisms who inhabit it may very well cause and order themselves, a condition which, empirically, appears to hold among animals and other living organisms. This is, in effect, the conclusion drawn from the Darwinian concept of natural selection; and Hume reinforced his point by mentioning that the adaptations of the parts and organs of animals to their purposes would either have occurred or the animals would not exist. The Darwinian theory, thus, fills in the evidential gap suggested by Hume's logical comments upon the design argument. In this sense, evolution specified what in Hume's view was a theoretical possibility, and in so doing exploded the ancient view that the means-ends adjustments and adaptations of animals, and of the parts or organs of animals, among and within themselves, necessitate a designer-purposer. The old saw, no purposes without a purposer, which we found to often depend upon an equivocation between purpose (intention) and purpose (process-product or means-ends relations), is further driven beyond the rational pale. Thus Hume set the logical stage for the profound effect that the doctrine of evolution had upon the traditionally accepted design argument. To make matters worse, the doctrine of evolution could be applied to the origin and development of religious doctrines themselves!

Another aspect of Darwin's view reinforced a point made by Hume in the *Dialogues*.

> That which we have discovered in the way of inexactness and imperfection in the optical machine and in the image on the retina, is as nothing in comparison with the incongruities which we have just come across in the domain of the sensations.[21]

The universe is *disorderly*. Here was scientific support for the not-too-beautiful, not-too-orderly view of the universe, which, by a logic similar to that of the design argument, implies that the transcendent cause of the world might not be unified or intelligent or even very able or powerful. Hume's direction setting is again obvious.

Reeling from these buffets, religion during this period had still other forces to contend with, among them the new science of anthropology. Perhaps the most important and famous of its practitioners was Sir James Frazer. In *The Golden Bough*, Frazer developed a naturalistic interpretation of religion which, in its researches into the origins of religion, showed a high degree of similarity between the rites and superstitions of primitive peoples and the ceremonies and religious convictions of civilized peoples. In consequence, doubts were raised concerning the truth of any religion, including Christianity. The anthropological argument, in common with the utilitarian argument, does not directly aim at showing religious beliefs to be false or true. Nevertheless, a profound doubt was cast upon Christianity simply because it had so much in common with primitive religions whose falsity had for centuries been proclaimed by Christians. An even more odious practice of the anthropologists was to view religion as merely another behavioral phenomenon characteristic of humans—a phenomenon of no more intrinsic importance, say, than eating habits. Frazer, somewhat like Comte, felt and expressed the belief that intelligent minds in modern civilization should reject the religious view of the world as inadequate. Science, for him, not religion, would supply the funds for progress. In addition, of course, his work showed the remarkable variations in religious conceptions, all claiming absolute validity on very similar nonobjective grounds. And this further undermined accepted religious views.

[21] Charles Darwin, *The Origin of Species* (6th ed.; London, 1890), p. 163.

His method is of interest, particularly since we will shortly turn to the ways in which Hume's approach is comparable to it and to those of other anthropologists. Frazer's reasoning assumes that all religions are *natural phenomena* which are produced by interrelationships among physical surroundings, material cultures, contacts with other cultures, and the basic needs and desires of human nature. For instance, the comparison of Christian Eucharistic notions with the primitive conception of the scapegoat, and with the primitive habit of partaking of the flesh and blood of the sacrificial victim, seemed to many to indicate little if any difference between the primitive and modern in matters of religion; and, of course, the conclusion drawn was that religion as a whole is primitive and hence mistaken.[22]

In case this material seems far afield of the design argument, I should agree, in a sense. In another, however, it is not. For we have seen that Hume found it necessary to combat the claim that the design of the world triggers an intuition, a felt presence, of the hand or voice of God. We will also recall that part of his response was to explain how religious belief in fact arises—that is, to give an alternative explanation of the admittedly compulsive effect of the design argument. Hume was, from the beginning of his career, extremely interested in religion. And even while dying he was quite fearful that his last pronouncement on the subject, the *Dialogues*, would not be published. This interest was historical as well as philosophical, and the two came together in his *Natural History of Religion*, which, while attacking the design argument, was basically concerned with the comparison of religious beliefs and their origins. The notion of supernatural beings, of providence, of the afterlife, and of divine being, all these topics concerned him—and one of his greatest preoccupations lay in the ways in which religions began. He consistently compares Christian and pagan religions. Like Frazer, he regards religion as a product of human nature at certain stages and under certain conditions. Having decided that religion in any of its received forms is cognitively preposterous, he was interested in why people believe in it.[23]

But to these doctrines we are so accustomed, that we never wonder at them: Though in a future age, it will probably become difficult to persuade

[22] Sir James Frazer, *The Golden Bough* (3d ed.; London, 1911), III, vi. See Baumer, *Religion and the Rise of Scepticism*, p. 152.
[23] See *Hume's Dialogues Concerning Natural Religion*, ed. Norman Kemp-Smith, p. 11.

some nations, that any human, two-legged creature could ever embrace such principles.[24]

Religion has no rational source. A comparison of various pagan religions, and their comparison with Christianity, brought Hume to the conclusion that primitive man—a barbarous, tortured, tired animal—was so pressed and beset by his needs and his environment that he had no time for the speculation or contemplation which would give rise to some more sophisticated form of religious belief. The origin of all religions, like the magic which was of such interest to Frazer, lies in man's attempts to ease his situation, to call on unseen powers by means of gifts and flattery. And out of all this grows modern religion:

> Thus the deity, who, from love, converted himself into a bull, in order to carry off Europa; and who, from ambition, dethroned his father, Saturn, became the Opticus Maximus of the heathens. Thus, the God of Abraham, Isaac, and Jacob, became the supreme deity or Jehovah of the Jews.[25]

Note the objective, uncommitted tone, the anthropological and comparative view that religions are simply another, unsacrosanct form of human behavior, growing out of natural conditions. The whole power of Hume's argument, where it is not directed at strictly logical problems in the design argument, lies in this anthropological and historical element. It is among ignorant and barbarous peoples that notions such as prayer, miraculous events, and other superstitious elements abound. Written in the 1750's, *The Natural History of Religion* is quite modern in tone and in attitude. Human nature, essentially arational, produces many things, including religion. Hume, in his application of comparative methods, in his conclusions, and in his view of the origin and development of religion, is one with the modern anthropologists.

This brings us to the fourth of the major nineteenth-century criticisms of religion. It is the psychological criticism. Again, as with the case of the anthropological critique of religion, the truth of religious belief does not come under attack; rather, its origins and causes are explained. Again we find religion viewed as nothing sacred, as just one of the ways in which man responds to his environment—a product of his subconscious needs, desires, anxieties. It is a form of wish-fulfilment, a product of dream and phantasy. This, anyhow, was the view of Feuerbach.[26] Prodded by his

[24] David Hume, *The Natural History of Religion*, ed. H. S. Root (Stanford: Stanford University Press, 1957), p. 56.

[25] *Ibid.*, p. 44.

[26] Baumer, *Religion and the Rise of Scepticism*, p. 153.

restless subconscious, man creates gods in his own hallucinatory image. Marx agreed with Feuerbach, up to a point, but insisted that the individual simply reflects his society, and his society reflects the control of the means of production.[27] Religion is but one aspect of an ideology.

Now how does Hume's work stand with respect to this perspective on religion? Was he, although dead, a spiritual citizen of the nineteenth century in this respect also? I have argued that Hume's work is the grave marker of a number of Enlightenment ideas, particularly the attempt to square science and religion. I have also argued just above that he is the harbinger of the modern era in several ways. My view is that here again we find that Hume was, if anything, even more in keeping with the twentieth century—i.e., not only does his analysis of religion in the psychological sense presage those of the nineteenth century: he was perhaps even ahead of them.

In the first place Hume's views, as developed in the *Dialogues*, in *The Natural History of Religion*, and in the sections devoted to religion in the *Treatise* and the *Enquiry*, all reject the contention that traditional religious doctrines can muster any rational support. This, in effect, throws religion back upon other sources, such as mysticism, intuitionism, and emotion. And in the twentieth century the reigning philosophical schools have reduced all such sources to the vagaries of emotion. These schools include positivism, instrumentalism, and ordinary language philosophy. Thus religious beliefs and doctrines turn out to be irrational expressions of emotion. Hume's consistent explanation of mystical and intuitional claims as species of emotion produced by man's psychological and social conditions is quite clearly in keeping with nineteenth- and twentieth-century interpretations of religious beliefs. According to these psychological doctrines, religion is not a product of reason: not even of the great design argument. Ask any woman or man, asserts Hume, why he believes in an omnipotent creator and he will not offer reasoned evidence,

> He will tell you of the sudden and unexpected death of such a one: The fall and bruise of such another: The excessive drought of this season: The cold and rains of another. These he ascribes to the immediate operation of providence. . . .[28]

Deities are *personifications*—projections of man's interests, powers, desires, fears, terrors, needs. ". . . he was apprehended to be a powerful,

---

[27] Karl Marx, *Theses on Feuerbach* (New York: International Publishers, 1939), Nos. IV, VI, VII.

[28] Hume, *The Natural History of Religion*, p. 41.

though limited being, with human passions and appetites, limbs and organs."²⁹ From this base even exalted religion arises; but it never, in any popular sense, loses its original essential character.

> But a barbarous, necessitous animal (such as man is on the first origin of society), pressed by such numerous wants and passions, has no leisure to admire the regular face of nature. . . . A monstrous birth excites his curiosity, and is deemed a prodigy. It alarms him from its novelty; and immediately sets him atrembling and sacrificing, and praying.³⁰

> . . . the first ideas of religion arose not from a contemplation of the works of nature, but from a concern with regard to the events of life, and from the incessant hopes and fears, which actuate the human mind . . . the anxious concern for happiness, the dread of future misery, the terror of death, the thirst of revenge, the appetite for food and other necessaries. . . .³¹

Hume depicts the origin of religion in dismal strokes of human phantasy and terror—such are the occasions of man's first glimpse of divinity. And as for the shape of these divinities, these projections:

> There is a universal tendency among mankind to conceive all beings like themselves, and to transfer to every object, those qualities, with which they are familiarly acquainted. . . . We find human faces in the moon, armies in the clouds; and by a natural propensity, if not corrected by experience and reflection, ascribe malice or good-will to everything, that hurts or pleases us.³²

The mind, sunk, according to Hume, into diffidence, terror and melancholy, has recourse to every method of appeasing those secret intelligent powers, on whom our fortune is supposed entirely to depend.³³ The world is populated with invisible powers and spirits. The unknown causes of nature's beneficent as well as maleficent events and phenomena are linked to these powers, which are vaguely analogous to human powers. Little by little, through social and political analogies (say of princes or monarchs), one god or goddess is separated out as the most important. Finally, on similar analogies, he is looked upon as the sovereign creator, the immediate author, of all that occurs. A natural psychological tendency common to all mankind, then, and not demonstration or proof, is the source of religion.

It can be said, therefore, that Hume's explanation of the origins and development of religious beliefs is very similar to those of modern psychology. They differ only in the specifics of psychological theory. I should like to recall to the reader's attention that all of this material,

²⁹ *Ibid.*, p. 24.   ³⁰ *Ibid.*   ³¹ *Ibid.*, pp. 27–28.   ³² *Ibid.*, p. 29.
³³ *Ibid.*, p. 31.

which seems so far afield of the design argument, is Hume's response to Cleanthes' claim that there must be something to the design argument, since it has such psychological compulsiveness, and since it retains this convincing character in the face of counterargument. Hume's claim, in whose detail we are immersed, is that the design argument is simply a rationalization of conclusions about deity reached upon other grounds. The present object is to spell out the sociological and psychological motives behind the rationalization. Of course Hume has not the "ids," "egos," "super-egos" of Freud or the stimulus and response of behaviorism, although he is close to them; he *does* have the association of ideas; he does not have a Jungian psychological inheritance; but none of these theories would be contrary to Hume's conclusions, and he had stepped, clearly, in their direction. The house of religion may have a reasoned, if leaky, roof; but its foundations are the emotions, which are always shifting in their support.

We can say with assurance that Hume did not presage the Marxian view that religion is purely a function of economic causes. It is probable that any such "single-cause" theory of history would attract from him only a tired smile. But our last basic source of skepticism in the nineteenth century, the historical, was of some interest to Hume. It is well known that Hume was one of the great historians of his age. History, as a method or approach shared by almost all of the above trends in religious criticism— the scientific, the evolutionary, the utilitarian—seeks to understand things in terms of their origins and development. The discussion of Hume's *Natural History of Religion* showed a type of research carried on almost in a spirit of disregard for the question of the specific truth or falsity of religious beliefs. Not the question, "Is it true?" but "How did men come to take it for true?" became the question.[34] Marx, Frazer, Troeltsch, Morley, all recognized the profound import of this approach to religion— as, we claim, did Hume. Else why the title "Natural History of Religion"? Hume early became convinced of the spurious character of received religious beliefs; witness his remark, as told to Boswell, that he had lost his belief in religion as a youth, upon first reading Clarke and Locke.[35] Thus his interest in religion went far beyond the destruction of key theological arguments in the *Dialogues* and elsewhere, and lay in the question "Why do people believe it?" We have already seen his answer

---

[34] See Baumer, *Religion and the Rise of Scepticism*, p. 157.
[35] See *Hume's Dialogues Concerning Natural Religion*, ed. Norman Kemp-Smith, Appendix A, p. 76, Boswell's interview with Hume, July 7th, 1776.

to the question. Hume seems not to have embraced historical relativism—in the sense of ideological historicism as instanced in Mannheim. But with respect to religion, he searched for its explanation not in its truth, finally, since he had rejected such a possibility, but in its historical development. Religious opinions were, to Hume as to Lord Morley, in the last analysis simply phenomena to be explained.[36] As Troeltsch put it, ". . . a religion, in the several forms assumed by it, always depends upon the intellectual, social, and national foundations among which it exists."[37] It is only a short step to the *Weltanschauung*. Renan, Lecky, Strauss, and Sidgwick only continue clearing the path laid out by others before them, applying historical techniques to the Old Testament, the New Testament, to ethics, to morality. An earlier pathfinder was David Hume.

Therefore, when Hume blew up the inner citadel of religion in his sustained, if well-mannered and sometimes obsequious, attack upon the design argument, he had not only used the ancient weapon of logic, the early modern one of empiricism, and in addition the very modern one of the principle of the verification theory of truth—he had begun to forge some new ones. He used the pragmatic or utilitarian mode of attack in a form which was little, if any, advanced by posterity at the hands of the utilitarians. He applied the technique of the modern theory of verification, and the empirical test of proof, in a way that is still accepted with small variation by many modern philosophers and logicians, and is still being developed in its full implications. His criterion of a priori proof—that a tautology or analytic statement is true unless its denial implies a self-contradiction—used so effectively against Demea and Cleanthes in the *Dialogues*, is yet undiminished in its respect and use. His explanation of the acceptance of religious belief as based upon sociological and psychological conditioning, and upon projection arising from man's emotional reactions to fear and terror of the unknown, is the kernel of a considerable part of modern psychology and sociology of religion. His historical and comparative approach to religious belief reads in a remarkably modern way, with remarkably modern tone.

Now as Hume said, analogies between man, man's productions, and the universe—likenesses and differences—can be found among any two objects in the world: and this is, one can suppose, true of all peoples and

[36] John Viscount Morley, "On Compromise," in *Works* (London: Macmillan Company, 1921), III, 14. "Recollections," *ibid.*, I, 65. See Baumer, *Religion and the Rise of Scepticism*, p. 157.

[37] Ernst Troeltsch, *Christian Thought: Its History and Application*, ed. F. von Hugal (London: Doran, 1923), p. 6.

of all ages. But I should like to resurrect a rather older mode of interpretation in the following remarks upon Hume's place in the history of
thought. And I should like, at the same time, to criticize the "climate of
opinion" sort of view, as offered, say, by Basil Willey and Carl Becker,
who find, as mentioned above, that people like Hume so conveniently "fit"
their ages. I have been endeavoring to show that in many respects Hume
did not fit into his age—that he destroyed the design argument in its
pseudo-scientific form, the most pervasive and satisfying form of theology
during the Age of Reason, and the most strongly shored support of the
accepted form of Christianity. No sooner had the new science, so gloriously
espoused by Newton, been wed to traditional theology in an apparently
indissoluble union, than along came Hume to destroy it. No wonder
Hume was consistently careful, no surprise that he attacked the "Alcoran"
and not the Bible; little reaction to the discovery that he lost several valued
and desired positions, academic and otherwise, because of his religious
beliefs. No wonder Boswell hadn't the courage to walk in his funeral train.
No wonder Millar and Strahan and Smith were horrified at the thought of
publishing his theological and religious essays. It was rather as if the
crew, viewing in satisfaction the house they had just finished building,
suddenly saw the trickle of water, heralding the stream, which had begun
to wash away the foundation. Hume was not a deist, not a theist. He was,
if anything, an agnostic in the most modern sense, one who maintains that
the limits of human observation and logic make it impossible to establish
certain metaphysical claims—among them being the theological. In treatments of natural religion, of the design argument, of theology in general,
contemporary philosophers merely repeat Hume's arguments and cite his
materials.

CHAPTER 11

Epilogue

The Contemporary Context of Natural Theology

It would not appear possible for the design argument, along with natural theology, to escape the grievous wounds suffered at the hands of eighteenth- and nineteenth-century thought. In the eyes of sophisticated audiences, Hume's logic has more and more taken on the character of a definitive refutation, with even the strategic retreat of intuitive self-evidence, so marked a part of Cleanthes' attempts to defend himself, no longer finding its traditional acceptance. Despite such buffetings, however, the design argument has exhibited in the past the tenacity of a hardy perennial, suffering obscurity only to rise in full flower again, an indication of its continued existence in scattered and secluded corridors of academic and popular thought.

Was the design argument, so to speak, "done in" by Hume and by modern skepticism? How does it and natural theology fare today—in the twentieth century? It is difficult not to see the design argument, as any human object or institution or tool, as a sort of organic entity, struggling for existence, evolving and changing in response to forces directed against it, or as a kind of mechanically responding object, describable in terms of pendulum swings of action and reaction. Let us consider, then, the finality of Hume's refutation of the design argument in the historical sense. And at the same time let us discover if modern logic has come forth with any new armaments with which the design argument may defend itself against the skeptical onslaught; let us see if modern philosophy has produced any techniques which will enable it to reconstitute the scattered remnants of its forces. Such consideration will show, I think, that the pendulum has swung in the opposite direction, or at least in an oblique direction, from natural religion of both the Newtonian and the ancient variety, for at present there is no living interest among theologians in natural theology, or in the design argument, as they were formulated in the eighteenth century by Newton, or by the ancients. Natural religion and with it the design argument, in any traditional sense, is as dead as the proverbial doornail.

I must again emphasize the term "traditional" in the last sentence. It is not that natural religion in a number of attenuated senses is not alive; as we shall shortly see, it lives on in the thinking of a number of active and profound formulations of theology such as those of Henry Nelson Wieman, and in humanism, pragmatism, and idealism. These views of theology, however, will be seen to have very little in common with traditional natural theology. Indeed, they represent a shift made in response to critiques such as Hume's and to the advance of scientific method, removing from religion almost all its traditional mystical and supernaturalistic elements.

Further, it is not that theology and religion in general have shared the fate of the design argument. It is for this reason that the "oblique" direction of the pendulum was mentioned above. On the contrary, theology and religion in general have experienced a considerable resurrection, although the character of that which has been reborn is at present quite vague and variegated. There is a rebuilding, so to speak, but the nature of the foundations, as well as the superstructure and design, are not yet clear. None seeks to refute Hume's analysis of the design argument. Existentialism, neo-orthodoxy, mysticism, and the efforts of linguistic philosophers are among the significant trends at present. But only the last-named attempts to revive any sort of traditional natural religion, if even this can be said. Not only do few if any of these contemporary theologies attempt to refute Hume, most of them insist upon the essentially irrational character of religion, although ordinary language theorists as well as existentialists tend to change the meaning of "irrationality" in such contexts by broadening the term "rational" so as to include mental operations not ordinarily comprehended under inductive or deductive methods. As is so often the case, we may initiate our discussion with a verbal tangle. Throughout this essay I have attempted to describe some traditional kinds of natural theology. It has, with respect to the Christian era, been the traditional conception of God and His relations to the world, His characteristics, that has been under scrutiny. Supernaturalism, transcendence, omnipotence, omniscience, omnibenevolence, providence, unity, intelligence, the creation of the universe and all that is in it, including its laws, are among the main notions that make up this traditional conception. And "natural religion," "natural theology," the "design argument," have traditionally been associated with it. My particular thesis has been that this sort of natural theology and its prime argument, the design argument, has met its logical end.

Modern discussions of natural theology, however, might include the claim that it is very much alive, particularly in the work of thinkers such as H. N. Wieman or F. R. Tennant; and it might even be the case that modern humanism and "natural piety" would be comprehended under such a heading. I think that these proposals are correct, but that they do not contradict my position, since "natural religion" in the work of these men does not connote the traditional supernaturalistic conception of God outlined above. For this reason, among others, modern humanists often refuse to call themselves Christians—witness Bertrand Russell. Humanism quite often, as in Julian Huxley and Sidney Hook, is precise in its rejection of supernaturalism. Unlike supernaturalism, humanism locates man's goals and values in his interests, that is, in his biological, psychological, and social nature, in his potentialities for experience. As a result it is difficult to distinguish modern humanism from some variety of ethics, or from some kind of moral system involving dedication to ideals. This seems true of Dewey, who designates a pragmatically inspired humanism a "religious" creed. He retains the term "God," but it does not mean an omnipotent, omniscient being; it refers to a two-fold interaction of man with his environing universe, through which commanding ideals emerge and guide action toward their realization.[1] "It is this active relation between ideal and actual to which I would give the name 'God.'"[2] Neither does he insist that the term "God" be used for this concept. Hence humanism, while it is assuredly "naturalistic" in that scientific method is the keystone of its epistemology, and in that it redefines "religion" and "God" in terms of man's nature and his functional relations to a natural environment, and, finally, in that it rejects any traditional sort of supernaturalism, it is most assuredly not "religion" in the traditional sense.

The work of other modern theologians might, however, seem to fit more appropriately into the proper, traditional connotation of "natural theology." Henry Nelson Wieman and F. R. Tennant, for instance, are often called natural theologians. Their thought reflects the ideas of a group of theologians who attempt to revise the elements of religion so as to remove it from the list of beliefs which conflict with scientifically established truth. They are typically called "modernists," and their allies include Whitehead,

---

[1] E. A. Burtt, *Types of Religious Philosophy* (New York: Harper and Brothers, 1939), p. 405.

[2] John Dewey, *A Common Faith* (New Haven: Yale University Press, 1934), pp. 48 ff.

Dewey, Alexander, and others whose philosophies contain the notion of creative evolution. Religion stakes its claim, for these philosophers and theologians, in the field of the realization and preservation of human order, value, harmony.

It seems clear, even from this brief and summary note, that such thinkers are indeed natural theologians. Nevertheless, their work does not represent the traditional variety of natural theology which we have followed, in the pages above, down through the ages. For Wieman, knowledge of God is identical in human experience with an observable process which works beyond human control and plan; it is the creative source of human good; and it is found in concrete personal application.[3] "God" is "that character of events to which man must adjust himself in order to attain the greatest goods and avoid the greatest evils."[4] In its empirical orientation and in its respect for science, in the consistent reference of its key terminology to matters of natural fact, it appears obvious that Wieman's theology is naturalistic. Yet God is not for him a supernatural being—indeed, God is not very much like God, at least not like Newton's God, or even like the Gods of Catholicism and modern Protestant fundamentalism.[5] Thus the tradition of modernism, as represented by Wieman, exemplifies neither a resurrection nor a continuation of the type of natural theology so abused by Hume in his *Dialogues*.

For the rest, no important modern theological persuasion remains naturalistic in the traditional sense. On the contrary, the most renowned and famous theologies of the present are markedly anti-naturalistic and anti-rationalistic. They exemplify a return to past notions: to biblical authoritarianism, to personal revelation, to certain philosophical views which began, most clearly, in the work of that melancholy Dane, Søren Kierkegaard. As we shall see, these points of view, if anything, represent a wholesale reaction to natural theology. I should like to treat a few major figures in these camps, briefly, in order to indicate the ways in which they have retreated from natural theology.

Perhaps it would be best to begin with the "new supernaturalism," or, as it is often named, "neo-orthodoxy." Its famous proponents include Karl Barth, who is probably the best-known figure among other well-known

[3] D. D. Williams, *Interpreting Theology, 1918–1952* (London: SCM Press, 1953). This book was also printed under the title *What Present Day Theologians are Thinking* (New York: Harper and Brothers, 1952).

[4] H. N. Wieman, *The Wrestle of Religion with Truth* (New York: Macmillan Company, 1929), p. 14. See also H. N. Wieman, *Man's Ultimate Commitment* (Carbondale: Southern Illinois University Press, 1958), pp. 12–13.

[5] Burtt, *Types of Religious Philosophy*, p. 443.

practitioners, such as Emil Brunner, Reinhold Niebuhr, and a host of literary figures including T. S. Eliot. All reject any kind of "rational," "logical," "scientific," or otherwise reasoned view of God and religious belief, a rejection which includes all of the traditional arguments for God's existence and attributes—ontological, cosmological, teleological, design. In addition, their notion of God is the traditional one. Replacing reason and argument for knowledge of God with some variety of mysticism or intuitionism patterned after revelation, they usually claim that human logic is incapable of delivering to us knowledge of God or even knowledge of the solutions to human problems. Faith and personal revelation alone are the channels to knowledge of, and the proper relationships to, God. As D. D. Williams puts the point with respect to Barth, ". . . he has tried to establish this Christian faith on grounds which cut away all 'natural theology.'" [6] For Barth, then, the "intellectual respectability" of religious belief is not a matter of concern. In this, of course, there is a radical departure from most other modern attempts to deal with religion, which represent if nothing else a continuing and profound effort to do just that— to establish religious belief on respectable intellectual grounds. For the theological question which faced Newton and Locke and other eighteenth- and nineteenth-century thinkers: "How can the Christian faith be made intelligible within and in harmony with the highest idealism and scientific thought of our generation?" (a question which Newton believed had been answered by the design argument), Barth substitutes a new question: "What is there in the Christian faith which gives us such an understanding of ourselves that we must assert our loyalty to the Holy God above all the splendid and yet corrupt values of our civilization?" [7] The question-begging character of this assertion exhibits clearly Barth's low opinion of human reason.

Barth marches, therefore, at the head of a legion of modern theologians whose banners are emblazoned with the ancient religious mottoes. For scientific thought, for reason, for inference, for what modern logical thought calls "cognitive language," Barth substitutes faith and revelation. Acquaintance with God comes through "confrontation." For these modern Tertullians, not only are logical techniques inadequate to the acquisition of knowledge of God, they are also inadequate to the knowledge of the moral order. According to such a view, therefore, there is no salvation of any kind in the logical order, and this position is buttressed by the extreme claim that to place faith in the logical order, in reason, is to commit the

[6] Williams, *Interpreting Theology, 1918–1952*, p. 45.
[7] *Ibid.*, p. 12.

heretical sin of pride. This "theology of crisis" includes many other important ideas. Carried along in the current of crises is a group of cónceptions which seeks to provide a bridge to religious belief. Reason, logic, the design argument, are methods of crossing which have been swept away in the flood of skepticism, and are replaced by the "leap of faith," by "I-Thou" relationships of confrontation between man and God, if we follow Brunner. In Barth this anti-rational development is extended into a well defined biblicism. Although it may be interpreted, and although its expansion and analysis is the main task of theology, the Bible remains the absolute word of God. Revelation, sin, redemption, atonement, faith, transcendence, all the traditionally supernaturalistic ideas of revealed religion have been brought back into theology. Does this type of theology escape Hume's criticism? Certainly—but only at the cost of literally excising reason from the body theological. There is no natural theology here, no design argument.

Among the modern trends in theology, none is more influential than that of existentialism. Markedly skeptical, existentialism claims that a scientific or rational criterion for man's decisions is impossible, and emphasizes the irrational character of his deepest feelings and choices. Unable to base his choices rationally, man is forced into error, and consequently into fear, anxiety, and terror. Existentialistic concentration upon these concrete, personal, unique aspects of man's experience, aspects unchartable by means of scientific or logical processes, forces theology to have recourse to a "leap of faith" of some variety or another. This means, of course, the rejection of natural theology, although not, as we have seen in Barth, the rejection of philosophy. Rather, it produces a different kind of philosophy, one which is not naturalistic. Rudolph Bultmann dips into the well of existentialism for his philosophical inspiration, and concludes that theology has in the past been too closely tied to the particular myths of the Old and New Testaments. Barthian biblicism is therefore rejected. Christianity, according to Bultmann's lights, must be "demythologized," and interpreted in terms of the anxieties, guilts, and fears of modern life, all of which are expressions of absurdity and irrationality. There is little if any evidence of natural theology here.

The philosophical approach to theology and religion is marked in the work of Paul Tillich. We have already seen that neo-orthodoxy stakes its claim far outside the boundaries of philosophical or scientific reasoning; Tillich rather overlaps such characterizations. Deeply philosophical, and yet critical of the scientific claim to all the territory of truth, he shows the influence of existentialism in his view that man's existence, fraught with discontinuities, doubts, anxieties, fear of death, cannot be eased by any scientific knowledge of God—by any rational knowledge.[8] Following Kierkegaard, Tillich reaffirms the view that, ultimately, men must make a "leap of faith." We cannot look to philosophy for the real truth about God or the way of salvation.[9] The search for the divine can be completed only in a "mystical and ecstatic unification."[10] This sort of theology takes a direction which ends not only in the rejection of traditional natural theology, but, further, in a stress upon the limitations of human reason with respect to many decisions. Again we find the claim that reason can solve man's problems regarded as a sin of pride. How such "leaps" of faith solve men's problems is never made particularly clear, nor is it clear how theologians such as Tillich (and Barth and the rest of them) can develop such rationally sophisticated positive and negative theological systems without themselves falling prey to the heresy. In order to avoid being thus hoist by their own petard it could be claimed that the theology involved represents a sort of revelatory inspiration; but even this seems somewhat less than humble.

Nevertheless, existentialistic thought undoubtedly forms the basis of much contemporary theology. Its kernel seems to be as follows: whatever meaning and value man can find in his life must be the outcome of man's choices, man's inventions. This "decision" character of his existence forms a core of meaning for existentialism which is projected, so to speak, upon the cosmic plane. It is man's freedom which is fundamental, since "existence," on the level of concrete life, means *unique* choice, and choice means freedom.[11] Within the unique and personal level of existence, scientific categories such as classification, generalization, objective observation and experiment, prediction and verification, are useless; they are useless with respect to the peculiarities of personal problems, each of which is different, difficult, and incomprehensible in terms of scientific generalization and abstraction. "Existence" is concrete and personal; "essence" is abstract and general. With these choices, choices unavoidable in practical life, come a host of problems. Responsibility, for instance, appears. And with it, because our choices and decisions are allied with ignorance and

[8] Paul Tillich, *The Courage to Be* (New Haven: Yale University Press, 1952), pp. 139–140.

[9] Williams, *Interpreting Theology, 1918–1952*, p. 53.

[10] *Ibid.*, p. 56.

[11] Abraham Kaplan, *The New World of Philosophy* (New York: Random House, 1961), p. 106.

unpredictable consequences, comes the crushing sense of failure which is anguish, anxiety. Our choices are made, according to Kierkegaard, in "fear and trembling." Life is full of absurdity, is irrational, is inexplicable, is unexplainable, is incongruous, is meaningless.[12]

It is difficult to overstate the difference, the disparity in attitude, in method, and conclusions, between this sort of theology and that of Newton and modernist theologians. It is a disparity which is not limited to the methods employed, but includes in addition a complete attitude towards life and the world. Newton, Locke, and their followers felt no fright at the development of science and reason, at the unfolding of new knowledge. Newton's theology reminds us of an inexperienced virgin—theology in its youthful hope; Barthian theology reminds one of theology as the old jade who has got religion again. A far cry, then, from the optimism of eighteenth-century English gentlemen, or even of Victorian gentlemen, such as Bentham and Mill. With neo-orthodoxy and existentialism reason has been thrown off; it was just a light cloak anyhow, as we have seen, and it had always smothered many things dear to the elect. Existentialism harbors an ultimate skepticism which infects every plane of human life. The crises of modern national and international politics, two dread world wars, and the threat of another which promises even greater feasts for the vultures, have all, no doubt, contributed to the development of pessimistic attitudes. Notwithstanding the obvious response that such catastrophes are due to the lack of reason rather than its application, we see in most modern theologies a return to some sort of revelation—to a "hope" that provides the springboard, the power, for the "leap of faith." Whereas the world was once construed as a beautiful piece of workmanship, a superb and intricate machine working for man's benefit and expressing the glory, goodness, and intelligence of God, it is now not even the "neutral" machine of Bentham and Mill. Nor is it the "situation" or "environment" which Dewey and Russell take to be the arena for the development of man's potentialities. The world is again a hostile place—and, if Barthian views are added, a place peopled by demons. Demons, it appears, are never finally exorcised.

The fact that most modern theologies, at least the most vital appearing ones such as neo-orthodoxy and theistic existentialism, have staked out a claim that does not on the surface violate any scientific territorial rights does not mean that there are not intra-party squabbles within the ranks. But such internecine strife does not militate against the dominant note among thinkers of such inspiration—the basic irrationality of human

[12] *Ibid.*, p. 116.

existence. A cross section of modern theologians, literary figures, and philosophers, indicates an often passionate skepticism with respect to reason and science in their relation to man's life and problems. Tillich, Niebuhr, Jaspers, Eliot, Berdyaev, Kafka, Koestler, Auden, Camus, all reject reason as the source of salvation for the human predicament. Alternatives to reason are offered, to be sure—leaps of faith, mystic unifications, confrontations—offered, in the sea of man's troubles, anxieties, and despairs, his sense of the vacancy of modern life, as anchors of quiescence. Page after page is devoted to the "pathology" of disbelief, the loneliness and despair, the vacancy, of modern life.[13] Even when the conclusion is atheistic, as it often is in literary figures and in philosophers like Sartre, nevertheless there is evident a pervasive and profoundly skeptical and pessimistic mood which describes the human scene in terms of hollowness (Eliot), thirstiness (Eliot again), alienation and anguish (Kafka, Koestler, Auden). Wherever one looks in modern theology, there is found the constant rejection of the methods of science, of reason, whether inductive or deductive, as pathways to knowledge of God, to man's right decisions, to the solution of man's problems. A profounder skepticism concerning the role of reason, a profounder rejection of natural theology, both in fact and in attitude, would be difficult to conceive. And, of course, there is the side product, the corollary, of such rejection: the return to religion's ancient sources—to mysticism, revelation, faith, scriptural authority, to all that had been, perforce, more or less rejected by natural theology. It is almost as if, when observing a team of white-coated scientists working with their microscopes, a change takes place, and there, standing in front of the bench, which is still covered with the paraphernalia of science, are a group of reconstituted witch-doctors. Of course, these witch-doctors have moved only into part of the laboratory. It is simply that the scientists are from now on to be restricted to another part of the building. Whether or not the witch-doctors remain in theirs, however, has yet to be seen—they have never done so in the past!

One of the most significant trends in modern theology appears to be developing among the linguistic philosophers, who, in recent years, have begun to pay attention to theology and religion. With positivism, religion and theology were relegated to a position outside the pale of cognitive acceptance, mainly because the fundamental theses of these fields are not subject to empirical verification, and, in addition, do not appear to be self-evidently or a priori true. Theological statements, according to this

[13] Baumer, *Religion and the Rise of Scepticism*, pp. 205 ff.

philosophy, are to be parked along with those of metaphysics in the limbo of "non-cognitive" or "non-sense" utterances—pseudo-statements, or of some variety of emotive language. In A. J. Ayer, Russell, and the philosophers of the Vienna circle, there is a strongly anti-theological, anti-religious strain. Propounding the verification theories of meaning and truth, positivism rejects then as "pseudo-propositions" any beliefs which cannot be indirectly or directly verified by observation and experiment. This thoroughgoing experimentalism, with its Humean roots, resulted in the drastic rejection of theological utterances where they are said to denote any sort of supernatural beings or super-mundane powers or laws. As A. J. Ayer says, "The theist . . . may believe that his experiences are cognitive experiences, but, unless he can formulate his 'knowledge' in propositions that are empirically verifiable, we may be sure that he is deceiving himself."[14] A great deal more could be said about this type of philosophy and its relationships to theology, but my particular problems do not necessitate it.[15] The rejection by positivists of any natural religion in the traditional sense is as complete as it was in their spiritual father, David Hume.

The most recent practitioners of linguistic techniques in philosophical analysis, often called the "ordinary language" school of philosophy, vary considerably the approach of positivism. The ordinary language people are "sippers" where the positivists, like the Barthians, might be called "gulpers." On the one hand the members of this loosely connected group emphasize the fact that statements making cognitive claims in the sense of the natural sciences are subject to verification analysis, both with respect to meaning and to truth. This is generally taken to involve the rejection of claims that supernatural beings or events—say miracles and God—are scientifically provable. To this extent the ordinary language point of view tends to support positivism. On the other hand, it is often insisted that traditional formal and inductive logical principles do not exclude all the possible logical characteristics of human utterances—language has a multitude of purposes and functions, among which are various nonscientific uses which are not necessarily nonlogical just because they are nonscientific. In the view of Wittgenstein, from which so many of these ideas flow, language is "functional." There are many language "games" of which the

[14] A. J. Ayer, *Language, Truth and Logic* (2d ed.; London: Victor Gollancz, Ltd., 1946), p. 119.

[15] Frederick Ferré, *Language, Logic and God* (New York: Harper and Brothers, 1961), Chaps. 2 and 3.

scientific model exemplifies only one, although a very important one indeed.

The upshot is that ordinary language philosophers tend to grant to many forms of belief and statements much more respect and appropriateness than would be granted by the positivists. And among the many traditionally accepted and respected beliefs which had come into a time of troubles with positivism, and are being refurbished and placed again among the accepted, are those of theology. I shall give some attention to this approach to the body theological, although I am not sure whether it has effected a resurrection, or whether it has dismembered the body and buried it in different and hard-to-locate places. It appears, on the surface, to be a form of naturalism.

All linguistic utterances, according to this view, have in common some social context and some practical effects. It would seem to follow that language, since it is a complex social instrument having many legitimate uses, cannot be construed entirely in terms of the scientific use or model.[16] Now, in line with this direction of thought, the question becomes "What is the use or uses, the functions, of theological discourse?" When different uses of language are confused, or when the different models are mistaken for one another, troubles or confusions ensue, and the task of philosophy is to analyse the "meaning" of the statements, to "clarify" them, so as to get rid of the difficulty or difficulties. In our case, it would be the difficulties of theological discourse when it is construed according to scientific uses. To apply to theological discourse the criteria, say observation and experiment, of science, results in the relegation of such discourse to the classification of "pseudo-statements." The resulting theological statements look like objective assertions but in fact they are not like them at all in that they are not verifiable. In general, ordinary language philosophers employ two related techniques: one is called the *paradigm case method*; and the other, following the excellent analysis of Ferré, might be called the *method of comparison*. The former seeks to clarify a confused utterance, word, or phrase by exhibiting an example which is clear in its use. For instance, for one who claims on grounds of modern physics that the term "solid" no longer has any meaning because everything is composed of whirling electrons, a rebutting paradigm case would be the use of "solid" with respect to stone walls and dishes, showing that there are perfectly clear and meaningful uses of the term "solid" which do not contradict the claims of modern physics. A stone, in other words, can quite easily both be "solid" and "composed of electrons."

[16] *Ibid.*, p. 61.

The method of "significant comparison" is used to clarify a muddled phrase or sentence by comparing it with other phrases or actions which do a similar job. A woman's statement "I hereby declare the ship X in commission" has the same function as hitting the prow with a bottle of champagne. It is ceremonial. Obviously the woman does not build, float, or operate the ship, although her face, as did Helen's, might "launch" a thousand ships.

The question is, does this type of philosophical endeavor provide hope for theological discourse in the sense of natural theology or the design argument? The answer is, sometimes yes, sometimes no; yes for some, no for others. Ordinary language philosophers disagree. Some say that theological discourse has no meaningful or appropriate use or uses. On the other hand, many seem to believe that theological language has many valid functions. It is almost universally held that theological discourse is not cognitive in the scientific sense, that theological assertions cannot be demonstrated or proved in the ways that scientific propositions are proved. Therefore, one of the major original claims of natural theology—that theological statements are scientifically provable—is given up without a struggle; the design argument is not, as Newton and his ancient and modern cohorts believed, experimental or logical in its proofs and methods.

Nevertheless, some interesting analogies remain. I shall attend only a few of the better-known instances, but they will suffice, I think, to make my points. What are some of the legitimate functions of theological language? In seeking among the "linguistic diseases" will we find any logical drugs which will cure our theological "mental cramps"? If there is an "appropriate" use of, or function of, theological discourse, it might be possible to avoid Hume's dilemma, the dilemma which concluded that theological statements are either emotional expressions or dogmas based upon some sort of faith or revelation—that they are never scientifically validated beliefs. It should be mentioned at this time that the attempts offered by the following thinkers to avoid this dilemma give this writer the feeling that ordinary language offerings have less therapeutic value than its practitioners believe—a situation similar to the Chinese method of treating one pain by creating another. This may take one's mind off the first pain, but it rarely effects a cure. It is curious that those to whom the "cramp" is of such a miserable nature are those who, I think, are the least satisfied with the relief offered. But more of this later.

It should be made clear at the beginning that not all linguistic philosophers of this general persuasion conclude that there are any "appropriate" or "unqueer" functions for theological utterances. Applying the "treatment" to such common theological assertions as "God exists," or "God designed the world," Professor Findlay claims not only that we cannot prove God's existence: we can prove that no God (a necessary being) could possibly exist.[17] Surely this is more than mere agnosticism. No necessary (a logical term) being can be shown to exist (an existential term)—to combine necessary and existential terms is to proffer a contradiction in terms. Hence the existence of a necessary being is impossible. "Necessarily existing being" is a contradiction in terms. J. J. C. Smart says that none of the traditional arguments for God's existence, including the design argument, are even of limited validity. In his view the design argument is "good" (appropriate) only for those who already believe in God's existence on other grounds.[18] Antony Flew, in a famous discussion, says that the traditional notion of God, and traditional statements about Him, are dogmas since no possible evidence could disconfirm them and no existential statement is proper unless its opposite is possible, i.e., unless it is disconfirmable. Theological statements suffer, in his words, the "death of a thousand qualifications" in the futile attempt to fit their meanings into scientific molds and to claim validity or truth for them according to scientific criteria. The design argument would represent an example. No evidence of nondesign suffices to reduce the theist to the admission of defeat. No set of circumstances, such as the assertion that no gardener is seen, heard, smelt, touched, suffices to disconfirm belief that there is a gardener at work designing the garden and keeping it up. Flew, Smart, Mackinnon[19] all agree that the type of analogical reasoning which characterizes the design argument is logically indefensible—always there is the mistaken application of finite words to the infinite, of naturalistic terms to the supernatural.

R. M. Hare argues that the question "Does God exist?" is not a proper question.[20] Belief in the existence of God represents a "blick," or a sort of assumption which determines the way in which we look at things or construe them. His paradigm case is that of the lunatic who believes that

[17] J. N. Findlay, "Can God's Existence Be Disproved," in *New Essays in Philosophical Theology*, ed. Antony Flew and Alasdair MacIntyre (New York: Macmillan Company, 1955), pp. 47 ff.

[18] J. J. C. Smart, "The Existence of God," in *New Essays in Philosophical Theology*, pp. 29, 45–46.

[19] D. M. Mackinnon, "Death," in *New Essays in Philosophical Theology*, pp. 262–263.

[20] R. M. Hare, "Theology and Falsification," in *New Essays in Philosophical Theology*, pp. 101–102.

someone is after him, and no explanations, arguments, or evidence will shake his belief.

What, then, are the "appropriate" uses of theological statements such as "God exists" or "God loves all men?" Since it would seem to be almost universally agreed that Hume was right in his contention that such utterances are not to be confused with scientific beliefs, or even with common-sense empirical discourse, is the theologian or believer who utters them left any cut of the cognitive pie other than that of nonrational faith or emotion? The answer to this question is difficult, since most linguists, barring those mentioned above, seem also to be saying both yes and no to it. Emphasizing the above-mentioned "multiple uses" of language, they appear to assert that theological utterances serve functions which are in some senses "like" cognitive ones but in other senses unlike them. This peculiar approach can, I think, best be seen in some examples. I might put in here my view that the question is not simply whether or not there are likenesses per se, but whether or not the likenesses discovered are significant or trivial, relevant or irrelevant, since everything is in some sense like anything else. A man and a pile of sand are alike in that they occupy space.

J. J. C. Smart, who, as we have seen, denies that design theology is cognitive in the empirical or scientific sense, nevertheless says that this "doesn't endanger theology." [21] It is this sort of puzzling statement that we run up against so often in the works of linguistic philosophers, and it is interesting to construe it, to see its implications. There is, he says, a "theological necessity" which is different from "logical necessity." If one is (already) a Christian believer, then for him it is "necessary" that God exists. God's existence is a presumed constant, somewhat like the notion of the constancy of the velocity of light in a vacuum is a presumed constant for the physicist. Such is Smart's paradigm. The design argument is, while not an argument in the strict sense, "a potent instrument for heightening religious emotions." [22] Hare's "blicks" are quite similar in status to the "presumed constant" of Smart. Theological assertions and beliefs are not logical "explanations" at all. [23] Also similar is John Wisdom's [24] case of the untended garden—no gardener is perceived or perceivable, but his active presence is affirmed by some viewers who say the garden is nevertheless

[21] Smart, "The Existence of God," pp. 28–29.
[22] Ibid., p. 45.
[23] Hare, "Theology and Falsification," pp. 101–103.
[24] John Wisdom, "Gods," in Logic and Language, ed. Antony Flew (New York: Philosophical Library, 1951), pp. 187 ff.

being cared for. The facts, the condition of the garden, the nonperception of any gardener, are the same for both parties in the dispute. There is no "scientific" way of settling the disagreement, but nevertheless one person insists that there is a gardener—this is his "way" of viewing or construing the facts.

Hence for Wisdom theological utterances serve an "attention-getting function."[25] Facts are not, therefore, exactly irrelevant, since the utterance and its attendant beliefs sort of "form" our way of looking at the facts. One man looks at them as if they constitute a designed and cared-for garden, another man does not. In somewhat of a circumscribed sense, one "sees" what the other does not see.

I. T. Ramsay sees theological discourse as serving a "penny-dropping" or "ice-breaking" function.[26] Following out other examples, in which we find that our paradigms multiply like philosophical rodents, Willem Zurdeeg[27] proposes the view that theological expressions make up a "convictional language" which turns upon an "I-Thou" relationship. For Smart, they are characterized by "worshipful assent." For Alasdair MacIntyre they constitute "expressions of self-commitment" to an authority.[28] (We see, in a number of these examples, the influence of existentialism and neo-orthodoxy.) For J. B. Coates, theological statements "help one feel at home," cause one to feel that the world was "created by a helping hand."[29] For Phillip Leon they function as "inspirational" elements which do not represent any sort of reality.[30] For R. B. Braithwaite Christian discourse "indicates commitment" to the emotional attitudes of a Christian.[31] For D. M. Mackinnon it represents "confident affirmations by one-who-must-die."[32] Old bodies in new clothing! Under new management, so to speak, we find the ancient traditions, the opiates, goads, evincements, prods, expressions euphoric and capitulatory, lacking, of course, since this is a genteel and predominantly British tradition, the thunder and lightning and mountaintop.

[25] *Ibid.*, p. 181.
[26] Ian T. Ramsay, *Religious Language* (London: SCM Press, 1957), pp. 27–28.
[27] *Ibid.*, p. 137.
[28] Alasdair MacIntyre, "The Logical Status of Religious Belief," in *Metaphysical Beliefs* (London: SCM Press, 1957), p. 185.
[29] J. B. Coates, "God and the Positivists," *The Hibbert Journal*, L (1952), 226.
[30] Phillip Leon, "The Meaning of Religious Propositions," *The Hibbert Journal*, LIII (1955), 151.
[31] R. B. Braithwaite, *An Empiricist's View of the Nature of Religious Belief* (Cambridge: Cambridge University Press, 1955), p. 11.
[32] Mackinnon, "Death," pp. 261–263.

By this time the theological reader may be thinking that he is drowning in a philosophic liquid not of his own mixing. Theological utterances, if this kind of thing keeps up, may come to mean everything and thus nothing. A somewhat maddening scope begins to exhibit itself, producing a problem of deciding whether there are *any* statements outside science which are not theological! Austin Ferrer [33] believes that theological assertions are parables. Thus the notion of God's creation reflects the parable from human invention; "redemption," in like manner, arises from various types of deliverance and restoration in human life and experience. Divine love is parabolic of human love. Note the lack of any strictly cognitive claim. As I. M. Crombie puts it, "Often it has been held to be the task of natural theology to prove the existence of God. This seems to me to be a task which cannot, in any strict sense of 'prove' be accomplished." [34] Macpherson [35] follows Wittgenstein and says that religion simply belongs to the inexpressible. Ferré [36] says that theological sentences are "paradoxical" and "inconsistent," often, in other words, illogical and unverifiable, but that nevertheless they serve the function of producing a "richer awareness" of religious beliefs.

Now the conclusion would seem to be this. Few if any of the major writers considered hold to a view which claims that theological arguments and assertions are scientifically "appropriate." When the attempt is made to cast them in such a mold, the intended theological drama turns into a logical comedy. Since it is admitted, even emphasized, that theological utterances cannot be formulated in the inductive and deductive mold of science and common sense, they are, indeed, "odd" or "queer." Thus for our original question: Does linguistic philosophy attempt a reformation of "natural theology" in the traditional sense? we have a clear answer—no.

Nevertheless, such an answer is an inadequate description of linguistic attitudes towards theology, mainly because so many of these philosophers insist that it does not constitute a criticism of theology, once the nature of the functions of theological statements are properly understood. A better way of putting the situation might be as follows. Theological utterances

[33] Austin Ferrer, "A Starting-Point for the Philosophical Examination of Theological Belief," in *Faith and Logic*, ed. Basil Mitchell (Boston: Beacon Press, 1957), pp. 21-25.

[34] I. M. Crombie, "The Possibility of Theological Statements," in *Faith and Logic*, p. 56.

[35] Thomas MacPherson, "Religion as the Inexpressible," in *New Essays in Philosophical Theology*, p. 142.

[36] Ferré, *Language, Logic and God*, p. 55.

do serve legitimate and logical, though nonrational-in-the-traditional-sense functions. Hume's logical points are granted, even underscored, but it is claimed in counterpoint that such points score for only one sort of game. Thus Hume and his followers are wrong if it is concluded that theological utterances are nonsense or useless. This would be a "category" mistake, to use one of Ryle's more famous terms. And so, while we are in fact left with theology refused entrance into the inner chamber of honored logic, truth, and fact, nevertheless the building of accepted statements is being expanded in order to form another valued room wherein theological statements may abide. In essence, such philosophic construction extends the term "logic" in order to include utterances in addition to those of the inductive and deductive sciences. Such efforts are quite similar to those initiated with respect to ethics by Toulmin, Nowell-Smith, and others. This, then, is the manner in which ordinary language philosophers are tending to treat the "mental cramps" occasioned by the exposure of religion and theology to the disease of modern scientific logic and epistemology.

It is, unfortunately, by no means clear to me that the "mental cramps" occasioned in both philosophic circles and in common life, as well as in religion and theological circles, will be removed or cured by this sort of mental massage. Whether one regards these linguistic treatments as "explanations" or "justifications" of theological statements, it leaves both the believer and the unbeliever with the vague feeling that whatever theological assertions are, such views of them are curiously castrated ones. I suppose that in the last analysis what I mean by the present line of comment is that the linguistic approach to theological assertions does not produce a satisfactory justification of theology and religion in the sense of supplying them with a cognitive basis. They proffer no reason for the uncommitted to believe religious beliefs or to accept their theological justifications. The statements of both science and empirical common sense, on the other hand, are admittedly quite different. Put in another way— such views provide explanations of the ways in which, psychologically and otherwise, theological utterances might perhaps function—but they provide no reason for choosing such beliefs, or for choosing one set of beliefs, say the Christian, over those of Mohammedanism, or over none at all.

It is often if not always argued that having a function implies fulfilling a need. Modern theology, as we have seen above in its neo-orthodox, existentialistic, modernistic, and fundamentalistic varieties, as well as in its linguistic formulations, almost universally maintains that there are deep and complex fears and needs in man's nature. These needs often escape scientific formulation, description and explanation, and even were they explained by science, the explanations would not resolve the problems they engender. The pressures and tensions of life in modern western culture, the wars and hatreds, the rather widespread sense of aimlessness; the grinding, dulling, and seemingly unremovable poverty of most other cultures; the shock and pain of disease, unexpected and incurable; the inexplicable and ineluctable fact of death and the implied absurdity of a life of struggle whose conclusion is inorganic dissolution; the constant and unjustifiable inequities of social and political life—all these are pointed to as contributing to the recurrence of, and the profound need for, what have been called religious beliefs. And thus we have the "leaps of faith," the "I-Thou" relationships, the "worshipful attitudes," the sense of a "helping hand," the "inspirational elements," the "heightening of religious emotions," the "expression of self-commitment," the "penny-dropping," "ice-breaking" feelings, the "affirmation of one-who-must-die"!

But does all this really improve the position of the theologian in his search for a justification of his beliefs and for the claim that one who is nonreligious should accept them? The theological battles, some of whose strategies and tactics, advances and retreats have been reported in this book, and whose final and inescapable logical defeat is recorded in Hume's *Dialogues*—all, it appears—dealt with the profound question as to whether or not the beliefs and assertions of theology and religion are *worthy* of belief in the way that scientific and practical assertions are worthy of acceptance. I think that the sophisticated ordinary language "explanations" of the "functions" of theological discourse have made it abundantly clear that the answer is no. I shall point out some additional reasons for this statement.

In the first place, our discussion of the work of these writers makes it plain that not one of them has provided a bridge over the epistemological chasm dredged out by David Hume, the gulf between empirically derived matter-of-fact statements and relations of ideas, the cognitive sort of statement, on the one side, and on the other side the variously various emotive expressions and evocations. None of our writers, it seems to me, wishes to claim that theological statements significantly compare to, or are justifiable in the same manner as, the statements of common sense and science.

The justification, if it is a justification, therefore is driven back upon the old cry that there has been a confusion between scientific utterances and theological utterances, a "linguistic" confusion, and the claim that the criteria of the former do not apply to the latter. Now surely this is not a correct analysis of the work of Hume and his followers. Hume was most certainly pointing out just this very fact, as were and are most skeptics. They have always insisted that the attempt to claim scientific status for theological beliefs is doomed to frustration. Herein lies the very kernel of the believer's "mental cramp"—in precisely the fact that theological assertions are different from scientific ones. Hence the distinctions made by the ordinary language philosophers tend, to my mind, to be trivial, simply because they *do not remove the cramp*! A. C. Ewing has hit the nail squarely, and with a blow struck it home, with the remark that "Emotion . . . requires some objective belief, true or false, about the real to support it for long . . ." [37] Theologians have been struggling for cognitive support, a support they felt they had found in Newtonian theism. Linguistic philosophy has not provided this. If, while wrapped in a fancier cover than that provided by Hume, the distinction remains withal, linguistic philosophy has made a poor present to the religious believer who suffers from cognitive doubt. If it is insisted, as often is the case, that the term "cognitive" is herein applied too narrowly, the answer is that such a charge renders the issue purely verbal; call it what you will, none of the proffered analyses makes theological utterance cognitive in the most accepted senses of cognitive justification, the empirical and the scientific. And this is just what is lacking in and is desired for theology. Rather than claim some peculiar "commitment" talk, or "heightened emotions" talk, the believer would, I am certain, rather again strongly embrace doctrines of faith and revelation as sources of religion—as true beliefs. This, of course, is precisely what Barthian neo-orthodoxy and existentialism have done.

Hence the justification must of necessity turn into a "pragmatic" appeal. If the question of truth is beside the point in matters theological, and by this is meant scientific or empirical truth, then the only real bone of contention left lies in the question whether or not theological and religious beliefs have a "use," whether psychological, sociological, or moral, and whether or not they serve as an efficient instrument for resolving the problems initiated by such basic "needs." Put another way, (1) are theology and religion useful? and (2) even if it is admitted that they are, as I am sure they are, it might be asked, do their good consequences outweigh their bad ones? And (3) are they better than other alternative systems of persuasion? Chewing on these bones of contention has, I

[37] A. C. Ewing, "Religious Assertions in the Light of Contemporary Philosophy," *Philosophy*, XXXII, No. 122 (July, 1957), pp. 207–210.

am sure, toughened the teeth of the disputants; but I'm not certain that any nourishment has been derived from the repast. It does seem that these questions are empirical ones, at least in principle, but it also appears that it is unlikely that they are the sort of questions that can be finally resolved. For at least a great many religious people, whether religion is useful or not may be considered irrelevant. In addition, the criteria of usefulness (i.e., this world, or the next one?) are not likely to be agreed upon. That theological assertions and religious beliefs function to express feelings, moods, emotions; that they do in fact function to help people who are tense and anxious because of the innumerable personal problems of life, goes without saying. It also goes without saying that they do not help those who *for cognitive reasons* find it impossible to believe them. But note again: this approach opens theology up to comparison with other possible avenues of resolving such problems, psychological, sociological, political, humanistic, etc. Indeed, the door is opened to the traditional pragmatic justification for religious belief which was argued above in some detail both in Hume's *Dialogues* and in nineteenth-century skepticism. Peculiar, is it not, that after all the sophisticated verbal hair-splitting of linguistic analysis, we find ourselves forced back to the common way of putting the problem, and the same old arguments. My feeling is that religion can do no more than break even in such a comparison, particularly in that the reasons for which most people give up religious beliefs lie in the fact that they no longer regard them as true.

Let us briefly point up these contentions again. The attempt to support theology on pragmatic grounds grants the fundamental criticism made against religion—that religious and theological utterances are not true, or are neither true nor false, or that they are not assertions at all. In comparison with scientific models, the best that theology can do is to end in agnosticism, i.e., in the view that religious beliefs are not demonstrably false. But, it is claimed, their cognitive questionability notwithstanding, religious beliefs are needed in order to "bolster morality" (Cleanthes in Hume's *Dialogues*), or to allay psychological problems, needs, tensions. This contention, however, is not by any means self-evidently true, and puts the question out for inspection. Does religion do all these things for man? Lucretius said no; modernists say no (remember that it is traditional religious belief that we are considering); agnostics and atheists do not, apparently, find such beliefs necessary; and if behavior indicates belief, most of those who claim to believe actually do not. And one can thus argue either that other avenues, such as the application of psychological, sociological, and humanistic techniques, would do a better job; or that even if theology and religion do the job, which is arguable, they bring with them attendant fanaticisms and stupidities, such as religious wars, cross-cultural hatreds and misunderstandings, persecutions, private and public conflict and misunderstandings, that far outweigh any advantages to be gained by their acceptance.

Another strand of thought consistently appearing in our ordinary language theologians is the view that theological statements are *like* scientific ones in that they provide what might be called "models" for the interpretation and organization of facts or experiences. The reference is to those overlying axioms and assumptions which provide us with ultimate categories for organizing and relating facts. This sort of thing was evident in John Wisdom's "attention-getting" function of theological discourse, in Hare's "blicks," and in Smart's paradigm of the velocity of light in physics. Now it is true that scientific thinking involves such "blicks." But it is simple, I think, to dispose of this line of argument. The "blicks" of science, including "wave" analogies, etc., are supported by their success in enabling scientists to predict and control natural sequences of events. The models of scientific operations are expansible, coherent, indirectly verifiable and fruitful, subject to public criteria, and are usually given up when other models prove more advantageous. They tend to be quite dynamic. This is not true of theological and religious beliefs nor of the statements that make up the fundamental axioms of theological and religious discourse in the traditional sense. Hence, as Flew has pointed out, they tend to be dogmas, or circular statements which admit of no possible disconfirming evidence; no evidence would serve to shake the acceptance of such beliefs on the part of their believers. Finally, the sense of fruitfulness is clearcut in scientific discourse. The evidence is in and grows with each cure of a disease. But, as we have seen, theological utterances either are not subject to such criteria, or, as in the case of fruitfulness, the evidence is not in or there is doubt that it supports theology. Even an appeal to the fact that the uniformity of nature and the principle of noncontradiction are unprovable will not do—they are necessary adjuncts to scientific proof, which stands upon its own, and they draw their support from the success of scientific endeavor.

But even were we to find that this problematic theological route seems to be at least open to empirical argument and to evidence that it might be more fruitful to have theological discourse and religious beliefs than to not have them, or to the claim that religions provide the most effective

response to man's more profound and "deeper" necessities, I am nevertheless sure that the traditional theologian and believer would find this an
obnoxious support for his views. Of course, paradox and inconsistency
often excite curiosity, the heightening of emotions, expression of commitments, worshipful attitudes, are useful—but to what? Push these delight-
fully sophisticated analyses to their conclusions, and religion nevertheless
is left in an insecure status. As Flew puts the point succinctly with respect
to theological discourse: "The first reason is that religious talk seems so
often not merely deceptive, like, say, ethical or scientific talk: but as if it
really is in some way failed science or fraudulent ethics . . . a misguided
attempt to do super-science . . . about the cause of everything." [38] Since the
only cure for the wounds of traditional religious belief is the bandage and
medication of truth and cognitive status, such attempts as those attacked
by Flew are actually irrelevant. The cauterization wished by the theologian
is that of truth, and this is what he has not been able to get, and it is not
provided by ordinary language analysis. At best it provides an anaesthetic
for the pain.

With this series of comments, our travels are practically ended. No
modern theology is pursuing the path of natural theology or its prized
argument—the design argument. It is as if we had looked under the
tombstone which Hume placed over the burial plot of the family "natural
theology," one of whose members was the design argument, to see if it
were still dead; or as if we in a sense were checking to see if the family line
has continued, on some distaff side, transported, so to speak, to an alien
shore—modern philosophy and theology. But no. As has been seen, the
ghost of natural theology is laid, at least in any recognizable traditional
sense. We have briefly viewed a number of modern theological tendencies.
They might be construed, if we continue our somewhat macabre simile, as
throwbacks (neo-orthodoxy, whose "orthodoxy" is more proper than its
"neo," would be such a return), or as different species (modernism and
humanism, which are really ethical theories with a glaze of consecration),
or as distaff productions (ordinary language theology). Among them there
is faint support for design theology—indeed, it provides no "argument"
for God's existence and attributes in any traditional sense of "reason,"
whether inductive or deductive. There is agreement, even insistence, that
religious beliefs are not rational, but are intuitional, or are emotive
expressions or evocations, commitments, persuasions, ceremonial utterances, or something else. And last, even ordinary language theologians

[38] Antony Flew, "Creation," in *New Essays in Philosophical Theology*, p. 185.

are uniform in the contention that theological utterances are not existential, not of a scientific character. And so to Cleanthes' claim that theological beliefs are grounded in the same sorts of evidence and the same sorts of inferences as science and practical thinking—the response of modern philosophy is in the negative. The pendulum of natural theology has not swung back in any recognizable form. Indeed, its old enemy, the pendulum of revealed theology, is gathering strength.

The *Dialogues* as a Work of Art

"Any question of philosophy, on the other hand, which is so *obscure* and *uncertain* that human reason can reach no fixed determination with regard to it—if it should be treated at all—seems to lead us naturally into the style of dialogue and conversation."

—Pamphilus to Hermippus[1]

"Art rests on the fact that deep feelings pattern themselves in a coherent way all over our life and behavior."

—Richard Wollheim, *Art and Its Objects*[2]

In this essay I will take seriously the fact that Hume chose to produce his ultimate work, the *Dialogues Concerning Natural Religion,* as a work of art. This is not, I think, to do what is ordinarily done with this great work. I will not, therefore, analyze the *Dialogues* as an argumentative essay that is in an external fashion rhetorically embellished, and thus made more "artful," in order to manipulate the reader and to hide or distance the author from the opinions therein. Such views, I believe, impoverish both Hume and the *Dialogues.* For one thing, they severely limit his intentions and imply that he is deceitful. For another, they severely limit the rich character of the *Dialogues.* I assume that Hume's decision to set the religious and theological arguments out in dialogue form was a rational act in a deeper sense, a sense tied to the things a successful work of art can do; things that a scientific essay, or even an "artful essay," cannot do, or do so well. It goes without saying, of course, that borderline cases abound.

There is not sufficient space to say more than a small part of what should be said about the concept of art I shall employ. Like all such, it is controversial.[3] However, the concept, or variants of it, is widely enough accepted to serve more than parochial interests. Its main constituents

will be roughed in and briefly related to the *Dialogues,* with elaboration
to come as needed. First, uncontroversially, a work of art is the product
of an intentional act (or set of related actions) and is an artifact. It is also
generally conceded that art serves a wide range of intentions, including
the celebration of unity and the expression of beliefs, feelings, and
attitudes that cannot be captured in the desired ways by other forms of
presentation. Human beings are responsive to the formal aspects of their
experiences of objects and events. And it is generally believed that
another of the reasons that art is of interest to audiences and to artists as
well lies in its expressive capacities. And although it is not necessary to
my present purposes, I would make a stronger claim: that a major
interest of art lies in its capacity to reflect inner states, which are in some
sense or senses recapitulated by the spectator, reader, listener. There are
no abortive problems here. Hume labored diligently over the *Dialogues*
for years. This shows his deep emotional involvement in them. And his
profound desire to make them public is clear from his letters, which
express the pathos of his frustrating attempts to gain the aid of friends in
the effort, even if only after death, which proved to be the case. And
Hume gave deliberate attention to the artistic aspects of his later works,
in the belief that one of the reasons for the failure of the *Treatise of Human
Nature* lay in its aesthetic inadequacies. (See n. 6, below.)

The important point is that in electing the dialogue form for a work of
such significance to him, Hume chose to produce this artifact, the
Dialogues, under the concept of art, and other features are thus involved.
First, works of art are characterized by certain kinds of differentiation
among their elements. Such features, when used recurrently, constitute
form or structure. Given a type of formal arrangement, the elements
require each other. (Any complex object, of course, has internal differentiation). The most general formal unities lie in what I shall call
structures, following Beardsley. In literary works these can be divided
into aspects relating to the beliefs and attitudes of the speaker or
speakers. First, there are structures that involve perspectives of place and
time. Then there are those exemplifying changes in the beliefs and
attitudes of the speakers; changes relating to logical or cognitive aspects;
and changes relating to dramatic and expressive aspects. Since the
Dialogues make up an episodic, fictional narrative, these elements are
related sequentially as well as logically—and thus will be called "developmental sequences." I will also make use of some other analytical
devices, again appropriating Beardsley's terms. Thus I will make a
distinction between implicit and explicit speakers, and between primary

and secondary (implicit) meaning, often embodied in abstract argument. [4] In the *Dialogues* a set of explicit arguments and beliefs are set out, in a series of linked episodes, by a group of explicit speakers. By processes of abstraction we can discover an implicit argument that is not wholly identical with any explicit ones, and an implicit speaker not identical with any one of the explicit speakers. I hope to identify both the implicit argument and the implicit speaker with David Hume. Indeed, among the things a literary analysis of the *Dialogues* should make plain is that a number of common problems with respect to their interpretation are linked to the attempt to identify Hume's beliefs with one or the other of the explicit speakers.

A number of other formal features, of varying degrees of importance, can be discovered in the *Dialogues*. First, they exemplify the Neoclassical unities of place (Cleanthes' library), and time (one day). Second, and more importantly, they exemplify the classical complex plot structure—scenes of recognition and reversal of situation. Each character is forced to recognize deficiencies in his argument, and to make accommodations that may be characterized as reversals of a logical or conceptual situation. Such defeats and changes, of course, characteristically involve surprise and other emotional accompaniments.

One of the most interesting formal features is the "adversarial" model or paradigm that, in tandem with the other formal devices, governs the dramatic as well as the logical or cognitive flow of the episodes. Sometimes called the "strife" model—its origins are shrouded in antiquity— it has been deeply involved in the intellectual presuppositions of western culture, from the Socratic dialogues, through scholasticism, Hobbes, Darwin, Hegel, Marx, to the modern concept of the competitive free-market system. The characters in the *Dialogues* may thus be viewed as adversaries, since therein each puts forth claims and is attacked or supported by one or more of the others. Each contestant can win, lose, or draw with one or more of the others; and can do so by more or less—that is, the contest is dimensional (which again relates to the emotive-expressive potential of the form); there is a sort of "natural" set of options, which are higher or lower on the scale of emotive intensity, in relation to the images and other expressive devices. It is important to be clear on this point; the model carries expressive capacities by virtue of its form. Understood by author and reader alike, it thus serves to focus attention, and generates feelings of excitement, anticipation, frustration, depression, satisfaction. The deep Hegelian ironies consequent on the use of this and other formal devices in the *Dialogues* are profound and unsettling.[5] No character wins much, and each loses a great deal; and thus, at the close of the discussion, the atmosphere of Cleanthes' library is laden with exasperation. This inconclusiveness of arguments and ideas, their tendency to generate contrariety and contradiction, is characteristic of certain aspects of philosophical thought. These large-scale elements of form are supported by a number of "small-scale" formal devices. Irony, imagery, diction, metaphor, are implemented as recurrent elements, mainly for expressive purposes. They help to tie positive or negative emotional associations to arguments and related claims. Demea is horrified, for instance, (as would be any orthodox Christian), by the image of a bumbling God producing the world by means of sexual intercourse.

The cognitive aspect of the work, the message or messages, is contained partly in the logical or conceptual developmental structure. The expressive and emotive aspects relate to the propositional content, the claims and counterclaims of the logical structure, and to the small-scale devices of irony, imagery, etc. As noted above, the adversarial model itself carries emotive force. Thus the emotive and expressive features are viewed as functions of the descriptive features of the cognitive materials, and of the formal features as well. Taken together, there is the rise and fall, the development and resolution of tensions, that we designate "dramatic sequence."

Now what do we hope to gain by this aesthetic analysis of the *Dialogues*? I can here only block them in. First, I hope to show that both the cognitive and emotive features of the *Dialogues*, including the explicit and implicit proposals and endorsements Hume makes therein, can only be understood by viewing the *Dialogues* as a work of art. Second, I think that it shows, as conclusively as this sort of thing can be shown, that Hume's thoughts and attitudes toward theology and religion, particularly natural theology and natural religion, cannot be identified with those of any one of the explicit speakers, such as Philo or Cleanthes. Rather, they must be identified with those of an implicit speaker, and the concept of an implicit speaker is a function of suggested or implicit meaning. And this last, of course, is a concept of art and aesthetics. I will also argue to a number of points relating to the general theses just set out, among them that Hume showed in the *Dialogues* that certain philosophical, theological, and religious concepts are dialectical — that is, that they generate counterexamples in virtue of their conceptual structure, if they are applied in certain ways. (Kant, of course, who cannot have not been influenced by the *Dialogues*, called these phenomena "antinomies"). I will attempt to show that Hume considered belief in a designer-cause (although one almost vacuous in content), like belief in the uniformity of nature and the existence of external objects, to be based upon common sense natural propensities, an instinct of sorts.

Perspectival Elements

I will begin with a brief consideration of the perspectival structure. I have noted that Hume employed the Neoclassical unities of place and time. He was familiar with the main dramatic fashions of his time.[6] He held to a "sentiment" theory in terms of beauty and aesthetic experience; and "moderation" in regard to rules of decorum and art. Philosophically, Hume was in the empirical tradition, and was conversant with the main philosophical theories, both ancient and modern. He was interested in the new natural sciences, epitomized in Newton; and he reflected extensively over the relation of scientific methods to epistemological problems, and over the exploitations of Newtonian and other scientific ideas by theologians. Excluding Pamphilus, the youthful narrator, each of the characters in the *Dialogues* exemplifies a set of opinions and attitudes, philosophical and theological, that were common at the time. Demea is orthodox in religion, and essentially a continental rationalist in philosophy. Cleanthes is more open-minded about religion and of an "accurate philosophical turn of mind." He represents "Newtonian" theism and the empirical philosophical traditions of Locke, Butler, and Hume himself. Philo is a "careless" skeptic, appearing to oscillate in his arguments between extreme and mitigated skepticism, rooted in both ancient and modern concepts (Pyrrho and Descartes); and, of course, he also represents Hume's empiricism. It is important to understand that Hume was able to express his attitudes, beliefs, emotions, in the *Dialogues* in part only because he had these conceptual repertories available to him. In order to understand him, to recapitulate his thoughts and related feelings, the reader must also have an understanding of them. The analogy here is to other arts. The repertory of an abstract expressionist, say for example Hans Hofmann, includes such things as the use of each of the prime colors in each of his paintings, the use of contrasting warm and cold hues in order to produce a "push-pull" effect; the combination for contrast of flat, hard-edge rectangles with loose, spontaneous swings and splashes. One must be able to perceive these elements, and their positive and negative relations to the traditions of modern art, in order to understand what he is about. The adversarial dialogue form, the ironies, the clustering of visually oriented images, the satire, the philosophical conceptions of impressions and ideas, the modes of skepticism, were bequeathed to Hume in part by his tradition; of course, as was the case with Hofmann, he uses them in his unique way and varies their interrelations in creative combinations.

First Developmental Sequence

In this analysis, I will assume familiarity with Chapter 9 of this book.[7] Thus I will not repeat quotations except in those cases in which I neglected ideas I now believe to be important. I will develop the logical relations in terms of three intersecting aspects: (1) The ways in which the statements of the speakers, implicit and explicit, are related by implication, contradiction, assertion, denial, etc., and (2) the basic thread of the argument, including aspects relating to the existence and nature of God and to the types of argument and evidence involved. This "abstracted" argument, which I will also call the "implicit argument," as noted above, is implied by the statements of the explicit speakers taken together, but is not necessarily identical with those of any of them. This "dialectical flow" constitutes what might be called the secondary meaning, the implicit meaning, of the *Dialogues*. (3) I will argue that this implicit argument, and the related beliefs, are those of the implicit speaker.

In Part I, we will remember, the discussants set out, consequent on preliminary civilities and initial skirmishing, the ground rules of the discussion. The kinds of reasoning to be employed are to be those of ordinary life and the sciences; and thus, although Demea and Philo cannot resist belittling reason, all hands agree to resist the "abstruse" and "refined" reasonings of unmitigated skepticism—in the main because its conclusions are inconsistent with the presuppositions of action. Thus here, as in the *Treatise* and the *Enquiry*, belief in the reality of the external world and the uniformities of nature is held to be irresistible, and is presupposed by action. The irresistibility of these beliefs is due, in Hume's view, to natural propensities or instincts, and the beliefs are the product therefore of neither matter-of-fact experimental reasoning about causal relations, nor of unaided (demonstrative) reasoning. The contestants also agree, as we have noted, to discuss the nature, and not the existence, of God.

Given these ground rules, Cleanthes with gusto delivers the design argument. It is held that the world and its parts are machines. Both feature orderly relations or design, and both feature purposive or means-ends relations—"adjustments." (Any scientific law exhibits order.) The world and its parts are similar to human artifacts, "contrivancies"—"resemble them exactly"—and therefore share with them a further characteristic observed in connection with, as a cause of, human artifacts—wisdom, intelligence, thought. Taking into consideration the several statements made by Cleanthes, science is held to contribute to this theological enterprise in two ways: (a) its inductive and experimental (a posteriori) methods; and (b) knowledge of the orderly relations (causal, mechanical, purposive), among objects in the world and its parts. Cleanthes thus seeks to exploit Newtonian science for theological and religious purposes. The argument rests, of course, upon Hume's principle of induction, that "like objects, plac'd in like circumstances, will always produce like effects."[8]

The argument runs as follows. In cases a_1 a_2 a_3 human machines have been observed to (x) exhibit order, (y) means-ends adjustment, (z) intelligence as a cause. Thus (probably) any (A) objects that exhibit order and means-ends adjustments (x,y) have intelligence (z) as a cause. The world and its parts (B) are very similar to human contrivances with respect to x and y (order and adjustment), and therefore (probably) are z (have an intelligent cause). Both premises, in that they rest on limited observations and admit of "contrary" instances, are probable. Thus the argument concludes that there is, probably, a designer-cause of the world characterized by human intelligence, wisdom, great power, and (by courtesy at this point) beneficence and goodness, beauty, justice, compassion, mercy—the standard Christian tenets regarding God's character. A further part of Cleanthes' argument is that it is an instance of a posteriori (Newtonian) scientific methods—since it explains something by showing it to be an instance of an inductively or experimentally established law. Finally, it assumes that the degree of conviction ("vivacity") of a belief should be proportioned to the evidence (repetition, degree of similarity).

In our "adversarial" sense, Cleanthes has made his move in the contest, and the reader, a complicitor in such practices, is excited with anticipation, whether an orthodox believer or a Newtonian natural theologian. The attack, as we know, comes quickly in Part II, and is generally conceded to be devastating. It begins with Demea, who complains that the argument only affords probability (he desires certitude), and that it predicates of God the anthropomorphic traits of men—intelligence, etc. For orthodox Christians this demeans God, makes Him unworthy of worship and adoration, a major future problem for Demea and Cleanthes. Cleanthes, it should be noted, is satisfied, though not joyous, with this situation. But, as we have seen, Philo is not so kind. He attacks both premises of Cleanthes' argument. Abstracted from Philo's statements, the outline of his argument is: (a) the similarities between men's contrivances and the world and its parts are quite weak (hence affording very low probability); and (b) the presupposed general causal laws, which require the repeated observation of the conjunction of the objects (classes of objects) are lacking. In other words, the causes have not, as required by such argument, been observed. This is "regular" Newtonian experimental reasoning about causes and effects, as designated by Hume. The order and adjustments of human machines, for example, have been observed in innumerable instances to have been produced by intelligent human contrivers, but no one has observed the origin of worlds. Thus, although the point does not arise at this particular place, the argument must be considered to be an "irregular" causal argument, in which only resemblance, but not constant conjunction, holds (T. 142–50, 192–98, 203–15, 242, 269–73). Thus since there is limited similarity, while it affords a low probability that the world has an intelligent designer, attribution of other traditional Christian traits of God are suspect; and the claim that the design argument is an instance of scientific method is completely refuted. Since this critical argument is later accepted by Cleanthes, it can be conceived, in the abstract, as one part of the view of the implicit speaker. It is, of course, part of the abstracted argument. The "irregular" character of the design argument will occupy us again shortly. It has not received the attention it deserves.

So—Cleanthes is now on the ropes: devotees of Newtonian design theology are shocked; unmitigated skeptics, agnostics, atheists are pleased; the orthodox, along with Demea, are ambivalent and anxious. As Philo points out (D. 24) they wish for certain reasons to be mystics, but nevertheless they are displeased by the failure of theistic proofs. The uncommitted probably enjoy the show, and with excitement await Cleanthes' response, for he appears to have lost the major elements of his argument—that is, both the proof of a designer-cause, and the claim to a scientific methodology.

He responds (in Part III) with a reformulated argument, which I had noted, but had not clearly understood when I wrote the first edition of this book.[9] And commentators still find this section puzzling and controversial. As will become more clear as we proceed, a considerable amount of the puzzle follows from the failure to see that the dialectical and adversarial form requires at this place a recognition scene, and the beginning of a reversal of situation, for Philo as well as for Cleanthes. There is a kind of preamble, as usual, that helps to set the stage for a recurrent theme of the *Dialogues,* in both the dramatic and cognitive senses. Cleanthes complains that Philo's position is that of an unmitigated skeptic, producing the kinds of "cavils" and "abstruse reasoning" that were ruled out of the game at its beginning. And he says that he will not seek to refute Philo by "serious argument" (D. 33–34), but rather by examples and instances. The first goes as follows.

> Suppose, therefore, that an articulate voice were heard in the clouds, much louder and more melodious . . . and spoke to each nation in its own language and dialect . . . [and] the words . . . not only contain a just sense and meaning . . . (but) instruction altogether worthy of a benevolent Being superior to mankind — could you possibly hesitate a moment concerning the cause of this voice, and must you not instantly ascribe it to some design or purpose? (D. 34)

We infer to an intelligent mind as cause when we hear an articulate voice speak understandable utterances. And we would do so in the above case, although the degree of loudness, and other aspects, would make the object much dissimilar to an instance of human speech. A second example, of a library of vegetable books, is similar in purport. It also is related to language, although of the written variety, and inference by analogy to an unobserved cause. Cleanthes next brings forth the example of the anatomy of the eye (D. 36), and claims that the belief in the "idea" of a contriver in this case (and that of the mechanics of sexual procreation) is even more forceful than would be the heavenly voice and vegetable library. He uses one further example in this section: the fact that "Some beauties in writing" we meet with seem "contrary to rules, and gain the affections and animate the imagination in opposition to all the precepts of criticism." (Serious arguments seem to be those that conform to the rules of matter of fact or demonstrative reasoning.) Even if the argument is contrary to the principles of logic, says Cleanthes, "its universal, its irresistible influence" proves clearly that there may be arguments of a "like irregular nature." Further, were Philo not to suppress his natural good sense by abstruse philosophy, he would agree (D. 36–37). We have already noticed that Cleanthes consistently attempts to identify Philo with the abstruse cavils of the absolute skeptics. At this point the explicit narrator, Pamphilus, states that Philo is embarrassed and confused (D. 37).

It is of great importance that we see that the dramatic as well as the logical or cognitive sequence of the *Dialogues*—*i.e.,* the climax, the resolution (for the time being) of the tension—requires that this formulation of the design argument by Cleanthes in Part III be different and not just a repetition of that of Part II. The recognition and reversal of situation of the plot demand it, and the dialectical character of the cognitive elements demand it—each of the cognitive positions generates its contradiction. Philo says we do not experience the cause; Cleanthes says, "Look round the world. . . . force like that of sensation"; in other words, he appeals to experience. Cleanthes' argument must serve several purposes. It must be of such a logical nature that it (a) responds in some way or ways to Philo's critique; and it (b) should explain Philo's embarrassment and confusion; and, finally, (c) it should set the stage for the following cognitive and dramatic sequence. My view is that the reformulated argument involves an appeal to natural propensity, or natural instinct; and does so in a way analogous to the views found in the *Treatise* and the *Enquiry Concerning Human Understanding.* There, the "careless" and "inattentive" skeptic finds belief in the existence of the external world and in the uniformities among its objects to be irresistible. Such beliefs are matters of "primitive," "natural instinct," based on "irregular" causal arguments. My position on this matter has in part been anticipated and supported, originally, I think, by R. J. Butler; and also by Nelson Pike.[10] (D. 224–29, Pike's commentary, which has been invaluable to me.) Something similar has been supported, tentatively, by Penelhum. (See n. 10, above). Opponents of the view are J. C. A. Gaskin,[11] and Pheroze Wadia.[12]

There are several important aspects of this rendition of the argument. First, notice that Cleanthes has reached back to the ground rules set out in the beginning—a person may not use abstruse caviling argument in order to refute beliefs resting on commonsense irresistibility; and this irresistibility rests on (a) the necessities of action, and (b) the fact that denial of the beliefs produces "great violence" to natural propensities. I do not as yet clearly understand how this latter notion is related to or distinguished from "irresistibility," *i.e.,* self-evidence, or the "vivacity" of an idea or impression.

These "natural propensities" have an important place in Hume's general position with regard to skepticism (T. 183–87; E. 151, 158–65). In the *Treatise,* (T. 242, 150, 195–97) in relation to possible knowledge of an unperceived immaterial soul (or external objects), Hume points up that only by means of an argument of an *irregular* kind (my italics) can reason discover anything independent of impressions, and in a footnote the reader is referred back to Section 2 of Book I. And what we find there is Hume's consideration of cases of imperfect causal reasonings, based on ideas derived from consistency and coherence. One of the main issues there considered concerns the existence of external objects and relations that can be thought of as causes of our impressions (taken as effects). Now proper reasoning concerning causes and effects requires, by the rules, that *both* be repeatedly experienced in conjunction. And external objects are not experienced independently of the impressions they thus seek to explain. And yet, the vulgar, and those who hold to common sense, presuppose, to the contrary, that there are such independent objects, with uniform relationships, that cause our impressions (T. 193, 269–73). Such beliefs appear, on skeptical philosophical grounds, to be unreasonable. What is it that causes people to believe in the existence of objects, and in their uniform relationships, which are external to our sense impressions? Imagination, Hume informs us (T. 150, 193, 197–215, 242). We experience consistency and coherence in our impressions—and upon this basis imagination produces, by a kind of reasoning about causation, the opinion that they have continued independent existence (T. 195–98). Such inferences appear to be like regular reasonings concerning causes and effects, that is, based on resemblance, and "derived from custom, and regulated by past experiences"[13] (T. 197). But they are not—this kind of "inference arises from the understanding, and from custom in an indirect and oblique manner" (T. 197). It is interesting, since one of our quotations relates to the arts, that in *Of the Standard of Taste* Hume talks of "irregular writers" (poets) who transgress the "rules of art." And when they do so, it is because the "force of these beauties" in their works has the power to overcome censure.[14]

Very well, an irregular argument, since it is an inference to a cause in which the cause is not an instance of an experienced object, or a member of a class of experienced objects, is not therefore an argument that qualifies as experimental, or scientific, or reasonable. But it may be the kind of argument that seeks to establish the existence of the exterior world of nature and the uniformity of nature, which Hume has said are beliefs rooted in irresistible natural instincts. Hume notes that as resemblance between objects is diminished, the force and vivacity of the impression is weakened, and, of course, so is that of the related reasoning. There are also "unphilosophical probabilities," reasonings that tend to produce errors. Among them are those derived from general rules supporting prejudices (T. 147). Like all judgments of cause and effect, they too are rooted in custom. Where the imagination moves from experienced objects and limited similarity to causes, the imperfect analogical reasoning, referred to above, comes into play.

And so Cleanthes' second argument appears to be an instance of an irregular argument and to conclude in a belief whose source is similar to those concerning external objects and their uniformities. What does Hume say further about these beliefs in the *Treatise* and the *Enquiry,* and are the views expressed there of any help with respect to understanding the reformulated argument in Part III of the Dialogues? In the *Treatise* and the *Enquiry,* Hume claims that such skeptical doubts are overcome by carelessness and inattention. "Carelessness and inattention alone can afford us any remedy. For this reason alone I rely entirely upon them" (T. 218, 273). Carelessness here relates to one's not carrying skeptical principle through in practical life. This is of interest because we will recall that Philo is introduced as a "careless skeptic." And in the *Enquiry* (156), such a "careless" view is a matter of common life. It seems that "carelessness" and "inattention" are not, thus, general features of skepticism, but rather relate to the failure consistently to carry skeptical principles over into practical life.

Indeed, as Hume said, one cannot do so and continue to exist. In the words of Cleanthes, Philo will leave through the door and not the window. He will, in other words, act as if nature is uniform and admits of laws. If we did not have such propensities, we would perish (E. 38, 40–41, 151, 158–65. T. 183–87). "The great subvertor of Pyrrhonism or the excessive principles of skepticism is action, and employment, and the occupations of common life" (E. 158–59). Since nature is so obstinate, and skepticism cannot produce conviction, Hume follows his desires, and dines, plays cards, converses with friends as if the doubts are unfounded (T. 269).

There is another very interesting point in connection with these examples. It was noted by Pike, whose view in relation to it is rejected by Wadia and Gaskin. Pike notes, rightly I think, that the "linguistic" examples are unusual. Hume had in other places cited reasoning about the relation between a voice heard and a person as its cause as an example of causal reasoning (E. 27, 50). In these examples both the sounds (effects) and the persons (causes) and their relations are items of repeated prior experience—a situation that does not obtain where the cause inferred is a designer-God. What makes these examples unusual, as Pike notes, is that the relation between heard or read sentences, understood in accordance with shared rules of grammar and vocabulary, is noncontingent (criterial). When we so hear or read, we do in a sense "know" in a "self-evident" manner that the source (if not the cause—controversy abounds here) is an intelligent mind. Thus Cleanthes (Hume) is in a sense correct in these examples; but, unfortunately, the relationship is intentional and nonextensional (intensional), and therefore the propositions which designate such relations do not qualify as instances of the kind of scientific reasoning relating to causes that Cleanthes desires. Pike suggests that Cleanthes might agree with viewing this as a "criterial" relation. Wadia thinks, rightly I suppose from a psychological standpoint, that Cleanthes (Hume?) would be baffled by the notion.[15] It would certainly create a problem for Hume, whose view is that the relation between causes and effects is independent, or, as we would say, external and contingent; it cannot be a "relation of ideas." I think it does not matter whether Hume or Cleanthes would be baffled, any more than it would matter that Shakespeare would be baffled by the claim that Iago in *Othello* exhibits homosexual traits.

Would it be appropriate to *interpret* Cleanthes' examples as indicating that the second formulation of the design argument involves a noncontingent relationship between the premises and the conclusion? Would it be appropriate to interpret Iago's behavior toward Desdemona as motivated by homosexual urges? These are interesting questions. It is argued by some modern aestheticians that since works of art are type objects, there may be an essentially ineliminable element of interpretation involved in their explication. The aspects of this view can only be suggested here. It appears to be true that (tokens of the) performing arts (drama, opera, music) must, by the nature of the type-token relation involved, admit or tolerate predication of non-necessary properties, *i.e.*, properties in excess of those necessarily predicated of the type object. If, as is often argued, the concepts employed in understanding *any* work of art constitute something analogous to a performance, then it is quite possible that any work of art may be subject to incompatible (contrary or contradictory) interpretations, each of which is consistent with the minimal (factually) descriptive features predicable of the work, and thus ineliminable. Works of art are continually seen from new points of view. Hume's *Dialogues Concerning Natural Religion* is a type object, and is a dramatic narrative, etc. These considerations suggest that it *may* be the case that the controversies over the interpretation of the *Dialogues* are related to the fact that the *Dialogues* is a work of art, and may, quite appropriately, be ineliminable.[16]

I must apologize for what may appear to be an extended digression; it is not. The philosophical analysis of these passages from Hume supports the contention that a shift in the argument is demanded by the formal and expressive character of the *Dialogues* as a work of art. The dramatic sequence of the first developmental sequence shows a climax at the end of Part III, and this implies that the revised design argument there mounted by Cleanthes, and which countered Philo's criticisms of the first formulation, is necessitated by the logic of the dramatic concepts involved, which also set in motion a new dramatic and logical sequence.

This interpretation is often denied. Gaskin, for instance, claims that the reformulated argument does not exemplify an appeal to an instinctive propensity or instinct. He systematically sets out the criteria for natural propensities found in Hume as follows: Such a belief is one of naive common sense; it must lack rational foundation; the belief is unavoidable in the crucial sense that no one could *act* in the world if he lacked the belief; it must be universally held. Gaskin holds that the application of the first criterion to the issue is indecisive. The second is contingent on the outcome of some of the other criteria. The application of the third and fourth criteria, he believes, leads to the conclusion that belief in a designer is not, in Hume's opinion (as set out in the *Dialogues*) a natural instinct or propensity. [17] His argument is, essentially, that the criterion of action is crucial; that it simply is not necessary to believe in an intelligent designer-God in order to act in the world; and that belief is necessary with respect to the uniformity of nature, and the existence of the external world of objects. Despite my deep respect for Gaskin's book—it is superb—I think he is mistaken on this very tricky issue. First, I think the irresistibility criterion is slighted in his treatment; but I have not the space to pursue the point, and it is not in his view the crucial one. But I believe that his argument concerning the relation of action to belief in a designer suffers from a key ambiguous term: *God*. I think his argument depends for its force upon using the term *God* with an essentially orthodox meaning—a person with powers, intelligence, etc. And of course we need not believe in such a being in relation to our actions in the way we need to believe in the uniformity of nature—in relation to prediction and expectation, for instance. But this is not the meaning the word *God* has at the end of the third dialogue. In the conclusion reached in the abstract or implicit argument at the end of Part III, *God* means only a cause remotely analogous to human intelligence; and the content of that intelligence is "adjustment," or means-ends relations. And I submit that belief in such means-ends relations in regard to natural processes, including the remote and proximate causal conditions thereof, does in fact require belief with respect to action. Could we act as if the heart does not pump blood, or that food nourishes, with any more success than we could deny that natural processes are uniform? Indeed, are not such means-ends relations simply species of such uniformities? Gaskin does not characterize *action* precisely enough. He characterizes *action* in relation to such things as belief in the uniformity of nature in the following way: "no one can act in the world if he lacks this belief?" And, "only too clearly men can and do live in a coherent and successful manner without belief in God."[18] But if God is identified with means-ends and process-product relationships in nature, then this is no more true of Cleanthes' God than it is of the uniformity of nature. After all, people *can* act against the uniformity of nature in the relevant sense: it is simply that, as Hume says, if they do so they will perish. The necessity of the beliefs is hypothetical; it is not "you cannot act against the uniformity of nature"; rather, it is "if you act against the uniformity of nature you will perish."

To return to the dramatic aspects of the *Dialogues*. It is important for us to realize that as it stands at the end of III, the abstract argument leaves much unsettled, since neither the design argument nor its refutation has clear command of the philosophical field. This reflects the fact that while one of the explicit speakers, Cleanthes, has not as yet received a response, or been refuted, it may yet come, and be conclusive. Thus, if we take the implicit speaker to reflect the unresolved opposing views, then he may be said to be cognitively as well as emotively ambivalent.

Formal Elements

Cleanthes has now thrown down the gauntlet, and we prepare for another round in the contest. He has won inasmuch as his reformed argument evokes no response from Philo, and a response from Demea does not refute his argument. Philo has won in that he has forced Cleanthes to give up the scientific pretentions of the design argument, and to appeal in their place to a kind of irresistible impulse. Demea seems to have gained the (probable) existence of God; but the gain is burdened with realization that the God so proved has unwanted features. Cleanthes, however, has lost the aspect of the design argument that gave it most of its force with eighteenth-century thinkers—its claimed affinity with Newtonian and other natural sciences. Philo has lost in that he has not convincingly refuted one limited form of the design argument. And he is forced to face the rejection of the suspension of belief that he had early recommended. Cleanthes has lost, by implication, something more. The limited scope of the reformulated design argument affords him no support for the attribution to the deity of the features Christians traditionally associate with it. And he had, in Part II, laid claim to some of them.

In terms of complexity of plot, therefore, Cleanthes and Philo have come to recognition scenes and related reversals. Cleanthes is forced to recognize that his argument is not a species of science and changes his argument. Philo, in that he does not (and will not) respond to the second formulation of the argument, recognizes that his skeptical arguments are not convincing in the face of natural propensities, and he changes the direction of the argument to the nature, as distinct from the existence, of God. And, as we know, he later reverses his situation and accepts the design argument.

Small-scale formal elements, as should be expected, parallel the larger ones. Images are introduced that will recur throughout the work. Receiving considerable attention are examples drawn from the sciences. Great scientists like Newton, Galileo, Copernicus, are repeatedly cited, together with famous ideas and discoveries, viz., circulation of the blood, the planetary systems, the mechanics of the eye. Also introduced are footprints, sexual reproduction, light, watches, houses. Machines in general are cited: the metaphor of the machine is omnipresent. These examples, ideas, images are for the most part used as positively or negatively charged emotive terms in order to associate the successes of science with whatever claim that is being made. Many of the images associated with God, however, are emotively negative, a feature increasing in intensity as the discussion proceeds. There is the recurrent characterization, attached both explicitly and implicitly to Philo, of the skeptic as deceitful—a caviler, a user of abstruse reasoning, a railer. Sooner or later, however, the ironies implicit in the concepts involved in the argument make it possible for each contestant to be charged with skepticism. Another recurrent image is that of the "vulgar," the common herd, characterized by ignorance, superstition, enthusiasm, unreflective action; and yet rightly resistant to extreme skepticism—again the irony. The scientific allusions are presented as positive, as good, praiseworthy, both in terms of scientific methods, which are taken as paradigmatic of good reasoning, and as derived information or knowledge. The "vulgar" views are often (but not always) presented as paradigmatic of bad reasoning. Other negative images are: absolute skepticism, with its cavils, and railery; superstition, enthusiasm, dogmatism (people who resist the "irresistible"); orthodox religion, priests, monks. All these attach negative emotive force to anything with which they are associated. Natural instincts, natural dispositions, common sense, are (usually) good.

Some interesting ironies have emerged; and they have, as expected, both cognitive and emotive aspects. The experimental methods of Cleanthes are used against him, as is the criterion of analogy—and such reversals will continue through the discussion. To set out some paradoxes: Cleanthes' method and criterion both prove and do not prove his case. Philo's "unmitigated" skepticism is shown to be a "mitigated" skepticism. Demea has an argument that implies something about the nature of God—intelligence—but it proves human, rather than the desired divine intelligence. One of the most pathetic ironies afflicts Demea and the orthodox, who wish to walk a tight line between predicating human properties of the divine, and thus losing the feature of divine transcendence and perfection, and not so predicating them, and thus making it (by implication) impossible to know God. Thus the orthodox, and Demea, wish to both predicate and not predicate things of God. We have the Hegelian vision of methodological and other conceptual categories that, when employed, produce counterexamples by virtue of their very structure. It is also quite difficult not to see Hegelian and Kantian antinomies herein. [19] Clearly, one of the main frustrations of the implicit speaker is that if one attempts to employ regular inductive causal reasoning in the explanation and proofs of objects and processes that are unobservable in principle, then one can, so to speak, prove or disprove the same claims or propositions. The explicit speakers appear to prove what is the case only at the cost of proving something they do not want to prove, or more or less than they want to prove. The propositions that their methods and arguments prove are not the propositions they wish to prove; and the propositions they wish to prove are not those that they are able by such arguments to prove.

The formal elements of the first dramatic sequence of the *Dialogues* indicate, profoundly, the dialectical nature and the related emotional associations of the metaphysical and theological issues involved. As Hume said at the beginning through Pamphilus, the issues are such that "human reasons can reach no fixed determination" with regard to them. Notice how the affirmations and denials of the propositional content of the claims, the successes and failures of the adversaries in relation to these logical sequences, the recognition and reversals of situation—how all conspire in this dialectical process. But at this place, the important point is to see the ways in which the artistic form of the *Dialogues exhibits* these features. Philosophy and art coincide.

Expressive Elements

At this stage Cleanthes and the design theologians have been whip-sawed. The large-scale form is expressive, in the main, of inconclusive-ness, frustration, dissatisfaction. In a dialogue, the emotive and express-ive elements tend to follow the give and take of the argument, *i.e.,* the cognitive or propositional content, as reflected in the constituent beliefs, affirmations, denials, and the formal interrelationships. In the adversa-rial situation, both Cleanthes and Philo have been on top and on the bottom. Each, along with readers who share their views, has won a round, with its attendant pleasures, and lost a round, with its frustra-tions; and each has a remaining bit of success. The unpleasantness, however, outweighs the pleasantness, because the losses so outweigh the gains. A draw, of course, is in most cases less than satisfactory. If we think of the views of the implicit speaker as in part those of Cleanthes, the loss of the claimed scientific support for the design argument is profound; for after a period of joyous optimism its proponents find their beliefs back among those tagged as irrational, or, at best, nonrational. It is easy to see why Hume, while rejecting absolute skepticism, excited such a high degree of negative feelings. On the other hand, the skeptic is similarly unhappy; although, since his views are perhaps less widely held, fewer followers are made unhappy. And if we think of the views of the implicit speaker as being in part identified with those of Philo, then the inability to refute the design argument conclusively leaves open the possibility that it will provide a support to the hated superstition and enthusiasm. Similar emotive elements can be related to the complexities of plot— each figure, as we have seen, has realized a failure, and either has made, or will make, a change in his stance. In both kinds of situation, there is dissatisfaction. Frustration is the standard.

The emotive and expressive aspects indicated above in relation to large-scale formal elements are supported strongly by the small-scale elements: the metaphor, imagery, irony. Irony in itself almost epito-mizes inconclusiveness. It here relates in the main to the inability to confirm or disprove a proposition, or to both the affirmation and denial of the same proposition. It also involves the inability to clearly satisfy or frustrate a desire; and in relation to the subjects of the *Dialogues,* there is the sense in which the same idea both supports and refutes the same religious or philosophical interests. The images of science and skepticism—the attractive and approved as against the negative and suspicious—carry positive and negative emotive freight to the persons and opinions to which they are attached. Deceitfulness is thus tied to Philo, confusion to Cleanthes, and vulgar superstition and mysticism to Demea.

Second Developmental Sequence

The second sequence begins with Demea. It will be recalled that Philo has not responded to the second formulation of the design argument. Demea concurs to a degree with Cleanthes' bizarre examples, even amplifies a bit the "linguistic" analogy. He is still troubled, however, by the attribution of human properties to God. This (repeated) reversion to mysticism provokes Cleanthes into the charge that such a view is scarcely different from skepticism and atheism, and Demea turns on him with some asperity. Tempers have heated up. The exchange focuses attention on problems relating to God's nature—how the (remote) designer may be characterized. This shift in attention sets the main issues for the remainder of the *Dialogues,* and provides an appropriate place for Philo to reenter the debate. A series of arguments ensues in which Philo makes use of the same methods employed by Cleanthes in the design argument in order to deduce a series of conclusions inimical to some of the basic tenets of traditional Christianity.

He begins with the proposition that causal arguments based on analogy cannot assign more features to the inferred cause than are discovered in the effect, a proviso Cleanthes cannot reject, for, as we have seen, there is no direct experience of a designer. Given this criterion, a number of things follow in short order. The causing mind cannot be (known to be) infinite, cannot be perfect, may be due to trial and error, may not be unitary (there may be more than one God), may be one of a family of mortal Gods, may be physical. In Parts VI–VIII, Philo pursues similar analogies. The world is as easily compared to organisms as machines, which suggests a God as a kind of world-soul. The world may be conceived as produced by vegetative seeds, or by sexual intercourse. It might even have been produced by a chance concourse of atoms—the order we discern, in other words, may be only a preserving force. None of these cosmic hypotheses destroys Cleanthes' position, but neither is it superior to theirs. At the end of VII, Cleanthes grants that he cannot counter the arguments, but repeats the antiskeptical point that such arguments ("whimsies") may puzzle but never convince. By the end of VIII, Cleanthes is down again; and Demea is very anxious, since Philo's arguments indicate that the world may not require a cause.

In IX, Demea, in despair, introduces the cosmological argument; and Cleanthes, joined by Philo, (who here deserts Demea), flattens it with Hume's "fork." One cannot prove matters of fact a priori, as the argument attempts to do, and it also fails to satisfy matter of fact empirical criteria. (See *Treatise,* Book I, Part III; and *Enquiry,* XII, Part III). This failure forces Demea in frustration and defense to return to an ancient but dangerous position: that religious belief arises from, and responds to, the inner needs of man, generated by human misery and helplessness. And with this the stage is set for the most signal indignity to be heaped upon orthodox religious beliefs — the view that even if we assume the existence of a designer-God, *it* may be nonmoral, or partly moral, or even morally malevolent. At this point Demea, having lost his ally, Philo, and able to protect neither his argument nor his view of God, leaves in disgust. Now what has happened in this sequence is clear. The abstract argument has reduced the meaningful content of the design argument to almost nothing, in terms of the nature of God. While it is still admitted that there is a low probability that the cause of the world is analogous to the mind of man, this affords practically no support to traditional Christianity. In essence, these sections separate God (conceived as a designer-cause) from morality, and this is a key general conclusion of the abstracted argument of this developmental sequence.

Although they differ in their attitudes toward these conclusions, Philo and Cleanthes in general agree with respect to the cognitive aspects of the abstract argument; and Demea leaves. These shared beliefs, and the related arguments, constitute the suggested or implicit meaning of the *Dialogues,* up to this point. If we take the abstract argument to reflect the conclusions of the implicit speaker, and this to be Hume, Hume rejects the cosmological argument, and rejects the view that the God afforded by the design argument provides a basis for human morality or the values of practical life.

Formal Elements

In the adversarial context of the plot, Philo is for the moment triumphant; Cleanthes is again on the ropes; and Demea has lost out entirely. In terms of complexity of plot, and the flow of dialectic, both Cleanthes and Demea have been forced to recognize the frailties of their views, and have thus suffered reversals in their religious beliefs as well as their emotions. Demea gives up entirely. Cleanthes has found it necessary to give up the Christian linkages of the design argument, including the most important, God as the basis of human morality. It goes almost without saying that the small-scale formal devices of these sections contribute to the cognitive and emotional features. The images of sexual procreation; animal and vegetable causes; and a malevolent, stupid, bungling God are horrifying to Christians. The ironies mount up. Every character, argument, belief is and at the same time is not something. The orthodox Demea's mystical "belief" is actually a result of a species of skepticism. Even Cleanthes is accused of skepticism. The analogical methods both prove and do not prove a God (a good one) in the standard sense. Philo is an ally but not an ally of Demea. All views and methods appear to be retortable upon themselves.

Expressive Elements

Both the large- and small-scale formal devices thus cannot fail, as ways of speaking, to exhibit basic expressive properties, and, by extension, the ideas and views of the implicit speaker.

The adversarial situation expresses frustration and anxiety. Conceptual features of the arguments, both with respect to their propositional content, and their methods, tend to generate counterexamples or absurdities. Neither Demea nor Cleanthes has been able to maintain his position.

This imagery, and the formal elements it supports, indicates deep contempt for orthodox belief in the beneficence or morality of a designer God, for orthodox religion, and for the cosmological argument. Cleanthes, at this point, is not out, but he is down enough for exasperation to show; and given our aesthetic assumptions, we may say that this is probably also true of the implicit speaker, Hume. And we must remember that from the beginning, in the views of both Cleanthes and Philo, there has been frustration, and consequent contempt, for the vagaries of certain types of metaphysical belief and argument. And it must also be kept in mind that the implicit argument (the intersection of the beliefs of Cleanthes and Philo, *i.e.,* the implicit speaker), is still committed to the (minimal) content of the reformulated design argument. In other words, the implicit speaker must yet believe in the remote probability of a stupid, perhaps malevolent, cause of the world. The implicit speaker is in no pleasant situation. In sum, then, at this point the two dramatic sequences express, with powerful paradox, contempt for (a) absolute skepticism in relation to religion; and (b) belief in some of the main tenets of orthodox religion.

Third Developmental Sequence

This sequence contains two main topics, and the first continues to astonish many commentators on the *Dialogues*. First, Philo appears to reverse himself and to join Cleanthes in the acceptance of the design argument. The second is an argument over the issue as to whether religion does or does not provide support for morality and moderation in human behavior. They will be considered in order.

After Cleanthes chides him for extremism, Philo confesses a lack of caution on such matters as religion, because (1) no one of common sense is affected (as before, skepticism does not produce conviction), and (2), people who know him know he is a man of common sense (D. 108). He avows religious belief, and in a long statement, elaborates his reasons for support of the design argument. A purpose, intention, or design strikes everywhere the most "careless, the most stupid thinker," and this cannot be rejected, even by a person hardened in the most "absurd systems." Just reasoning supports belief, and even though the arguments in its support are very weak, and not numerous, the (limited) conclusions so derived deserve "plain, philosophical assent" (D. 123). Astonishment may arise concerning the "greatness of the object," and "contempt" for the inadequacies of reason, and "melancholy" at its obscurity. There is a deep desire for a revelation to end the doubts and obscurities. But "That the works of nature bear a great analogy to the productions of art is evident; and, according to all the rules of good reasoning, we ought to infer, . . . that their causes have a proportionate analogy" (D. 110). Cleanthes agrees, as of course he would; and both share the conviction that withholding judgment on such matters is impossible.

An important idea is introduced here. According to Philo, the differences between them relate to attitudes and not to content, and therefore come to this: Cleanthes emphasizes the potential similarities between the designer's intelligence and that of man, while Philo emphasizes the differences. This kind of disagreement appears to involve assessing degrees of a property, rather than its presence or absence. Nor is verification of such predications possible; and their basis is a limited number of observations, and a limited number of similarities, and therefore there are no clear criteria to be applied in the resolution of the (conceptually necessary) disputes. It is, thus, essentially (in Hume's view) a verbal argument, unresolvable because key terms are, and cannot but be, vague or ambiguous. As with *greatness* and *beauty,* standards vary, and thus "Men may argue to all eternity whether Hannibal be a great, or a very great, or a superlatively great man, what degree of beauty Cleopatra possessed. . ." (D. 111). So, is the intelligence of the designer (the one proved, of course) similar, very similar, or superlatively similar, to the intelligence of men . . . ? This passage ends on an interesting note—again a transition—Philo's remark that he indulges in extreme arguments because to do so is to behave in a way proportionate to the arguments of bigots, and his "abhorrence of vulgar superstitions" (D. 114). In other words, Philo is extreme because he has a profound fear that the design argument will be exploited by the forces of superstition and bigotry.

Cleanthes responds with the statement that even religion so corrupted is better than none at all. He does not respond to the arguments of Philo concerning vagueness. He maintains that religious beliefs, in particular the doctrine of the belief in a future state, are necessary conditions for morality, because earthly rewards and punishments do not provide sufficient ethical motivation (D. 114). And this initiates Philo's last major attack. In a long harangue he iterates a battery of examples of the bad consequences of religious ("vulgar") superstition, ranging over its "dismal" effects in civil governmental affairs, the duplicity of the clergy, the bigoted credulity of the vulgar, and, in particular, the weakening of the "natural motives of justice and humanity" (D. 117). Even the admitted "fits" of joy connected with religious enthusiasm are balanced by the dejection and melancholy commonly associated with the terrors of anticipating the day of judgment. "True religion," of course, does not have such consequences, but then it is not commonly found in the world. Philo leaves few stones of religious horror unturned.

It is apparent that the conclusion of these arguments, taken together with those that came in earlier parts of the dialogues, leaves religion almost empty of significant content. What remains is contained in an ambiguous or undefined proposition "That the cause or causes of order in the universe have some remote analogy to human intelligence." No extensions concerning morality, life, etc., are possible. But, strangely, "To be a philosophical skeptic is, in a man of letters, the first and most essential step towards being a sound, believing, Christian" (D. 123). One must fall prey neither to superstition nor to skepticism. And so the abstract argument, and its constituent propositional contents, comes to its indeterminate, almost vacuous close. It contains the following: (a) There is a belief in the remote probability of the existence of a cause of the world bearing a similarity to human intelligence that is so potentially limited as to be shared with a rotting turnip or the generation of an animal; (b) The cause believed in has neither moral features nor moral implications; (c) Religious beliefs that go beyond this minimal level, such as traditional orthodox superstitions and enthusiasms, are evil in their consequences, not the least of which is the tendency to interfere with the natural sentiments that support reasonable human morality.

Formal Elements

Viewing this segment in terms of the dramatic sequence, with its adversarial content, it is clear that again no explicit character has made significant gains, and each has suffered losses. The last worthwhile traits of the designer-God, belief in whose existence Cleanthes originally sought to justify, are clearly beyond his reach. And therefore, although he has finally exacted concessions from Philo with respect to a designer, they are essentially worthless for Christianity; and he has failed to establish or obtain agreement even to the profoundly important proposition that religion provides sanctioning supports for morality. Philo, on the other hand, has found it necessary to concede that the cause of the world has some remote and perhaps brutal analogy to intelligence. Despite the shared impoverished conclusion, both agree that on such issues, given the many and marvelous adjustments and other orderly relationships of things, suspension of judgment is impossible.

Expressive Elements

The expressive elements tied to these large-scale formal features are relatively clear. No contestant is satisfied; indeed, each is dissatisfied. The conclusions here are even worse than they were at the ends of the other phases of the discussion, and again are productive of frustration and depression. The general tone of Philo's avowal of belief has an air of unreality—the skeptic is not a skeptic after all. But, note, since he grants the essentially vacuous character of the content of the (abstract) argument, Cleanthes is now a skeptic! Indeed, both are "careless" skeptics, by our earlier characterizations. Both accede to the "irresistibility" of the conclusion of an "irregular" argument. In their common acceptance of the limited design argument, they do not carry out the rules of scientific reasoning about causal relations, and they accept the dictates of an "irresistible" natural propensity.

Philo betrays some other concerns. For one thing, he is ambivalent about the implications of even such a limited design argument, for he fears that it might be exploited by orthodoxy, superstition, and enthusiasm—witness his admission with regard to his treatment of Demea. And, as is true of almost any "rational" skeptic-philosopher, he fears placing trust in beliefs founded on "irresistible" impulses, since all such thinking is irregular and unscientific. On the other hand, he cannot completely discount the fact that the religious views of design theologians, subscribers to "true philosophy," are supportive of moderation in all things. In this, again, we see the conflicts, the antinomies, engendered by theological concepts. In effect, we have another "draw," and the characteristic feelings of frustration and dissatisfaction associated with inconclusiveness in relation to important issues and desires.

Small-scale formal elements again share in these expressive labors. The images used by Philo in relation to the final content of the design argument are powerful: "rotting turnips" share with "sexual procreation" some kind of similarity to human intelligence. The negative images used in relation to the bad consequences for humanity of religious belief and institutions are equally strong: vulgarity, deceit and sophistry, zealotry, bigotry, stupidity. None of these characterizations is countered by Cleanthes. On the level of ironies, a very general one comes to rest in this last section. The conclusion of the cognitive content of the abstract argument, the intersection of beliefs about God shared by Philo and Cleanthes, either by avowal or default, differs very little from the "mystery" espoused by Demea, although the adjective *adorable* is beyond salvage for anyone. Religion is good but not good (philosophical, superstitious); the designer is intelligent but not intelligent (a rotting turnip is an "adjustment"). Philo is a "careless" skeptic, but is not a skeptic (he avows the design argument and religious belief). Cleanthes is a believer (in the design argument), but a (careless) skeptic in that for him its content has washed way to near vacuosity. These ironies express the inconclusiveness, the abortiveness, of theological disputes.

The expressive tone of Philo's avowals of belief, and the mass of evidence, repetitive of the material Cleanthes introduced earlier, only to have Philo impugn it, are features of a person who is agreeing to something against his will, with considerable reservations, and without pleasure or joy. This shows in his manner of speaking, his exasperation and frustration at the inconclusiveness of the debate. These feelings also lie at the root of his expressed desire for revelation, since he wishes it in order to resolve the inconclusiveness and to clear up the vaguenesses and ambiguities of the arguments and conclusions. Note that it is a future revelation he wishes for, rather than an endorsement of those of the past, and this desire must therefore be seen in the light of the dilemma formed by the combination of the failure of rational endeavors and the inability to suspend judgment. The elements of Philo's harangue about the evil consequences of religious beliefs and institutions combine to express deep contempt, anger, disgust, even fear, with respect to orthodox religion.

Cleanthes' ways of speaking in this section express the same frustra-tion and exasperation — since he shares with Philo the failure either to win a meaningful victory for his position or to completely lose it. His utterances, however, contrast with those of Philo in that they exhibit a deep tone of sadness, a defensiveness. The early optimism about the potential of the design argument, the shortness and irritation in relation to points made against it, have almost vanished.

If we combine the cognitive elements of the arguments made by the explicit speakers, and incorporated in the final conclusions, we see that they are essentially identical with the intersection of the beliefs of Cleanthes and Philo. These beliefs constitute the secondary meaning of the dialogues, constituents of the abstract argument that ends in a remote, vacuous analogy. If we construe this conclusion as constituting the beliefs, and the related attitudes and emotions, of an implicit speaker, we have a person whose beliefs, attitudes, and emotions toward natural theology (and its attempted exploitation of the scientific method and religion in general), are deeply ambivalent, characterized by conflict in both the cognitive and emotive senses. There is, thus, a reconciliation scene, but it is one that features at best the dubious joys of resignation, with little celebration of positive achievement.

Conclusions

The formal, cognitive, and expressive features of the *Dialogues* combine to present a picture of ambivalence, frustration, and despair in relation to eighteenth-century theological and religious issues, in particular those concerning the relationships between science and theology. This point may be put in a more general way. By means of characterization, plot, and imagery, Hume in the *Dialogues* expresses the inconclusiveness, the incoherence, the confusion, of attempts to exploit scientific methods and knowledge for theological purposes.

Hume, viewed as the implicit speaker, has structured, formed, the work so as to express his feelings and emotions about some fundamental theological concepts and issues. Thus he expresses, with ambivalence, frustration, exasperation, depression, intensity, the inconclusiveness of the logical efforts related to the disputes; and he expresses, with anger and bitterness, his belief in the evil and other pernicious consequences of orthodox religion, with its constituent superstitions and enthusiasms. The features of inconclusiveness, ambivalence, are suggested by the adversarial form, the complexities of plot, the imagery and irony. The same formal features, in tandem with the imagery, irony, and character-ization, exhibit and suggest intensity, depression, frustration, exaspera-tion, anger, bitterness. The term *express* here takes as objects abstract properties such as frustration, exasperation, intensity, anger, inconclu-siveness, confusion, etc. Used both for works of art and for mental objects and processes, the terms used for such properties are often designated as *expressive,* or *anthropomorphic,* predicates. Terms such as *characterization, irony, complex plot, adversarial plot, imagery,* and *metaphor,* when given suitable content, indicate how the artist goes about express-ing ideas and emotions, the "ways" he does these things. And these formal and expressive elements, as we saw at the very beginning, are among the characteristic features of works of art.

The work of art, from this stance, is construed as (the product of) a linguistic act that has predicable features also used for (nonartistic) bodily and vocal expressions.[20] Expressive features can be predicated of works of art in at least two related ways. First, as expressing ideas — that is, beliefs, views, opinions, on subjects, issues. In such cases the prop-erties are indicated by propositional content. Thus, "Hume expressed his belief and concern that contemporary theologians were misappro-priating scientific method and material for theological purposes; and his conviction that the designer-God has no moral character or interests." As we have seen, Hume expressed many opinions in the *Dialogues* — that religion has evil and pernicious consequences, that the design argument is mistaken, etc.

Sometimes, however, it is the whole work that can be said to express an idea describable by a *that* clause. Thus "In the *Dialogues,* Hume expressed his final judgments about natural theology, that traditional religious and theological beliefs cannot be proved by the experimental, and other rational methods, of the sciences; but that belief in a designer has an irresistible core in our natural instincts."

Such beliefs may not, in a simple sense, be "stated" in the explicit statements of the explicit characters. Often they are a part of the secondary meaning, the implicit line of argument abstracted from the statements of the explicit characters. It is clear that when one expresses an idea or feeling in a work of expository or argumentative as opposed to literary or dramatic discourse, one does not imply or suggest it—it is stated directly and explicitly. In such discourse, an attempt is made to avoid implied meanings and emotions.

The expression of beliefs, ideas, opinions, presupposes the expression of abstract properties, as indicated above. And, as is clear from our examples, actions and statements that incorporate the latter form of expression are always done in some expressively or anthropomorphically describable way. It is in this element that we get the expressive features of the work of art. So—in the *Dialogues,* Hume (the implicit speaker) expresses with intensity, ambivalence, exasperation, frustration, despair, the inconclusiveness and ambiguities of metaphysical and theological disputes (such as those in the *Dialogues*)—feelings he often expressed in relation to similar problems in the *Treatise* (T. 268–70) and the *Enquiries* (E. 8–13, 158–65).

Similar analyses are possible for the more limited expressive properties. Thus "Hume expresses contempt for the belief that the design argument exemplifies the experimental methods of science." Examples could be multiplied.

There is no question, then, but that the *Dialogues* is a work of art in the formal and expressive senses.

Who is Hume in the *Dialogues?* Hume is the implicit speaker, the person who expresses the beliefs and emotions (indicated above) related to the explicit speakers. And so we can make a fresh, but not completely original, attempt to settle an old problem. If in the *Dialogues* Hume is the implicit speaker who asserts the implicit arguments and expresses the emotions characteristic of the related images, ironies, ways of speaking, etc., *then he cannot be identified with any one of the explicit speakers.* He is the "persona" who sets out the abstracted argument; and thus he is all the characters insofar as the frustrations and dissatisfactions are concerned, and at the same time he is the ambivalent person who in one "self" holds the conflicting beliefs and attitudes of both Cleanthes and Philo.[21] The *Dialogues* may also be viewed as the autobiography, or the history, through characterization, of the arguments and emotions attendant on Hume's frustrating and often despairing efforts to make theological progress—as the march toward their ambivalent conclusion.

Why did Hume set out his religious and theological ideas, in their terminal form, as a work of art? For many reasons. Works of art intersect many intentions. Even without appeal to his other works on the same subjects, the *Dialogues* alone show a deep and powerful desire to express his beliefs and attitudes toward theology and religion; and he quite rightly knew that argumentative and expository discourse is not so well suited for the particulars of his purposes. One reason is that expressive and emotive predicates, when used for works of art, are intransitive, and hence one cannot provide descriptive equivalents for these predicates when they are used in relation to expressive properties. If I say that the last exchanges in the *Dialogues* are expressive of exasperation, of Hume's exasperation, and someone asks me "how do the *Dialogues* express exasperation?" I could not provide a description that could be substituted for the word *exasperation* in my sentence.[22] It is not, of course, that I could do nothing; I could direct his attention to the images, the interruptions, etc. It would be like someone asking me to provide a description for the term *spontaneity* as applied to a painting by de Kooning. The key point is this: the exasperation and disgust expressed in the *Dialogues* (and the other feelings as well) are not identifiable independently of the work itself. The philosophical point may be indicated in the following way: one of the ways in which it is possible to come to know the emotional features associated with philosophical reflection is by doing philosophy in the form of works of art, or by recapitulating such creative activities as a spectator. Art works *show* the feelings and the forms of thought.

A thinker might wish, as artists commonly do, to express more than meanings (beliefs and feelings) in his work.[23] Often, for instance, painters desire to affirm some formal characteristics of the materials with which they work—the colors, surfaces, etc. In certain of his paintings the modern painter Georges Braque, for instance, wished to affirm the texture of the surfaces of his works; and therefore he used sand, paper, etc., in them. Expressionists and hard-edge painters often wish to affirm colors, shapes, gestural spontaneity, etc. Hume, I think, desired to so make his readers experience directly the dialectical features, formal features, of certain kinds of metaphysical and theological disputes— their resistance to resolution, their tendency to generate counterexamples, the paradox, the irony so internally related to their conceptual constituents. Thus in the *Dialogues* he initiates a process whereby the reader, made attentive by characterization, plot, imagery, quite directly experiences these features. These tactics also may extend or increase the scope of the reader's attention to such features, or make him more deeply aware of one or the other of them.[24] In these ways the reader of Hume's *Dialogues* develops a heightened sensitivity to the ramifications of the design argument; becomes more aware of its implications with respect to the moral capacities predicable of such a vaguely conceived cause. Such heightened sensitivities on the part of the spectator are a profound consequence of any great work of art, and are rightly considered to be one of the great values of art. Such sensitivities, of course, also accrue to the artist in his creative endeavors. Here again, then, are things that can be done only, or at least most effectively, by means of art — and Hume did them well in the *Dialogues*.

A further, plainer reason for Hume's decision to use the form of a work of art, particularly the dialogue form, lay in his deep fear of orthodox religion, with its superstitions and enthusiasms. He wished to influence people, to make them aware of the pernicious effects of religion, make them more tolerant. And he believed that the formal structure of the dialogue, attending as it does (when done properly, as with Hume) to the articulation of all sides of the questions, was well suited to these ends. And he was right. Used honestly and intelligently, the dialogue form tends to be impartial in its generation of the appropriate feelings, since they are a function of the intentional objects, and the propositional contents, of the constituent sides of the arguments. Seen in this light, Hume's requests to friends for help in formulating strong arguments for his dialogues are appropriate and sincere and do not require the interpretation that he desired them because he was attached only to the views of one of the characters in the *Dialogues*.

Finally, the dialectical nature of many philosophical concepts makes the dramatic form of the adversarial dialogue most effective. The tendency of theological concepts, for instance, to generate counterexamples is apparent — for instance the attempted use by Cleanthes of the concept of similarity in a causal context in which the inferred cause is not observable. In the dialogue form this feature is *shown, exhibited,* as distinct from described, or inferred. It is presented. And this is a powerful tool for communicating both ideas and feelings. And thus again we have a reason for Hume to choose to express his deepest thoughts under the concept of art.

Is the *Dialogues Concerning Natural Religion* a good work of art? It is difficult to do justice here to the question. To be sure, it is. It is certainly among the greatest philosophical dialogues in literature, and one of the greatest in any subject. But the work is good for "good" aesthetic reasons. It is good, even superb, because of its formal, expressive, cognitive, and moral features. Certainly enough has been shown above to justify the critical claim that it has good form. The adversarial structure, the complexities of plot, are ideal for the exhibition of the difficulties, the frustrations, the inconclusiveness, of certain types of theological and philosophical disputes; in particular those that do not respond to typical conceptual and epistemic techniques. And it is a superb vehicle for the exhibition of the expressive properties relating to philosophical issues.

The characterizations associated with the persons in the *Dialogues* are admirably fitted to the exhibition of the types of persons who would use the types of arguments involved and suffer the types of emotions characteristically evoked by such disputes. And they are consistently articulated. The imagery, the irony, are well chosen in relation to expressive potential and for the evocation of the appropriate feelings in the readers who recapitulate the argumental flow. Cognitively, it is a philosophical masterpiece, perhaps the most conclusive example of philosophical criticism, of any kind, ever mounted. It is a philosophical work of art; and this means that it is creative in a number of senses, of which I can mention only a few. It brought sophisticated original philosophical techniques to bear on issues of compelling importance — the main one being the attempt to exploit the new sciences for religious purposes. A second, I think, is the tie of morality to religion.[25] It also involved the creative application of traditional conceptual techniques of philosophy to such problems. It is a signal use of artistic form in a philosophic endeavor, and implies, as some modern philosophers claim to be the case, that philosophy is more like art than science. The *Dialogues* reflect the fact that art works can be creative in at least two ways: one, in the use of traditional formal and expressive techniques in a new manner and, two, in the development of new techniques. Hume was a master of both. Now can anyone, in the face of such manifold considerations, yet believe that David Hume set out his thoughts about the design argument in the form of a work of art, the dialogue form, in order to hide his opinions and avoid criticism? It appears to me that to think so not only impoverishes Hume, it subverts him.

It is clear that the cognitive greatness of the *Dialogues* is dependent upon their dramatic and expressive magnitude; and thus their aesthetic character is a necessary condition of their philosophical achievement — how else could the inconclusiveness, the abortiveness, the Hegelian ironies of some kinds of philosophical concepts, have been shown?

Notes

1. David Hume, *Dialogues Concerning Natural Religion,* ed. Nelson Pike (New York: Bobbs-Merrill, 1970), p. 4. Further references will be abbreviated as follows: (D. page number).

2. Richard Wollheim, *Art and Its Objects,* 2nd ed. (Cambridge: Cambridge University Press, 1980), p. 112.

3. These concepts have been influenced in the main by Wollheim, *Art and Its Objects;* Joseph Margolis, *Art and Philosophy* (Atlantic Highlands: Humanities Press, Inc., 1980); Guy Sircello, *Mind and Art* (Princeton: Princeton University Press, 1972).

4. Monroe Beardsley, *Aesthetics* (New York: Harcourt, Brace and Company, Inc., 1958), pp. 237–54, 122–30. These citations concern structure, and implicit meaning, respectively.

5. Stanley Cavell, *Must we mean what we say?* (Cambridge: Cambridge University Press, 1976), p. 174.

6. Peter Jones, *Hume's Sentiments* (Edinburgh: University of Edinburgh Press, 1982), Chap. 3; Michael Morrisroe, Jr., "Rhetorical Methods in Hume's Works on Religion," *Philosophy and Rhetoric,* 2 (1969), pp. 121–38; and "Hume's Rhetorical Strategy: A Solution to the Riddles of the *Dialogues Concerning Natural Religion,*" in *Texas Studies in Language & Literature,* 11 (1969): 963–74; Christine Battersby, "The Dialogues as Original Imitation: Cicero and the Nature of Hume's Skepticism," in *McGill Hume Studies,* ed. Nicholas Capaldi, David F. Norton, Wade L. Robison (San Diego: Austin Hill Press, 1976), pp. 239–52. On tradition see Wollheim, "Criticism as Retrieval," *Art and Its Objects,* pp. 185–204, particularly pp. 194–95.

7. See Chap. 9 of this book, pp. 135–68. For excellent and recent analyses, see *Dialogues,* ed. Pike, pp. 128–204; James Noxon, *Hume's Philosophical Development* (Oxford: Clarendon Press, 1973), pp. 165–87; Nicholas Capaldi, *David Hume* (Boston: Twayne Publishers, 1975), Chap. 9; Terence Penelhum, *Hume* (New York: St. Martins Press, 1975), Chap. 8; J. C. A. Gaskin, *Hume's Philosophy of Religion* (New York: Barnes and Noble, 1978), Chaps. 8 and 10.

8. David Hume, *A Treatise of Human Nature,* ed. L. A. Selby-Bigge (Oxford: Oxford University Press, 1888), p. 105. Further references abbreviated as (T. page number). Hume's *An Enquiry Concerning Human Understanding,* 3rd ed., eds. L. A. Selby-Bigge and P. H. Nidditch (Oxford: Oxford University Press, 1975), will be abbreviated as (E. page number).

9. See this book, pp. 141–42, 161–65. On the nature of argument by analogy, see the following: Stephen Barker, "Hume on the Logic of Design," *Hume Studies,* 9, no. 1 (April 1983): 1–29; H. S. Harris, "Hume and Barker on the Logic of Design," ibid., 19–24; Wesley Salmon, "A New Look at Hume's Dialogues," *Philosophical Studies,* 33 (1978): 143–76.

10. Terence Penelhum, "Hume's Skepticism and the Dialogues," in *McGill Hume Studies,* pp. 270–78; R. J. Butler, "Natural Belief and the Enigma of Hume," *Archiv für Geschichte der Philosophie,* 42 (1960), 73–100; James Noxon, "Hume's Agnosticism," in *Hume,* ed. V. C. Chappell (Garden City: Anchor Books, 1966), pp. 361–83; Capaldi, *David Hume,* pp. 188–97; Cavell, *Must we mean what we say,* pp. 59, 325 n. 15.

11. Gaskin, *Hume's Philosophy of Religion,* Chaps. 8, 10; p. 181, nn. 10, 13.

12. Pheroze Wadia, "Professor Pike on Part III of Hume's Dialogues," *Religious Studies,* 14 (1979): 325–42. See also his "Philo Confounded," in *McGill Hume Studies,* pp. 279–90.

13. On resemblance and conjunction, see (E. 34, 36–38, 73–79, 104–108). See also Cavell, *Must we mean what we say?,* pp. 324–25.

14. David Hume, *On the Standard of Taste and Other Essays,* ed. John W. Lenz (New York: Bobbs-Merrill, 1965), pp. 7, 11.

15. Wadia, "Professor Pike on Part III of Hume's Dialogues," p. 342.

16. Wollheim, *Art and Its Objects,* Secs. 35–40; Margolis, *Art and Philosophy,* pp. 18–24, Chap. 4, *passim.*

17. Gaskin, *Hume's Philosophy of Religion,* pp. 134 et seq.

18. Ibid., p. 135.

19. Cavell, *Must we mean what we say?,* p. 174; Dorothy P. Coleman, "Hume's 'Dialectic,'" in *Hume Studies,* 10, no. 2 (November 1984): 139–54; Manfred Kuehn, "Hume's Antinomies," *Hume Studies,* 9, no. 1 (April 1983): 25–45.

20. Sircello, *Mind and Art,* Chaps. 3, 4, 5; Wollheim, *Art and Its Objects,* Secs. 15–19, 48–49; Margolis, *Art and Philosophy,* Part Two.

21. Penelhum, *Hume,* p. 193.

22. Wollheim, *Art and Its Objects,* Secs. 42, 48, 58; Ludwig Wittgenstein, *Philosophical Investigations,* ed. G. E. M. Anscombe (Oxford: Oxford University Press, 1953) I, Pars. 519–46); II, vi, ix. *Blue and Brown Books* (Oxford: Oxford University Press, 1958), pp. 177–85; *Lectures and Conversations* (Berkeley: University of California Press, 1967), pp. 28–40; Sircello, *Mind and Art,* pp. 40–43, 141–42.

23. Wollheim, *Art and Its Objects,* pp. 93, 139–40.

24. Ibid., pp. 120–28.

25. Capaldi, *David Hume,* pp. 188–98.

Index

Absurd, the, in Existentialism, 192; in Kierkegaard, 196

Academic Skepticism, 148

Ad absurdam, use of in Hume, 162–165

Ad hominem, use of in Hume, 152, 162–163, 168

Aether, 8. *See also* etherial medium

Agnosticism, 113–114, 118–123, 188, 208

Alexander, Samuel, 192

Alexandrine School, 111

Allegorical interpretation of scripture, 66

Analogy, in the Alexandrine School, 110–111; argument by, xxiii, 12–13, 16, 20, 22, 33, 35–36, 43–44, 56–57, 88–89, 95–99, 102–111, 113–114, 116–132, 138–140, 143, 148, 175, 187; as argument by example in Aristotle, 107; in Aristotle, 102–108, 129, 130; in Bacon, 43–44, 85; in Bentley, 58; in Berkeley, 60–62, 85; in Browne, 59, 85; in Butler, 63–64, 81, 85; definition of, 150–151; extrinsic, 120; in Galileo, 125, 132; to human purposes and intentions, 12–13, 20, 35; in Hume, 138–148; Hume's criticism of, 149–169, 189; as induction, 104; in King, 85, 86–87; of the machine, 8, 16, 20, 22, 33, 35, 36, 42, 61, 66, 74–80, 89, 95, 98, 125, 127, 137, 139–140, 150, 152–153, 155, 157–158, 161, 171–173, 176, 180; in Newton, 8, 16, 84; in Paley, 171–172; in Philo of Judea, 113–114, 130; in Plato, 95, 98–99, 129; proportionate, 99, 103–104, 106, 111; in St. Thomas, 59, 117–120, 122, 124–125; in science, 22, 125–128, 132; scientific, 22, 90–91; in Stoicism, 109–111, 130; substantial, 120; in Whewell, 174–175

Analytical philosophy, 170

Animal spirits, 54

Annet, Thomas, 75

Anselm, St., 117, 122, 123

Anthropology, and religion, 182–183

Anthropomorphism, 15, 113–116, 119, 121–123, 131, 174

Anxiety, in Existentialism, 194–196

Apocalypse, 17, 83

A posteriori, 20, 34, 41, 55; in Aquinas, 124; in Bentley, 58, 61; in Burnet, 36; in Butler, 64; in Clarke, 32; and the design argument, 8, 11, 13, 22–23, 89, 150, 151; in Hume, 135–143, 150–156; in Keill, 39; in Newton, 16, 24, 26, 31, 39, 84, 87; as scientific, 90; in Whiston, 38. *See also* empiricism *and* experiment

A priori, 31–32, 81, 98–99, 137, 180; in Aquinas, 86, 124; in Bentley, 58; in Herbert of Cherbury, 68; in Cheyne, 26, 84; in Clarke, 26, 84, 189; in Hume, 152–156, 187; in Locke, 89; in Logical Positivism, 197; in Paley, 172; in science, 90. *See also* mathematics

Aquinas, St. Thomas, 62, 106, 116, 117–124, 128, 131–132, 145; and analogy, 106, 117–123; in Berkeley, 62; in Browne, 59; in King, 59. *See also* Thomism

Archimedes, 132

Argument from design, Chapter 1, 8–16, 36, 38, 39, 42, 45, 58–59, 60, 63–64, 81, 86, 97–98, 108–109, 112–114, 126, 139–142, 142, 148, 151–152, 154–165, 171–172, 173. *See also* design argument

Argument to design, Chapter 1, 10, 12, 13, 16, 36, 38, 42, 58–59, 63–64, 81,

Argument to design—*continued*
86, 89, 98, 108–109, 112, 124, 139–
140, 148, 171–176. *See also* design
argument
Arianism, 18, 19, 37, 92
Aristotle, 4, 43, 91, 95, 99–107, 109,
112–117, 122, 124, 127, 129–130, 132,
146
Arminian controversy, 66
Arnold, Matthew, 177
Artificer, 11
Atheism, 14, 98, 113
Atomistic philosophers, 98, 113, 129, 131
Auden, William, 197
Augustine, St., 116–117, 123, 132, 161
Averroes, 70

Bacon, Sir Francis, 3, 20, 22, 43–44, 63,
70, 81, 85–86, 91–92, 112, 132, 143,
146
Balbus, 55, 137, 147
Barrow, Isaac, 11, 35
Barth, Karl, 192–194, 196, 207
Baumer, F. L., 178
Beauty of the world-system, 15
Becker, Carl, 188
Benevolence of God, 15
Bentham, Jeremy, 178, 196
Bentley, Richard, 3, 5, 6, 17, 36–37, 43,
57–58, 74, 89, 96
Bentley Letters, 6, 9, 10
Berdyaev, Nicholai, 197
Berkeley, Bishop George, 5, 22, 57,
60–62, 85, 86, 92, 102–103, 129–131,
137, 145–146
Bible, 39, 59, 69, 75–76, 82–83, 188,
192, 194. *See also* Old Testament *and*
scriptures
Bierce, Ambrose, 169
Blount, Charles, 67, 69, 70–71, 76
Bonaventura, St., 117, 122
Boswell, James, 186, 188
Boyle, Robert, 6, 17, 21, 27–33, 51,
55–56, 86, 89, 108, 171
Boyle Lectures, 32, 58
Brahmins, 158
Brewster, David, 18
Bridgewater Treatises, 173
Brown, Thomas, 67
Browne, Peter, 43, 57, 59–64, 85, 103,
106, 129, 131, 145
Brunner, Emil, 193, 194

Bultmann, Rudolph, 194
Burnet, Thomas, 34–36, 38
Burtt, E. A., vii, 24
Butler, Bishop Joseph, 22, 31, 57, 62–64,
78, 85–86, 96, 102, 137, 145–146, 176

Cambridge Platonism, 10, 11, 17, 21,
35, 45, 49, 51–57, 62, 64, 68, 75, 88,
97, 102, 112; and Berkeley, 62; and
Boyle, 86; and Locke, 85; and moral
theory 90; and natural religion, 90;
and Newton, 10–11, 55, 79, 80–81,
86, 91; and science, 85. *See also*
Platonism
Camus, Albert, 197
Caroline, Queen, 17, 31, 63
Cartesianism, 14, 30, 31, 36, 38, 46, 50,
53, 56, 69, 85. *See also* Descartes
Casirrer, Ernst, 56
Causes and causation, 9, 79, 88, 99,
121–122, 129, 147–148; and analogy,
8, 12, 16, 120, 146, 148; in Aquinas,
119; in Berkeley, 60; in Butler, 63;
and the design argument, 8, 12, 16,
89, 150, 155; efficient, 80, 89, 91, 120,
150, 153, 155, 160, 179; final, 16, 80,
128; first, 41, 53, 55, 119, 128, 144;
in Hume, 146, 148; material, 79–80;
mechanical, 30, 36, 79–80, 99, 128,
144; in Newton, 8–16, 30, 79, 144;
in Plato, 99; and similarity, 146, 148;
ultimate, 30, 36, 144
Celsus, 66, 70
Ceremonial language, 200
Chance, 99, 127, 129
Cheyne, George, 26, 28, 29, 31, 33, 84,
141–145
Christianity, 3–27, 75–95, 128, 189–211;
and analogy, xii, 3–27, 146; and
anthropology, 182–183; in Barth, 193;
in Bultmann, 194; in Deism, 65–78;
and the design argument, 82–83, 146,
158; emotion and, 167–168; and
evolution, 180–181; in Existentialism, 194–197; in Galileo, 125; and
Hume, 135–168, 187; and Newtonianism, xii, 16, 79–95, 146; and Neo-
Orthodoxy, 192–197; and Ordinary
Language Philosophy, 189–211; and
Russell, 191; and science, xii, 82–83,
125, 135–168, 181–183; traditional, 16,
167, 168. *See also* design argument

Chronological controversy, 66
Chronology, 16, 17, 19, 66, 82, 83
Chryssippus, 114
Chubb, Thomas, 67, 75
Cicero, 35, 50, 55, 66, 70, 101, 111; in Hume, 137, 147, 148
Clarke, Samuel, 5, 6, 11, 26, 27–33, 40, 41, 63, 75, 84, 89, 137, 171, 186
Climates of opinion, 46, 87, 90, 188
Coates, J. B., 203
Collins, Anthony, 37, 58, 67, 73–74, 76
Comparison, the method of significant, 200
Comte, Auguste, 179, 181
Confrontation with God, in Barth, 193; in Existentialism, 197

Daniel, 17–19, 83
Darwin, Charles, 177, 180. See also evolution and natural selection
Deduction, 48, 88
Definition, 104–105, 113, 130
Deism, 48, 49, 50, 65–78, 86, 87, 88, 90; criticism of religion, 73–74; and empiricism, 75; and Hume, 188; and laws of nature, 88; and Locke, 75; and moral theory, 90; and natural religion, 90; and Newton, 75–76; and reason, 48; and science, 70, 75–76; and theology, 76–86
Democritus, 11, 21, 51, 80, 127, 132
Derham, 27–28, 33–34
Desagauliers, 34
Descartes, 30, 31, 36, 38, 68, 76, 85, 91, 95, 155. See also Cartesianism
Descriptive Laws, 48, 173
Design Argument, 41, 49, 56, 79, 81–82, 89, 91–92, 95–96, 127–128, 132–148, 149–170, 180, 193; ad hominem character of, 162; and anthropology, 182; in Aquinas, 124; in Aristotle, 100–102, 129; in Bacon, 44–45; in Bentley, 57–58; in Berkeley, 60–61; in Boyle, 29–31; in Browne, 59; in Burnet, 35–36; in Butler, 63–64; in Cambridge Platonism, 52–57, 85, 87; in Cheyne, 33–34; in Clarke, 31–32; classical formulation of, xiii; and the cosmological argument, 150; in Deism, 76–78; and emotion, 184; Hume's criticism of, 132–169, 186–

188; in Keill, 39; limits of, 169–170; in Locke, 45–48; logical basis of, 8, 140, 164, 177, 183, 187; in Maclaurin, 40–42; versus materialism and skepticism, 95–96; and natural selection, 181; in Newton, Part One, 3–27, 84; and Ordinary Language Philosophy, 194–198, 201–202; in Paley, 170–173; in Philo, 113–114, 130; in Plato, 97–99; popularity of, 168; psychological compulsiveness of, 161–163; refutation of, 132–169, 186–188, 191, 194, 198, 201–202; as scientific, Part One, Part Three, 91, 125–126; in Stoicism, 108–112, 130; in Whewell, 170–176; in Whiston, 37–38
Despair, 197
Dewey, John, 191, 192, 196
Diogenes Laertius, 50, 101, 112
Divine Mind, 10, 91
Divine sensorium, 12–13, 55, 79, 80, 85, 91–92. See also sensorium of God
Dualism, 21, 50, 52, 56, 80, 81, 87, 91–92; in Boyle, 86; in Hume, 135; in Locke, 85; in Newton, 79, 84, 86

Eliot, T. S., 193, 197
Empiricism, 22–26, 38, 47, 57, 63, 70–77, 81–84, 85, 90, 132, 141–142, 150, 152, 154, 198, 202, 207; in Bacon, 92; in Bentley, 58; in Deism, 86–87; and the design argument, 21–26, 81–84, 141–157; and evidence, 155–157; and Existentialism, 91; in Galileo, 92; in Hume, 141–157, 179, 187; in Keill, 39; in Locke, 85, 92; in Maclaurin, 40; and natural theology, 192; in Newton, 13, 20, 21–26, 38, 81–85, 91–92; and religion, 179, 197–198, 205–207; and theology, 179, 187, 192, 195, 197–198, 207; in Whiston, 36. See also a posteriori and experiment
Epicureans, 66, 114, 131, 147, 178
Equivocal terms, 118, 121–123. See also univocal terms
Erasmus, 70
Etherial medium, 8, 15
Ethics, 47, 50, 65–66, 74–77, 85–86, 90, 110, 129, 166. See also moral principles
Evidence, external, 73

Evolution, 151, 153, 156, 180–181. *See also* Darwin *and* natural selection

Ewing, A. C., 207

Example, argument by, 43, 99, 106, 110–111, 129

Existentialism, 178–179, 194–196, 203, 205, 207; and anxiety, 195; in Bultmann, 194; and modern theology, 196; and reason, 194–196; and science, 194–195; and skepticism, 194–196; in Tillich, 194–195

Experiment, 11, 22, 23–25, 38, 48, 57, 81, 82, 87, 91, 142, 144, 150, 194. *See also* a posteriori, empiricism, *and* observation

Ezra, 69

Fact, matters of, in Hume, 146

Faith, 71, 87, 193–197

Ferré, Frederick, vii, 199, 204

Ferrer, Austin, 204

Feuerbach, Ludwig, 183–184

Final causes, 16, 30, 38, 58, 80, 100–101, 138, 148, 174–175. *See also* causes and causation, teleology, *and* purpose

Findlay, J. N., 201

First cause, 21, 79, 100–101. *See also* causes and causation

Flew, Antony, 201, 209–210

Forms, Platonic, 101, 114, 128. *See also* Cambridge Platonism *and* Platonism

Frazer, Sir James, 181–183, 186

Freedom, 195

Freret, 17

Freud, Sigmund, 186

Galileo, 4–5, 20, 21, 29, 68, 81, 92, 112, 125–126, 132, 150, 153–154; and analogy, 125–126, 140; and Hume, 139, 140–146

Games, language, 198–211

Gassendi, 30, 92

General consent, 76, 85, 88, 97, 161

General Scholium, 5–6, 8, 13, 14, 16, 23, 24, 58

Geometrical order, 7, 22

Gladstone, William, 177–178

Gnosticism, 66

God, in Anselm, 122–123; and anthropology, 182; in Aquinas, 106–107, 117–119, 120; in Aristotle, 100–102, 106; attributes of, in Medieval theology, 124, 130–132; in Bacon, 44; in Barth, 193; in Bentley, 58; in Berkeley, 60–62; in Boyle, 29; in Browne, 59; in Burnet, 35; in Butler, 63–65; in Cambridge Platonism, 52–55; in Cheyne, 33; in Clarke, 31; in Cudworth, 55; in Deism, 76–77; in Dewey, 191; existence of, Part One, Part Two, Part Three, Part Four, 7, 15, 81, 86, 113, 114, 124, 129, 130, 138–139, 153, 179, 196, 199–211; in Existentialism, 195–196; in Galileo, 126; in Hare, 201; in Hume, 137–168; intelligence of, 130; and laws of nature, 88; in Locke, 45, 85; in Maclaurin, 40; malevolence of, 159–165; in modern natural theology, 192; in Neo-Orthodoxy, 193–194; in Newton, Part One, 1–26, 30, 80–84; in Ordinary Language Philosophy, 199–204; in Paley, 171–172; perfection of, 119–122; personality of, 87; in Philo, 111–112; in Plato, 96, 129; in Positivism, 198; and providence, 64; in Russell, 192; in Scotus, 123; and space, 91–92; in Stoicism, 108–109, 130; in Tennant, 192; in Tindal, 75; in Whewell, 173–177; in Whiston, 37; in Wieman, 192; in Woolston, 74

's Gravesande, 34

Gravity, 12, 14, 37, 53–54, 58, 80, 87–88, 140

Gregory, 54

Grotius, 50, 88, 112

Hakewell, 35

Halley, Edmund, 5, 27, 33, 40

Hare, R. M., 201–202, 209

Hartsoeker, 14

Hedonism, 47

Herbert of Cherbury, 66, 67–71, 76

Hesiod, 158

Historicism, 187

History, 136, 182, 183, 187; and religion, 76, 83, 86, 166, 179, 186

Hobbes, Thomas, 32, 51, 53, 67, 69–70, 96, 127

"Homoiousios," 19, 83

Hook, Robert, 5, 17, 24

Hook, Sidney, 191

Hooker, 50

Horsley, 18
Humanism, 190–191, 208–210
Hume, David, 12, 40, 44, 92, 102, 132,
133, 135–168, 169, 171–172, 175, 176,
179, 189, 192, 202; and analogy, 57,
60, 64, 91, 135–168, 177; and anthropology, 183; and a posteriori argument, 22, 91; and climates of opinion,
188; and Deism, 77; and the design
argument, xiii, xiv, 22, 23, 91, 95,
135–168, 171–172; the historical importance of, xii, xiii; and the history
of religion, 186–188; and Maclaurin,
40; and miracles, 77–78; and modern
philosophy, xi, 23, 199, 205, 206, 207,
211; and natural theology, xii–xiii,
135–168; and Newton, 135–146;
Newton's influence on, 144; and
Ordinary Language Philosophy, 199,
205–207; and Positivism, 198; and
the psychological criticism of religion,
184–185; and skepticism, xiii, 22, 26,
178–180, 182–183, 186
Huxley, Julian, 177, 179, 191
Huygens, Christian, 5
Hypotheses, in Newton, 9, 15, 23, 24,
91; speculative, 15

Ideas, 72
Induction, 23, 25, 44, 48, 59, 63, 71, 86,
88, 104, 106–107, 147
Inertia, 11, 12, 21
Infinite space, 10
Innate ideas, 67, 68, 85, 88, 129
Instrumentalism, 184
Ionian science, 98

Jaspers, Karl, 197
Jesus, 74

Kafka, 197
Keill, John, 27, 33, 34, 39, 41, 86
Kemp-Smith, Norman, 136–137
Kepler, 4, 68
Kierkegaard, 192, 195, 196
King, Archbishop, 57, 59, 62, 63, 85,
86, 106, 145
Knowledge, 72, 86, 109, 118, 122, 123,
130, 193, 197
Koestler, Arthur, 197

Language, 198, 202; "Games," 198–
211; multiple uses of, 202; and logic

in Ordinary Language Philosophy,
198–211
Latitudinarian, 18, 168
Laws, causal, 80, 88–89, 91. See also
laws of nature
Laws of association, 144
Laws of motion, 12, 33, 36, 61, 80–81,
87–89, 100, 140, 144, 150, 165. See
also laws of nature
Laws of nature, 21, 22, 49, 79, 80–81,
82–86, 88–89, 140, 144; in Berkeley,
60; in Boyle, 86; in Burnet, 36; in
Butler, 64; in Cambridge Platonism,
56; in Cheyne, 33; in Collins, 74;
in Deism, 76–77, 88; descriptive, 48;
in Galileo, 4, 20; in Grotius, 88; in
Hume, 140–144; in Locke, 46–49, 56,
85–90; in Newton, 4, 20, 21, 22, 48,
79–80, 90; in Plato, 97; prescriptive,
48; in Pufendorf, 88; in Stoicism,
110; in Tindal, 75; in Toland, 72–73;
in Whewell, 174–176
Lecky, 187
Leibniz, 5, 14, 17, 29, 32, 171
Leucippus, 80, 127
Limborch, 51
Linguistic philosophy. See Logical
Positivism, Ordinary Language Philosophy, and Positivism
Locke, John, 17, 19, 20–21, 31, 37, 43,
44–48, 49–56, 57, 59, 64, 68, 71–72,
73, 85–86, 88, 90, 96, 112, 196; and
Bentley, 58; and Blount, 70; and
Butler, 63; and Deism, 60, 75–76;
and the design argument, 45; and
Hume, 137, 186; and laws of nature,
49–51, 88, 90; and theology, 85; and
Tindal, 75; and Toland, 71–73; and
traditional religion, 86
Logic, in Aquinas, 117–121; in argument by analogy, 8, 22, 95, 99, 102–
104, 105, 106, 140, 150–151, 154–168,
177, 187–188, 201; in Aristotle, 104–
105, 106, 107, 116, 132; in Bacon,
132; in Barth, 193; in Brunner, 193;
and the design argument, 16, 22,
135–168, 183; in Existentialism, 194;
in Hume, 135–168; in Linguistic
Philosophy, 198; in Neo-Orthodoxy,
193; in Newton, 26; in Niebuhr, 193;
in Ordinary Language Philosophy,
198, 205; in Philo, 113, 130; in

Logic—*continued*
  Positivism, 197–198; in Stoicism, 110–111; in Whewell, 176
Logical Positivism, 198–199
Lucian, 70
Lucretius, 70

Machine analogy, 35, 36, 42, 61, 64, 66, 74, 76, 78, 79, 80, 89, 95, 98, 125, 127, 137, 139, 140, 150, 152, 153, 155, 157, 158, 161, 171, 172, 173, 176, 180. *See also* analogy, mechanical causes, *and* mechanical laws
MacIntyre, Alasdair, 203
Mackinnon, D. M., 201
Maclaurin, Colin, 34, 40–42, 86, 141–142, 143, 144, 145
Macpherson, Thomas, 204
Mannheim, Karl, 187
Manning, Cardinal, 171
Marx, Karl, 179, 184, 186
Masham, Lady, 11
Materialism, 32, 51, 79–80, 87, 90, 116, 127–128, 130
Mathematics, 5, 22, 24–25, 31, 34, 48, 78–79, 83, 87–88, 103
Matters of fact in Hume, 146
Mechanical causes, 5, 22, 30, 36, 53, 78–79, 80, 98. *See also* mechanical, principles, mechanical laws, mechanical order, *and* mechanism
Mechanical hypothesis, 46, 80, 90, 98, 125, 127
Mechanical laws, 5, 6, 14, 22, 30, 31, 33, 39, 45, 52, 62, 66, 78, 79, 80, 86, 87, 89, 139, 174. *See also* mechanical causes, mechanical principles, *and* mechanism
Mechanical order, 7, 62, 64
Mechanical principles, 7, 21, 23, 24, 25, 48, 80, 98, 144. *See also* mechanical causes *and* mechanical laws
Mechanism, 50, 74, 76, 78, 79, 83, 95, 98, 127, 128, 129. *See also* analogy, machine analogy, mechanical causes, *and* mechanical laws
Metaphysics, 24, 32, 76, 79, 80, 85, 86, 87, 95, 100–104, 117, 119, 129, 130, 135, 138, 145
Methodology, in Newton, 20–26, 31, 81, 84, 87
Middleton, Conyers, 75

Mill, John Stuart, 171, 179, 196
Mind of God, 10, 80
Miracles, 19, 39, 71, 72, 74–78, 82–83, 86, 114
Models, linguistic, 199
Modernism, theological, 191–192, 206, 208, 210
Montaigne, 70
Moral principles, 47, 48–50, 73, 75–78, 85, 88, 90, 111, 173, 208–209. *See also* ethics
More, Henry, 10–11, 17, 35, 50–55
Morley, Lord, 186–187
Mossner, David, 137
Motion, laws of. *See* laws of motion
Mysticism, 18, 65–66, 74, 113, 115, 117–118, 123, 129; and Collins, 73–74; and Deism, 65–73, 76–78; and Existentialism, 194, 197; in Hume, 143, 152, 168, 184; and modern theology, 190, 193–194, 197; and natural theology, 96; and Neo-Orthodoxy, 193–194; and Newton, 18–19, 84, 86; and Philo, 130–132. *See also* natural theology *and* revelation

Natural causes, 14. *See* laws of nature
Natural law. *See* laws of nature
Natural philosophy, 16, 20–21, 36, 87, 88, 110
Natural reason, 46, 47, 56, 78, 83, 85, 87, 88, 110
Natural religion, 39, 45–49, 57, 65–68, 73–76, 83, 85, 87, 89, 90, 136–141, 187, 189. *See also* natural theology
Natural selection, 156, 180. *See also* evolution *and* Darwin
Natural theology, in Aquinas, 131; in Aristotle, 129; in Barth, 193–194; in Cambridge Platonism, 51–56; in Collins, 174; in Deism, 66–78; and Existentialism, 194, 197; in Hume, 135–168, 192, 211; in Locke, 46–48, 85; and modern thought, 190, 192, 197; in Newton and the Newtonians, Part One, xiv, 21–24, 48, 83, 90–96; in Ordinary Language Philosophy, 199–211; in Paley, 171–173; in Philo, 130; in Plato, 96–97, 129; in Positivism, 198; refutation of, 135–168, 176, 194, 197–198, 210; summary of,

Natural theology—*continued*
    Newtonian, 87–90; in Tennant, 191;
    in Tindal, 75; in Wieman, 191; in
    Whewell, 173–175; in Whitehead,
    191. *See also* God, natural religion,
    and physico-theology
Nature. *See* laws of nature
Neo-Orthodoxy, 190–194, 203, 205,
    207, 210
Newton, Arianism of, 83; and Bentley,
    57–58; and Berkeley, 61–62; and
    Butler, 64; and Cambridge Platonism,
    51–57, 80–82; empiricism in, 81, 87
    (*see* a posteriori *and* experiment);
    epistemology of, Chapter 1, 81, 87
    (*see* experiment, mathematics, *and*
    methodology); experimental method,
    7, 20, 22–24, 31; followers of, Chapter
    2, 77–78, 86, 90–97; and Hume, 135–
    168; latitudinarianism of, 18–19; and
    Locke, 47–50; mathematics in, 24–25,
    31, 87; metaphysics of, 21, 79, 81–84,
    87; methodology of, 20–26; and
    science, xi, Chapter 1; system of the
    world, 21; theology of, Chapters 1
    and 5, xii, 68
Niebuhr, Reinhold, 193, 197

Observation, 22, 23, 25, 38. *See also* a
    posteriori, empiricism, methodology,
    and experiment
Occam's Razor, 156, 180
Oldenburg, 54
Old Testament, 16, 28, 187, 194. *See
    also* Bible *and* scriptures
Ontological argument, xii, 61, 124,
    192
Order, geometrical, 7, 78. *See also*
    analogy, machine analogy, *and* mathe-
    matics
Order, mechanical, 7, 78, 140. *See also*
    analogy, argument from design,
    design argument, *and* machine
    analogy
Order, purposive, 36, 108, 138, 140.
    See also argument to design, final
    causes, purposes, *and* teleology
Ordinary Language Philosophy, 184,
    197–211. *See also* linguistic philos-
    ophy
Origen, 66

Paley, William, 136, 156, 170–173, 177,
    178
Pantheism, 13, 70–71, 114–115, 121,
    123, 130–131
Paradigm case method, 199, 201
Pardies, 24
Parmenides, 97
Pascal, Blaise, 16
Pelagian controversy, 66
Pemberton, Henry, 27, 34, 39, 86
Pentateuch, 69
Peripatetics, 148, 152
Philo of Judea, 95, 101, 112–115, 116,
    117, 123, 132
Philostratus, 66, 70
Physico-theology, 46, 65, 76, 87, 89,
    108. *See also* natural theology
Plato, 7, 11, 32, 93, 95–102, 107, 109,
    114–115, 124, 127–128, 130, 132,
    137, 149
Platonism, 10, 30, 50–53, 54–55, 79,
    80–86, 90–91, 114, 128, 142–152; in
    Boyle, 86; and Hume, 142–152; in
    Locke, 85; in Newton, 50–55, 79–81,
    91; in Philo, 114. *See also* Cambridge
    Platonism *and* Plato
Plotinus, 142, 143
Pompanatius, 70
Popkin, Richard, 178 n.
Porphyry, 66, 70
Positivism, Logical, 170, 184, 197–199
Pragmatic argument against religion.
    See utilitarian argument against
    religion
Prescriptive laws, 48, 173
Primary and secondary qualities, 31
Probability, 61, 81, 91, 108, 130
Prophecy, 76, 82
Proportionate analogy, 103–106, 110–
    111, 119–122, 128–129, 131. *See also*
    Aquinas *and* analogy
Protestantism, 18
Protoplast, 54, 80, 128
Providence, 37–38, 64, 79, 92, 109, 182
Psychological criticism of religion,
    183–185
Pufendorf, 50, 88, 112
Purposes, 8, 10, 15, 21, 22, 30, 35, 86,
    89, 108–109, 124, 128, 137–142, 148,
    155, 160, 170–172, 176, 180. *See also*
    argument to design, final causes, *and*
    teleology

Pyrrhonism, 96, 148, 178 n. *See also* skepticism
Pythagoras, 95

Ramsay, I. T., 203
Rationalism, 31, 32, 48, 50, 56, 68, 76, 84, 85, 87, 90, 97, 129, 131, 152; continental, 50, 56, 97; in Descartes, 48, 68, 176; in Herbert of Cherbury, 68; in Locke, 85; in Newton, 84; in Plato, 129; in Stoicism, 129–130
Rational religion, 49, 67, 71–72, 75–78, 83, 85, 87, 89, 90, 129, 193. *See also* natural religion *and* natural theology
Ray, John, 27–29, 33–35, 108
Reason, 46–50, 52, 55, 72, 78, 85–88, 110, 132, 168, 179, 183–184, 190, 193–195, 210
Religion, anthropological criticism of, 181–182; Deistic criticism of, 73–74; emotion the basis of, 167–169, 183–184, 190; historical argument against, 186–187; and inductive and deductive methods, 135–168, 190; irrational character of, 190; psychological criticism of, 183–185. *See also* natural religion, rational religion, *and* natural theology
Religion, natural. *See* natural religion, natural theology, *and* rational religion
Religion, rational. *See* natural religion *and* natural theology
Renaissance, 66
Renan, 187
Revelation, 67–68, 70–74, 76–79, 86–87, 113–114, 118, 129–130, 192–196
Robinson, 35
Rohault, 27
Ross, W. D., 100
Rousseau, 136
Royal Society of London, 27
Russell, Bertrand, 191, 196
Ryle, Gilbert, 205

Science, in Aristotle, 105; and Deism, 70, 77, 81, 84–85; and the design argument, Part One, 142, 150, 154; in Hume, 135; limits of, in Newton, 6, 13; Newtonian, Part One; and religion, 137–139, 169, 178–179, 180, 182, 192, 195, 200, 205; and theology, Parts One and Three, 3, 13, 14, 75–

76, 78, 81, 85, 86, 96, 130, 135, 137–139, 144, 150–154, 169, 178, 179, 180, 192, 195, 200, 205. *See also* scientific
Scientific, ambiguity of, 90; a posteriori as, 90; discourse, 199–211; laws, Part One, 48, 60–61, 76–77 (*see also* mechanical laws *and* laws of nature); method, 7, 22, 52, 81, 88, 135 (*see also* methodology); revolution, 20; synthesis, 4, 74; theism, xii; vagueness of, xii. *See also* science
Scotus, Duns, 123
Scriptures, 61, 66, 71, 76, 83, 114, 197. *See also* Bible *and* Old Testament
Seneca, 50, 66, 70, 101, 112
Sensorium of God, 12, 13, 55, 79, 80, 85, 91
Sextus Empiricus, 50, 101, 112, 147
Shaftsbury, 75
Sidgwick, Henry, 187
Similarity, 16, 110–111, 119, 122, 138, 145, 146, 148, 153, 154, 156. *See also* analogy
Skepticism, and the design argument, 98, 135–168, 176–178; in Hume, xiii, xiv, 135–168; and modern theology, 115, 170, 188, 194–211; and Plato, 97–98
Smart, J. J. C., 201–203
Smith, John, 51
Socrates, 9, 96
Sophists, 97, 127
Soul, 53, 54, 97, 129
Soul, world, 53, 54
Space, infinite, as the Sensorium of God, 10, 55, 91
Spencer, Herbert, 179
Spinoza, 32, 69, 70, 96, 127
Stephen, Leslie, 19, 179
Stobaeus, 50
Stoicism, 7, 43, 55, 59, 66, 68, 95, 97, 102, 108–112, 113–115, 124, 129, 130–132, 137, 146, 147, 148, 152; and the design argument, 108–112, 114–115
Strauss, 187
Suarez, 117
System of the world, Newton, 20–25, 36, 80, 84, 86

Teleology, 8, 12, 16, 30, 38, 47, 86, 100–101, 108, 124, 128, 142, 148, 155, 171–172, 174–176, 180, 193. *See also*

Teleology—*continued*
  argument to design, causes and
  causation, final causes, *and* purposes
Tennant, F. R., 191
Tennyson, 177
Textual criticism, 82. *See also* Deism
Thales, 79
Theism. *See* God, natural religion, *and*
  natural theology
Theology, natural. *See* God, natural
  religion, *and* natural theology
Thomas, St. *See* Aquinas, St. Thomas
Thomism, 59, 62, 86, 89, 96, 106, 108,
  117–124, 128–132. *See also* Aquinas
Tillich, Paul, 194, 197
Tillotson, 67
Tindal, 67, 75
Toland, 59, 67, 70–73, 76, 78
Trinitarian controversy, 66
Trinity, 18, 19, 82–83, 117
Troeltsch, 186
Truth, 67, 68, 87, 109–110, 114, 163,
  166, 178, 187, 198, 210

Uniformity of nature, 12, 23
Unitarianism, 92
Univocal terms, 118, 121, 122, 123,
  See also Aquinas *and* proportionate
  analogy

Utilitarian argument against religion,
  58, 161, 165–167, 176–179, 187,
  207–209

Varro, 111, 112
Verification principle, and religion and
  theology, 155, 187, 195, 197, 198
Verulam, Lord. *See* Bacon
Viret, 66, 67
Voltaire, 65, 171

Whewell, William, 156, 170, 173–177,
  178
Whichcote, 51
Whiston, William, 18, 27–29, 31–32,
  36–38, 41, 58, 86
Whitehead, A. N., 191
Wieman, H. N., 190–191
Willey, Basil, 187
Williams, D. D., 193
Wisdom, John, 202–203, 209
Wittgenstein, Ludwig, 198, 204
Woodward, 35
Woolston, 67, 74, 75
World soul, 53–54
Wren, 5

Zurdeeg, Willem, 203